Toxic Nourishment and Damaged Bonds in the Work of Michael Eigen

Toxic Nourishment and Damaged Bonds in the Work of Michael Eigen examines Eigen's rich phenomenological work on the Obstructive Object.

The contributors to this collection explore the core theme with reference to key Eigen works, including *The Psychotic Core*, *Psychic Deadness*, *Toxic Nourishment*, and *Damaged Bonds*. This volume seeks to elaborate on the *Obstructive Object* through essays and poems that include poignant clinical examples, the impact of exceptionally traumatized patients on their analysts, literature comparisons, and the more "mystical aspect" of Eigen's influence on working with the obstructive object. Essays draw from Virginia Woolf, Elena Ferrante, Wilfred Bion, D.W. Winnicott, Andrè Greene, Christopher Bollas, and Adam Phillips, among many others, in exploring injury-rage, unwanted patients, psychoanalytic faith, toxic nourishment, and damaged bonds.

Toxic Nourishment and Damaged Bonds in the Work of Michael Eigen will greatly interest psychoanalysts, psychotherapists, and those interested in psycho-analytic and spiritual psychology.

Keri S. Cohen is a Licensed Clinical Social Worker and a Board-Certified Diplomate in clinical social work. She is a psychoanalytic psychotherapist in private practice in Pennsylvania, USA.

Loray Daws is a registered Clinical Psychologist in South Africa and British Columbia, Canada. He is currently in private practice and is a senior faculty member at the International Masterson Institute in New York, USA.

Toxic Nourishment and Damaged Bonds in the Work of Michael Eigen

Working with the Obstructive Object

Edited by Keri S. Cohen
and Loray Daws

Routledge
Taylor & Francis Group

LONDON AND NEW YORK

Designed cover image: © Melanie W. Cohen

First published 2024
by Routledge
4 Park Square, Milton Park, Abingdon, Oxon OX14 4RN

and by Routledge
605 Third Avenue, New York, NY 10158

Routledge is an imprint of the Taylor & Francis Group, an informa business

British Library Cataloguing-in-Publication Data
A catalogue record for this book is available from the British Library

ISBN: 9781032346038 (hbk)
ISBN: 9781032346007 (pbk)
ISBN: 9781003322986 (ebk)

DOI: 10.4324/9781003322986

Typeset in Times New Roman
by codeMantra

Contents

Acknowledgments

We are deeply indebted to Routledge, especially Susannah Frearson and Saloni Singhania, for their enthusiastic support to the two volumes and Michael Eigen's work in general.

Routledge for their permission to re-publish Jeff Eaton's *Becoming a Welcoming Object: Personal Notes on Michael Eigen's Impact*, previously published in *The Living Moments: On the Work of Michael Eigen* (2015), and a section taken from Eigen, 2011 (pp. 86–87), *Eigen in Seoul: Faith and Transformation (Vol. 2)* reproduced in Daws' *Welcoming the Psychotic Core*, Chapter 5 in this volume.

Thank you, Jeff Eaton, for your permission to re-publish *The Obstructive Object*, originally appearing in *A Fruitful Harvest: Essays after Bion*, by The Alliance Press, 2011. An earlier version also appeared in *Psychoanalytic Review*, Vol. 92, 2005. From us as editors, thank you for your generosity in contributing no less than three papers. Your writings on Eigen and Bion serve as an anchor and a backdrop for these volumes. We are grateful for your creativity, ideas, and spirit. Like others in the volume, your work greatly supports the field.

Phoenix Publishing House Ltd for granting permission to reproduce Louis Rothchild's chapter "Abraham's and Isaac's Fear and Silence" from his forthcoming book, *Rapprochement Between Fathers and Sons: Breakdowns, Reunions, Potentialities*.

Dr. Stephen Mosblech, Managing Editor of the *European Journal of Psychoanalysis*, for the republications of Adam Schechter's article *The Join and Distinction-Union: A Resonant and Complex Oneness*.

Dr. Klaus Ottmann, Editor and Publisher, Spring Publications, for the republication of Stephen Bloch's *Music as Dreaming*.

Ms. Melanie W. Cohen for the exquisite cover art for both volumes. Your felt sense is greatly valued.

To all the writers who contributed to the volumes, your love of Eigen, unique creativity, and psychic wisdom are valued and appreciated. Reading your work and including it in our vision has been a rare privilege. Thank you.

Concerning the included case material, all efforts have been made to ensure permission from the analysands as well as to disguise the material included. As editors, and on behalf of all the writers included, we humbly and unreservedly acknowledge your contribution as the primal and vital background voices to the current work and the growth of psychoanalytic discourse in general. Although you will never be directly known, we extend our deepest gratitude for your presence.

Dr. Michael Eigen for his unending support and willingness to write the foreword to the volumes.

You remain our inspiration.

From Loray:

Keri Cohen for much support, humor, and creative perspective as we moved through the project over more than a year.

To my background of support: my family, many colleagues, too many to mention, and my analysts over 20 years (Drs. Assie Gildenhuys, A.C.N. Preller, and Janet Oakes). Autochthonous creation, inner freedom, and stepping forth are only possible through others. I remain deeply indebted and appreciative.

To the various analysands who graciously provided me with permission to include their inner work in this volume. Your work serves us all.

From Keri:

Thank you to Loray Daws for his vision and invitation to collaborate with him on these two volumes. His steadfast fortitude, generosity of spirit, and positivity accompanied this project with grace. I am very appreciative.

Thank you to Mike Eigen, who, at the beginning of the pandemic, predicted that there would be much creativity coming out of that world experience. These volumes are a testament to that prediction.

Thank you to my colleagues near and far, from whom I continue to learn and grow, including study, supervision, and dream groups, in which I am fortunate enough to be included. These welcoming spaces sponsor respite and growth.

Thank you to my husband and children. There are no words to describe the meaning and depth added to my life with all of you in it. You make it all possible.

About the Editors and Contributors

Gagandeep Kaur Ahluwalia is a psychodynamic psychotherapist based in New Delhi, India. She has been a student of literature and law in a previous avatar before arriving at psychoanalysis. While brewing and drinking endless cups of tea, Gagan often finds herself exploring the (un)bearableness of being, pondering spaces and their potential for creation and destruction. She is interested in philosophy, psychoanalysis, literature, music, movies, and intersections: roads, life, and feminism. Her areas of interest include the narratives people build about themselves and the stories they use to relate to their lives, gender and subjectivity and the nebulous affects that surround it, transgenerational transmission of trauma, and being and becoming.

Robin Bagai is a clinical psychologist in Portland, Oregon, who has been practicing psychoanalytic psychotherapy for over 35 years. His recent book, *Commentaries on the Work of Michael Eigen: Oblivion and Wisdom, Madness and Music* (Routledge 2023), adds to published work in edited collections: *The Spiritual Psyche in Psychotherapy: Mysticism, Intersubjectivity, and Psychoanalysis*; *Healing, Rebirth, and the Work of Michael Eigen* (Routledge 2021); and the *Jung Journal, Culture & Psyche*, Volume 16, 2022 – Issue 4: *Spiritual Psyche, Living Psyche … a Reverie*. Dr. Bagai has offered local and international seminars on over a dozen of Michael Eigen's books since 2014.

Rachel Berghash was born in Jerusalem. She has published a memoir, *Half the House, My Life In and Out of Jerusalem*, with Sunstone Press. Her poetry and poetry translations have appeared in numerous literary magazines, including *Chicago Review, Finalist in New Millenium Writings, Christianity and Literature, Forward, Psychoanalytic Perspectives, Colorado Review*, and in anthologies including *Living Moments* (Karnac) and *A Poet's Siddur*. In 2009, her poetry was nominated for the Pushcart Prize in poetry. Her book, *Psyche, Soul, and Spirit: Interdisciplinary Essays*, with co-author Katherine Jillson, has been published by WIPF & STOCK Publishers.

Keri S. Cohen is a Board-Certified Diplomate in clinical social work. She is a psychoanalytic psychotherapist in private practice in Lancaster, PA. Her work is with adults, adolescents, and children. She is a graduate of the University of Pennsylvania's School of Social Policy and Practice, and holds a certificate from the William Alanson White Institute's Online Intensive Psychoanalytic Psychotherapy Program. She has presented papers at national and international conferences on Bion, Ferenczi, and Eigen, and is a co-moderator of the international online Studying Eigen group. She teaches a private seminar and has attended Michael Eigen's Tuesday New York seminars for more than 15 years. Cohen is the co-editor of the 2021 Routledge book *Healing, Rebirth, and the Work of Michael Eigen* and has written published papers which include the works of Eigen, Ferenczi, and Bion. Cohen was asked to write the introduction to *Eigen in Seoul Volume Three: Pain and Beauty, Terror and Wonder* (Routledge 2021) and the foreword to Eigen's forthcoming Routledge book *Bits of Psyche: Selected Seminars of Michael Eigen*.

Françoise Davoine obtained an *Agregation* in classics (French literature, Latin, and Greek) in 1966, followed by a doctorate in sociology in 1981, before becoming a psychoanalyst. She worked for 30 years as a psychoanalyst in public psychiatric hospitals in France, as well as an external consultant, and is currently in private practice. With Jean-Max Gaudillière, she has published many volumes, such as *History Beyond Trauma, Wittgenstein's Folly-Mother Folly, Fighting Melancholia, Don Quixote's Teaching—A Word to the Wise, Don Quixote's Return to Fight Perversion*, and most recently *Shandean Analysis: Tristram Shandy, Madness and Trauma*.

Loray Daws is a registered clinical psychologist in South Africa and British Columbia, Canada. He is currently in private practice and serves both as a senior faculty member at the International Masterson Institute and as a board member at the Object Relations Institute in New York. Loray specializes in psychoanalysis and daseinsanalysis, and he is the editor of six books on psychoanalysis and existential analysis.

Jeffrey L. Eaton is a graduate and faculty member of the Northwestern Psychoanalytic Society and Institute, a member of the IPA, and a Board-Certified Psychoanalyst (CIPS). He received the Frances Tustin Memorial Lecture Prize in 2006 and has been the Beta Rank Memorial Lecturer at the Boston Psychoanalytic Society, the Margaret Jarvie Memorial Lecturer at the University of Edinburgh, a presenter at The Tavistock, London, and the 2017 International Guest Lecturer for the Australian Psychoanalytic Society. He has also been a frequent guest speaker at the International Frances Tustin Trust meetings as well as at International Bion meetings. For over a decade, he was a Senior Consulting Child Psychotherapist for the Gunawirra Foundation in Sydney, Australia, a project providing intervention for at-risk Aboriginal mothers, children, and infants. He was also the founder of The Alliance Community Psychotherapy Clinic, a project of The Northwest Alliance for Psychoanalytic Study. For over a decade, he

participated in INSPIRA, the International Seminar on Psychoanalytic Intervention and Research into Autism, and is currently on the board of the Frances
Tustin Trust, now based in Israel. He is the author of *A Fruitful Harvest: Essays
after Bion* and several chapters in edited collections. Information about his writing and practice can be found at www.jleaton.com. He provides consultation to
psychotherapists and psychoanalysts around the world, and is in private practice
in Seattle, WA.

Marlene Goldsmith is a clinical psychologist in private practice as well as a poet
whose work has appeared both in the USA and abroad. She is a published writer,
researcher, and lecturer in the area of women and creativity. Her writings and
presentations have focused on the artists Frida Khalo, Georgia O'Keefe, and
Martha Graham; the psychoanalyst Sabina Spielrein; and the film *Black Swan*.

Mila Kirstie C. Kulsa is currently a 5th-year PhD student in Clinical Psychology at the Gordon F. Derner School of Psychology, Adelphi University. Under
the tutelage of her faculty mentor, Michael O'Loughlin, Mila Kirstie recognizes the complexity of psychiatric care and a call for research to amplify the
voices and subjectivity of psychiatric sufferers. She aims to address this need
by receiving and working with individuals through the lens of psychotherapy
as an affirming, collaborative, and emancipatory practice. Mila Kirstie recently
published a peer-reviewed journal article discussing her dissertation research
methodology in the *International Journal of Qualitative Methods* (https://doi.
org/10.1177/16094069221143863), a peer-reviewed book review in *Psychoanalysis, Culture & Society* (https://rdcu.be/cRhvu), and an essay review with
Michael O'Loughlin in *JASPER* (Volume 5, Issue 1, pp. 91–109).

Michael O'Loughlin is a Professor in the College of Education and Health Sci-
ences and in the Ph.D. program in Clinical Psychology at Adelphi University,
New York. He has authored or edited many books, including, most recently,
Lives Interrupted: Psychiatric Narratives of Struggle and Resilience (2019)
and *Precarities of 21st Century Childhoods: Critical Explorations of Time(s),
Place(s), and Identities* (2023). Since 2018, he has been co-editor of the journal
Psychoanalysis, Culture and Society. He is also editor of the book series *Psychoanalytic Interventions: Clinical Social, and Cultural Contexts* and co-editor
of the book series *Critical Childhood & Youth Studies: Theoretical Explorations and Practices in Clinical, Educational, Social, and Cultural Contexts*. He
founded the Adelphi Asylum Project to train doctoral students in asylum evalu-
ation. He has a private practice for psychotherapy and psychoanalysis in Long
Island, NY.

Brent Potter, brings 30 years of direct clinical, managerial, and executive administration experience to his current behavioral health work. He is the author of the
existential psychoanalytic Amazon bestseller, *Elements of Self-Destruction*. He
went on to publish another Amazon-bestselling follow-up, *Elements of Reparation: Truth, Faith, & Transformation in the Works of Heidegger, Bion, & Beyond.*

Brent also published, with co-author Jacqueline Simon-Gunn, PhD, *Borderline Personality Disorder: New Perspectives on an Overused & Stigmatizing Diagnosis*. Dr. Potter's upcoming books, *Elements of Faith* and *The Myth of Sobriety*, are already garnering attention in the community. Brent has seats on numerous scholarly editorial boards and has published more than 100 professional articles, chapters, and reviews. Brent holds numerous degrees, including a BA in Psychology (Western Washington University) and an MA in Psychology (Duquesne University), a PhD in Clinical Psychology (Pacifica Graduate Institute), and a PhD in Psychoanalysis (Bircham University). He is a graduate of the Institute of Contemporary Psychoanalysis (ICP). The ICP awarded him his third clinical doctorate, a PsyD in Psychoanalysis, and a certification to practice as a psychoanalyst. He lives with his beloved wife, Gene Rose, and their adorable five-year-old daughter, Sumner. The Potter family grew by one, a year ago, with the birth of Sean. They live in the Philippines as well as in the great state of South Carolina.

Richard Raubolt is a licensed psychologist and certified psychoanalyst. He has published two books on trauma: *Power Games* and *Theaters of Trauma (Special Edition),* and one training manual, *Opening Hearts Opening Minds Therapeutic Group Consultation* (with Kirk Brink, PhD). Dr. Raubolt has produced five films exploring divisive social issues and ensuing traumas, for which he has been rewarded with four Gradiva Finalist nominations. He has also been granted membership in the Portuguese Association for Psychoanalysis and Psychoanalytic Psychotherapy in recognition of his work. Dr. Raubolt resides and practices in Grand Rapids, MI.

Louis Rothschild is a clinical psychologist in Baltimore County, MD. His publications have ranged from quantitative to qualitative, social-cognitive to psychoanalysis, and clinical to philosophical. Most recently, he completed his first book, *Rapprochement between Fathers and Sons: Breakdowns, Reunions, Potentialities,* with Phoenix Publishing House/Karnac. Additionally, he co-edited *Precarities of 21st Century Childhoods: Critical Explorations of Time(s), Place(s), and Identities* and also penned the epilogue for the book *Truth: Developmental, Cultural, and Clinical Realms.* Outside of his professional life, Louis has a fondness for tennis, triathlon, and chasing a rather elusive sourdough starter in the kitchen.

David Smith is a Belfast-based psychoanalytic psychotherapist with a background in therapeutic communities. With a particular interest in the creative use of culture to inform psychoanalytic thinking and clinical practice, his published writings include essays on Michael Eigen, Marion Milner, sea swimming, and Northern Ireland, in addition to writing credits for two short psychoanalytic films, *The Clearing* (2019) and *The Blind Sea* (2023). David has made clinical presentations in Belfast, Dublin, London, and New York City. He is Chair of the Northern Ireland Institute of Human Relations and former Chair of the Psychoanalytic Section of the Irish Council for Psychotherapy.

Stefanie Teitelbaum is a graduate of NPAP. She is a member, supervisor, training analyst, and faculty member of NPAP, IEA, and ORI. She serves on the Psychoanalytic Review advisory board. She has maintained a private psychoanalytic and psychoanalytic psychotherapy practice in New York City for 30 years. She was a staff psychotherapist at the Lower Eastside Service Drug-Free Out Patient Program. Her psychoanalytic papers are published in *The Psychoanalytic Review*, *Psychoanalytic Inquiry*, *The American Journal of Psychoanalysis*, and *Otherwise* – The online journal of IFPE.

Meg Harris Williams is a writer and lecturer on literature and psychoanalysis, as well a visual artist. She teaches internationally and is a visiting lecturer at the Tavistock Clinic and for AGIP, an honorary member of the Psychoanalytic Center of California, and editor of The Harris Meltzer Trust. Her books and papers have been translated into many languages and include: *The Apprehension of Beauty* (with Donald Meltzer; 1988), *The Vale of Soulmaking* (2005), *The Aesthetic Development* (2010), *Bion's Dream* (2010), *The Art of Personality in Literature and Psychoanalysis* (2017), and *Dream Sequences in Shakespeare* (2021).

Introduction to *Toxic Nourishment and Damaged Bonds in the Work of Michael Eigen*

Working with the Obstructive Object

Keri S. Cohen and Loray Daws

Introduction

Michael Eigen and his psychoanalytic work have been on the cutting edge of psychoanalysis for the last 60 years. With writers such as Henry Elkin, Wilfred Bion, Andrè Greene, and D.W. Winnicott, to name but a few transformational psychoanalytic figures, Eigen's psychoanalysis believes in holding an incubating space and time for the deadened psyche to begin to come back to life (1986, 1993, 1996, 2004). Opening this volume with Rachel Berghash's riveting poem introduces the range of feelings and imagery provoked throughout this current volume of work. Her work, similar to that of Eigen, is timeless with raw, searing beauty.

As articulated in the compendium volume *Primary Process Impacts and Dreaming the Undreamable Object in the Work of Michael Eigen: Becoming the Welcoming Object* (Daws & Cohen, 2024), Eigen's primary process of holding mimics the idealized, wherein the m'other' welcomes, takes in, and modulates raw feeling states that are too much for the infant, in time feeding them back to the infant in a digestible form. One can certainly call this empathy, or in Bion's terms, the conversion of Beta elements to Alpha elements, in effect, also taking "the edge off destructive feelings" (Eigen, 2011, p. 45).

In *Toxic Nourishment and Damaged Bonds—Working with the Obstructive Object*, another process of holding emerges. For Eigen,

> Bion asks what happens if this projection is *refused* and the full brunt of destructive fears are *sent back in raw form to the baby*, perhaps *compounded* with the mother's fears and aggression. To throw back the other's feelings may be an index of incapacity. Perhaps the mother cannot take it or doesn't know what to do with it, compounded by her own basic problems of destructive urges. The baby, then, is stuck with his annihilation anxieties un-assuaged. (Eigen, 2011, p. 45, italics added)

More specifically, "Picture a world in which projections have nowhere to go...or worse, met with emotional violence...How can capacity to work with destructive states grow without support? Bombs go off inside, and you freeze around them" (Eigen, 2011, p. 46).

In these ways, among others, the psyche becomes deadened, walled off, and isolated. One becomes subject to an internalized, *destructive object*. In the realms of psychic pain, indigestion, collapse, and despair, Eigen's psychoanalysis breathes new life into that which deadens, a space where psychic oxygen can flow between analysand and analyst. One could even view Eigen's work as a deep dive into holding and understanding the ego-destructive inner life of psychically deadened patients, aiding a recovery into life, or some semblance of life. Eigen intuitively understands these profoundly painful areas of the mind, and his tireless work with his patients eases the pain of the internal *obstructive object* (Eigen, 1992, 1998, 1999, 2001a, 2001b, 2005, 2006a, 2006b, 2007). In addition, he aids in the emotional transcendence from an Obstructive Object to a Welcoming Object. This volume seeks to elaborate on the *Obstructive Object* through essays and poems that include poignant clinical examples, the impact of exceptionally traumatized patients on their analyst, literature comparisons, and the more "mystical aspect" of Eigen's influence on working with the obstructive object. Essays draw from Virginia Woolf, Elena Ferrante, Bion, Winnicott, Greene, Bollas, and Adam Phillips, among many others, in exploring injury-rage, unwanted patients, psychoanalytic faith, toxic nourishment, and damaged bonds.

As may be known to many psychoanalytic readers, Wilfred Bion introduced the concept of The Obstructive Object to the analytic field, and in 2005, Jeffrey L. Eaton published an exceptional paper making Bion's idea of the obstructive object more accessible to the field in general and how he found the concept applicable in his reading of the work of Michael Eigen. Eaton (Chapter 1) writes about the obstructive object as "how another can be experienced as a projective identification rejecting object and how this breakdown in communication can be internalized as an ego destructive internal object" (Eaton, 2005, p. 355). Eaton offers that an analyst needs to "become a *projective identification welcoming object* that the patient can use interpersonally and ultimately identify with" (Eaton, 2005, p. 355). In this volume, Eaton's paper is republished as one effort to help the reader mentalize one of the many ways Bion influenced Eigen's life work. The concept is also furnished by Eaton's impactful writings on Buddhism, storytelling, myth, and rich clinical examples, taking the field further into examining the obstructive object. As mentioned, Eaton's chapter describes Bion's formulation as the product of intensive psychoanalytic treatment of psychotic and borderline patients, needing *a projective identification welcoming object*. In addition, Eaton creatively addresses the challenges encountered in the transference while serving as a welcoming other. Eaton's paper sets the stage for further development, opening the possibility of the analyst becoming a welcoming *inner object*, a notion central to Eigen's work through various volumes (Eigen, 2011, 2013, 2018, 2020). Similar to Bion and Eigen, Eaton's Bion-Eigen dialectic gives hope to a deadened inner psychic world.

Meg Harris Williams' (Chapter 2) paper is a beautiful rendition and review of Virginia Woolf's analysis, drawing on passages in her diaries, essays, and autobiographical writings. Harris Williams brings out the similarity between Wolf's own turbulence and Bion's (1970) idea of psychic turbulence and catastrophic change. This idea folds into the works and teachings of Michael Eigen with emphasis on the hidden, yet continuous traumas of everyday life, including the search for mitigation and transformation, but not necessarily a cure or expurgation. Harris Williams weaves together Bion, Woolf, and Eigen, emphasizing that psychic pain is not dismissed but suffered in a Bionian sense of how curiosity, or the K-link, is fueled by contrary emotions in the search for the thing-in-itself. Specifically, the core conflict of love and hate gives developmental shape to existence if it can be tolerated and brought forth. Harris Williams also reminds, as evident in Bion-Eigen and Woolf, that experiencing the core conflicts of love and hate involves more pain, not less.

Meg Harris Williams' chapter is followed by Michael O'Loughlin and Mila Kirste C. Kulsa's (Chapter 3) etiological exploration concerning ruptures and failures that underlie the Obstructive Object. Their chapter provides explanations and examples of how an infant becomes deadened, breaking from the symbiotic maternal relationship. They note, "Ruptures and failures involving unmitigated transferences of toxicity into a child directly relate to early and long-lasting difficulties in the child's construction of subjectivity and, subsequently, their capacity to sufficiently be in the external world" (in this volume). They draw on the work of Winnicott, Greene, Laplanche, Aulagnier, Mannoni, Lacan, and others to explain the infant's and child's withdrawal from the environment. Throughout their essay, case material from Eigen's Toxic Nourishment volume (1999) is added to "illustrate how *prescient* Eigen's writings on this topic are to… understanding… what gets subjectivity off to a good start, and how early occlusions can limit a patient's aliveness and thereby impair their capacity to live life fully" (in this volume).

Louis Rothschild's thought-provoking chapter (Chapter 4) seeks to work with Eigen's psychoanalytic observation that both ruptured and wounded unions have driven our archetypal myths. By this, Rothschild means that the idea that humanity has moved away from present-day violence in exchange for a linear movement from child and animal sacrifice to prayer is turning a blind eye to the realities of our day. He seeks to expand the notion of the Obstructive Object into society at large and encourages us to examine the societal myths proffered in an effort to disavow the reality of societal rupture (2006c). Rothschild uses Genesis 22, the binding of Isaac (Akedah in Hebrew), to articulate that the story is more than one that moves from aggression to compassion, but one that leaves an indigestible chronic wound. This represents not only the wound between parent and child, but also all of humanity. The author draws from Davoine, Derrida, Bion, Ferenczi, Freud, Laplanche, and many others. Rothschild highlights Eigen's work in that the violent reality of our human nature cannot be disavowed. Further, he notes, "through focus on what is damaged and indigestible or symptomatic in the Akedah exists a motivational emphasis toward avowal that labors to break the polarized representations and introjects of the Imaginary" (in this volume).

Marlene Goldsmith (Chapter 5) carries forward part of Rothschild's objective societal message in her chapter, exploring psychological breakdown and deadness to the point of "psychological paralysis" (page 1 of her paper). Goldsmith does this through two female characters in Elena Ferrante's Neapolitan novels. She highlights, among many other things, how the obstructive object is interfused within the sociocultural matrix and therefore also passed down throughout generations. Goldsmith relies on Eigen's *Toxic Nourishment* (1999) and *Damaged Bonds* (2001) work to provide the reader with a comprehensive understanding of the suffering of the characters in the novels, conflicts with obstructive objects, as well as related difficulties with projective identification and toxic nourishment. Further, Goldsmith's descriptive, insightful writing calls forth deep soul pain that can be felt throughout one's body as her work is read and digested. She calls on the reader to look deeply at how the obstructive object comes into play in nuclear and societal personal relationships.

In *Undreamable Dreams*, Françoise Davoine (Chapter 6) writes convincingly about proto-mental experiences rarely discussed in psychoanalytic circles. The experiences (if not patients) described by Davoine and her co-author of many books, Jean-Max Gaudillière, are usually deemed unanalyzable due to either a lack of transference or the presence of a narcissistic transference. Davoine, relying on her own unconscious and verbal slip as psychoanalytic instrument, reconstructs the reality and presence of "undreamable dreams," catastrophic dreams based on the Real in search of a "thinker" to dream the dream (Davoine's 'an embryo's dream'). A stunning exploration of the impact of "time-quacks" in search of an image/imaginal thinking/representation- Eigen's primary process processing in vivo, reminiscent of James Grotstein's *Orphans of the Real.* For Davoine, the non-repressed unconscious cannot be constituted by the signifiers of the symbolic chain, that is, Freud's secondary process, since the latter collapsed. Despite the collapse, proto-mental trauma may survive through images of words recorded by our senses – defined by Aby Warburg as "surviving images, *nachleben,*" surviving disasters, also evident in Robin Bagai's writing. That is, Robin Bagai (Chapter 7) offers the reader a striking poem to convey the deleterious effects and aspects of the Obstructive Object. His work in this volume seeks to actualize the intensity of feelings and images artfully in a condensed medium – a poem. In this poem, he uses two epigraphs and brief quotes to flesh out the context in true Eigenesque fashion, enlivening our senses by cultivating surviving images.

A theme throughout Eigen's work is his affinity for working with unwanted or demanding patients (Eigen, 1986, 1993). Several essays in this volume address multiple factors associated with this work. Often, these patients evoke such countertransference reactions that therapists and analysts struggle to survive the journey and the work necessary for some healing process to take root. Eigen models a holding process over time by supporting patients to transform their internalized obstructive objects. Time takes on a new meaning through this lens (Cohen, in Fuchsman & Cohen, 2021). Working with severely traumatized, neglected, and damaged patients may take decades. The following chapters in this volume speak painfully and clearly about working with these complicated patients.

Stefanie Teitelbaum's (Chapter 8) creative and beautiful chapter, 'Dreaming a Long Day with Michael Eigen,' draws from Eugene O'Neill's work and life, her own life, along with Eigen's unique thoughts on damaged bonds, damaged dreamwork, and the effort to dream the undreamable object. The painful reality that O'Neill himself was a *replacement child* is woven into the fabric of her exploration of both the simultaneous feelings of being wanted and unwanted in the complexity of our relationships. Teitelbaum relies on O'Neill's work to illustrate both the alternate and concurrent welcoming and obstructive elements as demonstrated in Michael Eigen's work, highlighted especially in his books *Toxic Nourishment* (Eigen, 1999) and *Damaged Bonds* (Eigen, 2001). Using these works, combined with the work of Bion ("no-thing"), Ferenczi, Freud, and Meltzer, Teitelbaum stunningly conveys how *intrapsychic life may become obstructed*. Despite the latter, such a journey may also serve as the search for transcending an inner life subject to obstructive forces.

David Smith's (Chapter 9) essay takes up a similar theme as Teitelbaum as he writes reflectively on Eigen's 1977 paper, *On Working with Unwanted Patients* (in Eigen, 1993). Smith draws theoretically from Eigen, Bollas, Thomas Ogden, and Adam Phillips. He discusses Eigen's interest in the use of the therapist's negative states, such as revulsion, irritation, and deadness. Smith eloquently illustrates this through a very rich, moving, and challenging clinical encounter from his practice. He emphasizes the importance of the therapist's ability to adapt to the patient. Through his clinical example, Smith also draws on Eigen's use of psychoanalytic faith, which sponsors the potential to foster mutual aliveness and growth.

Richard Raubolt's chapter (Chapter 10) illustrates Smith's view by clinically describing deeply painful and personal accounts of his psychoanalytic experience treating an injury-rage analysands. The chapter teaches even the most experienced among us how to survive, surrender, and sustain life in the therapeutic dyad while recognizing the saddening reality that often the patient-analyst journeys may fail. Eigen's writings on *Rage* (2002) serve as one of the many backdrops for Raubolt's chapter. Throughout the clinical examples, Raubolt compassionately attempts to contain his analysands' feelings of abandonment, prevent toxic mutual destruction, and remind us all that the analyst may feel forced to discontinue the treatment in order to preserve whatever "good" may be able to be salvaged. The reader will come to critically contemplate the cost of the Obstructive Object to both the analyst and analysand. In Raubolt's case, his very being was at stake. How much of the transference of the projective toxicity can the analyst hold? Raubolt's journey is a teachable moment that could be taught in graduate schools and institutes.

Fortunately, many clinical encounters with the Obstructive Object are not wrought with such harrowing impacts as described by Raubolt. However, the ego-destructive object remains alive and well in many patients to a greater or lesser extent, as it does for much of humanity and society writ large. Bion wrote on attacks on linking, which Eigen incorporates throughout his work, both an inner and outer attack on a link or links between self and people in relationships.

Keri Cohen's chapter (Chapter 11), *Transcendent Intuition: Linking Fragments to Psychic Attunement across Time and Space*, clinically explores a middle-aged analysand's painful, despondent feelings of growing up feeling unwanted, unvalued, and invisible. The loss of his marriage finds him facing greater isolation and injured trust in others. Andrè Greene, Arnoldo Chuster, Eigen, and Eaton's work provide theoretical moorings to support the analysand's coming-into-life after being subject to non-vitalizing inner and outer relationships. Given such obstructive developmental experiences, fragmented feelings and dissociated experiences add various challenges to forming a positive link between the analyst and patient. Through Cohen's descriptions, one learns to hold both the feeling of trauma and intuition as a guide toward *linking* the plethora of concurrent, emergent, affective feelings in the background. In time, within a holding environment, the analysand may begin to build a capacity to add links to experience, a mental space where the analysand gains freedom from the tyranny of the trauma, the environment, and the self. The analysand's psychological transformation enables an internal link, opening capacities for more profound intrapsychic healing work.

Part of the healing work for Eigen (2020) is his deep love for soulful prayer. Eigen has often been called a psychoanalytic mystic whose *life feeling* is deeply spiritual (2001, 2012, 2014a, 2014b, 2014c). Brent Potter's chapter (Chapter 12) explores, as a backdrop, the tenets of Christianity as he involves the reader in a deeply spiritually transformative psychoanalytically informed treatment with an analysand called Sarah. According to Potter, his analysand introjected a bad attacking object from childhood that she conflated with her son's sexuality. Potter's work weaves the reader through the pain of Sarah's internal obstructive object through dreamwork, faith versus no faith, and a feeling of brokenness that emanates throughout her sense of self. Fragments of her childhood could finally be integrated with what the Christian faith had taught her about homosexuality, being accepted in society, and what should and should not be tolerated. Through her analysis, Sarah developed the capacity to find an adaptive way to dialogue within herself about what it means to love, respect, and accept her son, whose life was not congruent with her Christian societal teachings. More profoundly, the analysis also facilitated her growing capacity to accept the unacceptable within her own history and self-feel in a transformative way.

Gagan Ahluwalia's (Chapter 13) essay brings palpable feelings to the reader concerning loss and grief, as it was written shortly after the COVID-19 pandemic. Ahluwalia reflects on the effects of virtual psychotherapy during COVID-19 as she simultaneously wrestled with self-disclosure to her patients concerning her own family dying from COVID-19. Ahluwalia uses both Bion's concept of the obstructive object and Eigen's welcoming approach as lenses to view grief and mourning, personally and collectively. Clinical vignettes from sessions and supervision bring together her transference and countertransference in an unprecedented manner as the world was coping with the pandemic – the Obstructive Object as found in outer *and* inner reality. Supervision was provided to Ahluwalia by Shalini Masih, whose contribution to these volumes can be found in the Welcoming Object book of this series.

Finally, closing the book with another poem by Rachel Berghash seems fitting. It carries forward some of Ahluwalia's themes of death and dying, albeit differently. Whereas the pandemic (similar to the obstructive object) was spread biologically, Berghash's poem, in contrast, speaks of purposeful death and dying that spread throughout human nature in its most vile form. Throughout his writings, Eigen never shies away from the infinite obstructive forces in/of our nature, confronting the beatific along with the incomprehensible of our psychic life without pause. Berghash does the same through her artistic voice, a poetic treasure for all.

It is evident from the various writings that our psychic work is never done, but perhaps through these authors, we may grow more self-aware of our influence on ourselves interpersonally, intrapersonally, and collectively; what we do to ourselves, we do to others. There are no boundaries to the destruction we unleash and the compassion and love we give. Neither Eigen nor his work offers to cure any of us; instead, he and his work provide a salvific place to explore when we are wounded, hurting, and in need (1986, 1993, 1995, 1999, 2001a, 2004, 2005). Eigen and his work also offer hope, faith, and the prospect of a better existence if only we can hold on to the unimaginable (2009, 2010, 2011, 2012, 2013, 2014a, 2014b, 2014c, 2016, 2018, 2020, 2021).

References

Daws, L., & Cohen, K. (2024a). *Primary Process Impacts and Dreaming the Undreamable Object in the Work of Michael: Becoming the Welcoming Object.* Routledge.

Eaton, L.J. (2005). The Obstructive Object. *Psychoanalytic Review*, 92 (3): 355–372.

Eigen, M. (1986). *The Psychotic Core*. Northvale, NJ: Jason Aronson, Inc.

Eigen, M. (1992). *Coming Through the Whirlwind*. Wilmette, IL: Chiron Publications.

Eigen, M. (1993). *The Electrified Tightrope* (A. Phillips, Ed.). Northvale, NJ: Jason Aronson, Inc.

Eigen, M. (1995). *Reshaping the Self: Reflections on Renewal in Psychotherapy.* Madison, CT: Psychosocial Press.

Eigen, M. (1996). *Psychic Deadness*. London: Karnac.

Eigen, M. (1998). *The Psychoanalytic Mystic*. London: Free Association Books.

Eigen, M. (1999). *Toxic Nourishment*. London: Karnac.

Eigen, M. (2001a). *Damaged Bonds*. London: Karnac.

Eigen, M. (2001b). *Ecstasy*. Middletown, CT: Wesleyan University Press.

Eigen, M. (2002). *Rage*. Middletown, CT: Wesleyan University Press.

Eigen, M. (2004). *The Sensitive Self*. Middletown, CT: Wesleyan University Press.

Eigen, M. (2005). *Emotional Storm*. Middletown, CT: Wesleyan University Press.

Eigen, M. (2006a). *Lust*. Middletown, CT: Wesleyan University Press.

Eigen, M. (2006b). The Annihilated Self. *Psychoanalytic Review*, 93: 25–38.

Eigen, M. (2006c). *Age of Psychopathy*. (http://www.psychoanalysis-and-therapy.com/human_nature/eigen/pref.html).

Eigen, M. (2007). *Feeling Matters*. London: Karnac Books.

Eigen, M. (2009). *Flames from the Unconscious*. London: Karnac Books.

Eigen, M. (2010). *Eigen in Seoul: Madness and Murder* (Vol. 1). London: Karnac Books.

Eigen, M. (2011). *Eigen in Seoul: Faith and Transformation* (Vol. 2). London: Karnac Books.

Eigen, M. (2012). *Kabbalah and Psychoanalysis*. London: Karnac Books.

Eigen, M. (2013). *Contact with the Depths*. London: Karnac Books.

Eigen, M. (2014a). *The Birth of Experience*. London: Karnac Books.

Eigen, M. (2014b). *Faith*. London: Karnac Books.

Eigen, M. (2014c). *A Felt Sense: More Explorations of Psychoanalysis and Kabbalah*. London: Karnac Books.

Eigen, M. (2016). *Image, Sense, Infinities, and Everyday Life*. London: Karnac Books.

Eigen, M. (2018). *The Challenge of Being Human*. Abington: Routledge.

Eigen, M. (2020). *Dialogues with Michael Eigen* (L. Daws, Ed.). London and New York, NY: Routledge.

Eigen, M. (2021). *Eigen in Seoul Volume Three: Pain and Beauty, Terror and Wonder*. London: Routledge.

Fuchsman, K., & Cohen, K.S. (2021). *Healing, Rebirth, and the Work of Michael Eigen*. Collected essays on a pioneer in Psychoanalysis. Routledge.

Foreword

Michael Eigen

The tendencies and states explored in these two volumes have a history going back to the beginnings of human beings' attempts to make contact with, communicate, and express themselves. Many vocabularies have been developed to deal with what it feels like to be a human being, and this current work's concern with obstructive and welcoming tendencies is a welcome addition, to use one of our vocabulary partners or siblings. I'm tempted to write obstructive-welcoming with a hyphen, the two are so much part of our makeup, and we will see in these chapters many angles, mixes, dissociations, and communions between them. The writings here open possibilities of human experience, relationships to ourselves, quandaries, and wonders.

To be welcoming, to be obstructive, to be welcomed, or obstructed – how many ways can you think of that you personally have felt these throughout a day? If you kept a diary, even for a short time, about feelings of welcome-obstruction, you would be touched by the realization of the ways and myriad moments they enter our psychosocial tapestry. If you make it even more personal and reflect on ways you welcome and/or obstruct yourself throughout the day and even moment-to-moment, awe as well as chagrin about our beings may grow.

I think of a car having an accelerator and brake – both needed for safety and speed. I learned very early that cars may be modeled on the human body in significant ways. And when I think of animals speeding up-slowing down depending on hunger and safety needs, a sense of having so much in common with all life spreads. One of the beautiful things about grammar school was learning about the needs of plants as well as people. Life everywhere – what will or can happen?

Obstruction is often associated with trauma, but it can also play a positive role making room for waiting, detour, and alternatives. One of the fun subjects in the first psychology class I took some 65 years ago was learning how an infant can grow by going around a blockage rather than going through it, especially when the latter was impossible. I once wrote (Eigen, 2018) about protecting our home from destructive squirrel invasion, and one time a squirrel caught in a cage kept banging its head against the bars until it perished. All other squirrels in that situation explored and waited and were left free in faraway parks. What different ways can we react to blockages, and what diverse functions can they have? Both welcoming-obstructive can have positive-negative consequences. There is even a long history of humanity welcoming and promoting destructive behavior. Positive-negative varies so many ways.

Freud linked death anxiety with birth anxiety. You can imagine and dramatize this in many ways. Will I survive being born? Going through a tight tunnel – does suffocation fear begin even before breathing? Winnicott felt when trauma hits as the self begins to form we can be left with fear of beginnings all lifelong. A lifelong fear of the self's existence. He places much emphasis on how the caretaking other responds to the baby's survival dreads. Can we be? How? With what quality?

Loray Daws and Keri Cohen have done a great service focusing on qualities of welcome and obstruction in growth. My work is used as an occasion to assemble significant explorations of these tendencies that are part of our basic makeup. The authors do much more than explore aspects of my work but use the former to stimulate, add, and open their own. It is a welcome compliment that one's own voice can help catalyze the creative voices of others.

Bion wrote of an "obstructive object," and Jeffrey L. Eaton contributed a growing dialogue with a "welcoming object" as well. Dualities have been with us ever since human beings tried to give expression to their multiple tendencies, an expressive momentum that, to my mind, has helped stimulate the evolution of experience in many keys and dimensions. I am more than hopeful that these two books touch obstructive-welcoming aspects of our psyche and humanity in ways that enable many readers to find more of their own voice and being as well. We are engaged in processes that can add to our appreciation of who we are and can be as we grow in learning how to support our lives and life itself.

Morning Blues

Rachel Berghash

"O night, my guide!
O night more friendly than the dawn!"
St. John of the Cross
my every moment is a moment of death
that partners with "all that is here"
my every moment is a moment of life
rising to join a luscious memory
my days pulse to a sad heartbeat
bonds are afflicted with sorrow
while nights are calm
dreams gleam with light
and soft leaves linger
at the periphery of my mind
                    Rachel Berghash 2022

Chapter 1

The Obstructive Object

Jeffrey L. Eaton

Introduction

In this essay, I explore the concept of an internal object that perpetuates an atmosphere of intense mental pain, violence, and self-attack. Chronic self-attack, including attacks on linking, blocks the growth of a sense of personal agency that would ordinarily allow a person to receive help and to cooperate in her own analytic transformation. According to W. R. Bion, some patients give evidence of living with an internal object that is ego-destructive and operates as *a projective identification-rejecting object*. Bion names this ego-destructive internal object an *obstructive object*.

In the following sections, I will describe some implications of Bion's obstructive object idea. First, I will explore the central theme of learning in Bion's psychology, giving special attention to the role of projective identification as a form of communication in early life. Next, I review Bion's ideas about the phenomenon of an obstructive object. I then offer a sketch of *an obstructive object scenario* as I am currently able to formulate it, offering a brief description of a case. Finally, I suggest that progress in working with the obstructive object scenario involves the analyst's capacity to become *a projective identification welcoming object* that the patient can use interpersonally and ultimately identify with.

The Scope of Bion's Work: The Importance of Learning from Experience

Bion's writing can be profitably read as the evolution of twin psychologies: one about the conditions that sponsor learning and emotional development, and another about the myriad obstructive forces and conditions, both internal and environmental, that lead to psychological stalemate, breakdown, or malignant transformation. A tension between learning (in the widest sense, *the evolution of the mind*) and obstruction to learning expands from Bion's early group work all the way through his final papers.

The roots of Bion's interest in learning are no doubt to be found in his own autobiography. Such a study is beyond the scope of this essay. However, even as a

DOI: 10.4324/9781003322986-1

little boy, Bion was a keen observer and a curious child. In his autobiography, *The Long Weekend* (1985), he gives us many moving vignettes about his curiosity, his sensitivity to his own emotional states as well as to those of others, his confusions over language, and his openness to impressions of all sorts.

Bion's war experience, which began when he was a teenager, provides a critical context for understanding the meaning that learning from experience came to have for him over the remainder of his deeply reflective life. He realized that groups (Bion, 1961) can become anti-learning assemblages, and that failing to learn – indeed, failing to think – can be a matter of life and death. The anti-learning forces observable in groups can also be inferred from the individual personality. What I want to emphasize is that for Bion, the theme of learning is not an academic one. Learning is about emotional experience. It can be detected in the movement from survival to creativity, from gathered information to personal realization, and from evacuative reaction to action mediated by reflective thought. Learning involves, in Bion's terms, the individual's relationship to the very fabric of life itself, attention (or its absence) to the emotional texture of truthful experience from which wisdom or folly may spring.

Bion explicitly distinguishes "learning from experience" from "learning about." For example, I may learn about psychoanalysis by reading books, seeing films, and listening to others who have been in analysis share their experiences. These experiences allow me to gather information and form impressions about which I may have strong feelings. I may even come to believe I know a great deal about psychoanalysis. However, such learning can, in no way, substitute for *the experience* of participating in psychoanalysis. These two kinds of knowing give rise to a personal "language of achievement" in contradistinction to the "language of substitution." The mind, according to Bion, only grows when nourished by contact with truthfulness. The task of maturation is to grow a greater and deeper capacity to explore experience, to become yet more truthful, to distinguish lies, and to make space to recognize the thoughts that are seeking a thinker. Experience, especially emotional experience, provides the building blocks of the mind.

How does this process of learning from experience take place? Projective identification provides one model of what sponsors healthy emotional development and learning from experience in earliest life. Extending Klein's work, Bion (1962) introduces the idea of normal projective identification as a form of communication between a baby and her mother (p. 37). The infant's facial expressions, vocalizations, crying, and muscular gestures signal his distress. By distress, I mean something familiar: a raw emotional experience at the level of sensation that obtrudes upon the infant's attention or awareness. This obtrusion may be of such intensity that it saturates the infant's experience through states of sensory-dominated arousal. Bion (1962) gives this familiar human experience a very abstract name. He calls such primitive sensory or emotional distress "beta elements" (p. 6). According to Bion, beta elements are suitable only to be projected, or, as he says, evacuated. This word – *evacuated* – speaks to the force and intensity of the process.

What is the fate of evacuated distress? Put more simply, what is the fate of the infant's cry of pain? For distress to be transformed, Bion suggests that it must find a home in the mind of another. Hopefully, a mind can be found to register the infant's pain. Still more importantly, that mind should belong to an individual who is more emotionally mature – someone with more experience of tolerating distress than the infant. If this is so, then pain can be more than registered; it can be recognized, reflected upon, and replied to creatively and compassionately.

Bion asks the question, what does this other mind do for the infant in distress? Something helps the experience of raw emotional distress become an opportunity to evolve in the direction of discovering meaning. Bion calls this something that helps "alpha function." The discovery of meaning depends upon the mother's ability to use her mind, including her attention, intuition, and emotional experience (all factors in her alpha function), to contain her infant's distress (the beta elements) and to transform that distress imaginatively.

In Bion's abstract formulation, beta elements are transformed into alpha elements. Alpha elements are, according to Bion, the building blocks of memory, dreams, and reflective awareness. The capacity to learn from experience (Bion, 1962) depends on a growing ability to transform beta elements into alpha elements. This transformation is sponsored as the infant internalizes and identifies with the mother as a containing object capable of alpha function.

According to Bion, an infant is dependent on the actual separate mind of another in a particular way. The infant's need for food, safety, proximity, and other forms of concrete care may be adequately provided for. Bion highlights another dimension of experience that he feels is an essential factor in the evolution of the infant's mind. An infant also depends on the quality of mother's attention and her capacity for reverie as a factor in alpha function. In short, the infant depends upon the unique qualities of the mother's own internal object world as expressed through the quality of her interactions with her baby. The quality of the mother's emotional presence helps her infant's mind to be born and to grow emotionally.

A mother sponsors the essential experience of transformation from beta to alpha, from distress to comfort, repeatedly. She picks her baby up, rocks her, sings to her, and speaks aloud about what might be troubling her infant. She allows her infant to disengage when overstimulated, and she reengages with her infant when her infant's gestures signal the desire to reconnect. The successful transformation of distress into comfort makes play and exploration possible. In essence, mother uses her own intuition, her unconscious memory of her own care as a child, and her emotional availability in the moment to investigate the experience of her infant and to reply to it.

According to Bion, the capacity to learn from experience is essentially characterized by an ability to tolerate and transform rather than to evade the inevitable turbulence and frustration of uncertain and painful situations. It also involves a *faith* that in states of distress – including even acute distress – one will not become totally trapped in an atmosphere of emotional catastrophe. Instead, this faith, based on the accumulated memories of the mother's repeated capacity to receive and transform distress into comfort, promotes a capacity for personal *reverie*, that is, a reverie for one's own experience as it arises and is lived through. This capacity for personal reverie can be pictured as the self's ability to turn toward and rely upon *internal projective identification welcoming objects* that can bear the turbulence of a new experience and can sponsor openness toward learning and exploration. The capacity for transformation from distress to comfort is the basis for motivated initiative. It requires continued rejuvenation, from both internal and external support, and must be widened, expanded, and continually consolidated as new experiences pressure the mind to grow.

The Obstructive Object and the Failure to Learn from Experience

By observing the phenomenon of the obstructive object, a model can be developed for understanding why learning from experience seems nearly impossible for some people. Bion introduces the term *obstructive object* in his "schizophrenia" papers (1993), particularly in *On Arrogance* and *A Theory of Thinking*. These papers, along with *Attacks on Linking*, form the background for several passages from *Learning from Experience* that describe the consequences not only of a failure of maternal reverie and absent or inadequate alpha function but also such important variables as an excess of envy as well as very low frustration tolerance in the infant. A constellation of factors of this kind can contribute to severe vulnerability in the mother–infant dyad. Such vulnerability may inhibit or obstruct the development of the container–contained relationship over time and make faith in the reliable transformation of distress into comfort impossible to realize.

The roots of the concept of the obstructive object are to be found in Klein's work on splitting and the paranoid-schizoid position. Klein focuses on the development of psychic reality through the mechanisms of introjection and projection. According to Linda Buckingham (2002), Klein theorized that

> Infants with an inherently low tolerance of frustration are likely to have phantasies of a bad, denying breast and will experience sadistic, attacking impulses towards it. This sets in train a negative cycle: fears of retribution, introjection of a bad, damaged breast, feelings of persecution which are projected back into the breast, and so on. Early disjunction between mother and baby can set in even if the mother is doing her best to counteract the baby's anxiety. Another baby, with high tolerance of frustration, may thus fare better under worse external circumstances, although a baby whose mother is not in touch with her needs will suffer. (p. 207)

A close reading of Bion finds him extending Klein's work and carefully addressing the intersection of interpersonal and intrapsychic variables that may give rise to situations that he names *infantile catastrophe* and *nameless dread*. Bion suggests that for some patients, distress is never reliably transformed and that dire consequences follow. In *Attacks on Linking*, Bion (1993) writes:

> Projective identification makes it possible for him to investigate his own feelings in a personality powerful enough to contain them. Denial of the use of this

mechanism, either by the refusal of the mother to serve as a repository for the infant's feelings, or by the hatred and envy of the patient who cannot allow the mother to exercise this function, leads to a destruction of the link between infant and breast and consequently to a severe disorder of the impulse to be curious *on which all learning depends.* The way is therefore prepared for a severe arrest of development. Furthermore, thanks to a denial of the main method open to the infant for dealing with his too powerful emotions, the conduct of emotional life, in any case a severe problem, becomes intolerable. Feelings of hatred are thereupon directed against all emotions including hate itself, and against external reality which stimulates them. It is a short step from hatred of the emotions to hatred of life itself. (p. 107, emphasis added)

Here, Bion is going a step beyond both Freud and Klein. Instead of positioning the individual's main conflict as arising between reality and fantasy, between love and hate, or between the life instincts and the death instinct, Bion describes how some patients are faced with a choice between emotion and anti-emotion. In the absence of maternal reverie or in the presence of excessive envy or frustration, hatred is directed toward emotional experience itself.

A critical feature of the obstructive object relationship is that the person feels overwhelmed by emotional experience. According to the *American Heritage Dictionary* (1981), one meaning of distress is "the condition of being in need of immediate assistance." This definition seems to capture the experience of the infant who feels a desperate urgency for relief when raw emotional experience (beta elements) obtrudes upon awareness. Bion (1977) writes:

If there are only beta-elements, which cannot be made unconscious, there can be no repression, suppression, or learning. This creates the impression that the patient is incapable of discrimination. He cannot be unaware of any single sensory stimulus: yet such hypersensitivity is not contact with reality. (p. 8)

It is at this very moment of distress and vulnerability that a containing object is so desperately needed. What kind of object will be there to greet the infant's distress? The obstructive object, as defined by Bion, is overwhelming in a quite particular way. An obstructive object is a projective identification rejecting object that has been internalized. Bion (1993) writes:

The [infant's] rudimentary consciousness cannot carry the burden placed upon it (by the experience of uncontained distress). The establishment of a projective-identification-rejecting-object means that instead of an understanding object the infant has a wilfully misunderstanding object—with which it is identified. (p. 117)

I want to unpack Bion's condensed language and try to bring closer to home what I think he intends to describe. What does a projective identification-rejecting object look like and feel like? In infant observation or in clinical work with mothers and infants, one can sometimes painfully observe the interpersonal origins of the obstructive object. Imagine, for example, an infant crying in his crib. Mother, for some reason, cannot bear her baby's crying. She does not pick her baby up and try to soothe him. Instead, she leaves the room, perhaps shutting the door to muffle her baby's cries. This is a literal description of a scenario in which the baby's distress is rejected. Bion suggests that this sort of scenario leaves the baby in a state of potentially unmodified distress. Drawing on the experience of infant observation, I can speculate about the sorts of experiences that a baby might have after its projective identification of distress has been rejected. Suppose that one could observe this baby, now left alone in its crib. Perhaps the infant will cry until exhausted and then withdraw into sleep. Perhaps he will adhesively identify with a pattern on the curtain or a shadow on the wall as a way of fixing his attention and subjectively pulling himself together. Perhaps we can imagine him finding his thumb, putting it into his mouth, sucking, and, in this way, gradually calming. Perhaps he will become muscularly tense and rigid, curling his toes, making his fingers into fists, stiffening his neck, arching his back, and finally settling into a different state. Now imagine that this scenario is repeated many times over several weeks or months without variation. A great deal depends, of course, on the complexity of the patterns of communication and rejection that are unfolding, evolving, or reifying between mother and baby over time. Somehow, these patterns are unconsciously represented by both partners in terms of unconscious relational expectations (Beebe and Lachmann, 2002).

It is from patterns of this kind that one can begin to appreciate what an obstructive object-creating scenario looks like and feels like. My contention is that an obstructive object scenario is a more extreme and chronic outcome of the repeated experience of meeting the other as a projective identification rejecting object. I want to be clear that I think the creation of the obstructive object scenario involves vulnerability at both the intrapsychic and interpersonal levels of experience. This scenario takes different forms with varying intensities for different patients. For the sake of brevity, I want to simplify the situation to its essentials. The obstructive object relationship, according to Bion, is "wilfully misunderstanding." I am interested in conveying the feel of this kind of link.

Imagine, now, a mother who cannot stand her infant's crying. She feels, for her own unconscious reasons, that her infant is *doing something to her* by crying out in distress. This mother cannot bear what feels too overwhelming. She screams at her infant to shut up. Maybe she shakes her infant to silence him. In the worst of all scenarios, she suffocates her infant with a pillow. *An obstructive object is experienced as someone or something actively hostile toward emotional experience, creating an atmosphere of escalating pressure and violence.* Though it is beyond the scope of this paper to describe, it is my experience that the obstructive object scenario is created anew again and again over generations.

Another way to picture the obstructive object is by turning to myth. For example, following Bion, the figure of the Sphinx is emblematic of an obstructive object. When we remember the Sphinx, we remember a monster. She is part woman, part lion, and part bird. We also remember her riddle. What is much more important than the content of her riddle, however, is the emotionally violent atmosphere evoked when the Sphinx stops Oedipus from continuing on his journey. There is an atmosphere of intense threat, confusion, and hatred. The Sphinx is not felt to be asking riddles playfully or in the service of learning, but in a bizarre and violent manner, as weapons to attack links and thinking.

Recall the images from the Oedipus myth. The Sphinx blocks the road to Thebes, stopping everyone who wishes to enter. She demands that they answer a riddle to pass. She threatens people by saying that if they answer her wrongly, they will die. The obstructive object sponsors an atmosphere of confusion and terror. The subject is faced with an unconscious choice between omnipotence and helpless collapse. This dire choice is symbolized by the Sphinx's own suicide when Oedipus guesses a plausible answer to the riddle. One is left in an atmosphere of horror.

With these images in mind, one can begin to observe a certain category of phenomena in the consulting room that superficially appear to be motivated by destructive impulses. It is very important to differentiate the consequences of violent projections, which are, indeed, often destructive, from their motivation, which may be very different. The intensity and pervasiveness of some forms of violent projection may be part of an unconsciously frantic search for a helping object that can transform pain and distress. If relief is not adequately found, the violence of the projection intensifies. Such constant and intense projections may then serve multiple simultaneous functions. The projection may serve to get rid of pain through evacuation; it may serve to communicate distress still more emphatically; or it may serve to try to control an object through an invasive fantasy, what Klein originally called excessive projective identification. Or it may serve to destroy the mental apparatus through a process described by Bion as "attacks on links." Since none of these functions can lead to an adequate transformation of distress into comfort, the self is faced with overwhelming emotional experiences that, over time, produce an atmosphere of intense ego-destructive dread.

Bion (1993) gives this description from his own clinical work in his essay, "Attacks on Linking":

Associations from a period in the analysis … showed an increasing intensity of emotions in the patient. This originated in what he felt was my refusal to accept parts of his personality. Consequently he strove to force them into me with increased desperation and violence. His behaviour, isolated from the context of the analysis, might have appeared to be an expression of primary aggression. The more violent his phantasies of projective identification, the more frightened he became of me. There were sessions in which such behaviour expressed unprovoked aggression, but I quote this … because it shows the patient in a different light, his violence a reaction to what he felt was my hostile defensiveness. (p. 104)

The Obstructive Object in the Clinical Encounter

Over the past several years, I have tried to observe what might be called an obstructive object scenario in my clinical work with children and adults. One feature I have noticed is the phenomenon of constant and intense projection, which serves a crucial function in perpetuating the overwhelming aspect of the obstructive object. Often, we think of projective identification arising as a discrete response to an overwhelmingly intense experience. However, in my experience, some patients rely on a kind of pervasive projective identification. Because distress cannot be transformed into comfort, some people act as if their minds have become machines for evacuation. Constant and intense projections blur the already tenuous boundary between self and other. This pervasive projection creates an atmosphere of confusion, hostility, and agitated frustration because intense distress is felt to be always present everywhere.

I have learned much about the obstructive object scenario by working with a patient I'll call Paula. Paula is a middle-aged woman who feels unable to sustain a loving sexual relationship with a man over time, to complete her professional and educational ambitions, or to earn a satisfactory income. She is highly intelligent but blocked in her capacity to learn from experience. She says she has no confidence in herself. Until recently, she had given little thought to her future.

Upon entering analysis, Paula characterized her daily experience as "scattered," "foggy," and "dreamlike." After several years of working together, Paula can observe how she "constantly distracts herself from the moment." She now reports finding some sense of being able to "be clear" and "to think straight." Paula still seems to oscillate between states of hyperarousal (sometimes reaching a level of panic) and hypoarousal (feeling exhausted, depressed, and sometimes overwhelmed with despair). She is still often exhausted by what feels to her like an unrelenting assaulting present from which she cannot escape.

Paula's early sessions were filled with fragmented descriptions of her feelings of deep rage and disturbance about the many atrocities occurring throughout the world. Paula seemed to repeat the same fragmented stories, often in detail, as if she had never seen me before or as if she could not believe I was listening to her or remembering our meetings.

Very quickly, I began to wonder if Paula could listen to me. Things I said seemed to be willfully ignored. Paula felt intensely disturbed by what she said was evidence of the corruption of the Bush administration. She also felt persecuted by the men in charge at her workplace. I understood these complaints at one level as a gathering of the transference, but Paula rejected transference interpretations as formulaic and "psychoanalytic bullshit." Paula insisted on the merit of her concrete concerns, especially of the shared social situation we were both living through.

I often felt intimidated, rejected, angry, and exhausted in the face of Paula's tirades. Her seeming unwillingness to accept my sincere attempts at understanding began to wear me down day after day. Over time, she became worried that I could not see or acknowledge her worries about "the real world." She implied that I was the one who needed analysis and that I was ill because I could not acknowledge reality.

Eventually, I began to recognize that Paula might unconsciously experience every emotional relationship as an obstructive object scenario. I began to discern that I might be enacting a role that seemed to feel to Paula like a projective identification-rejecting object. With self-analysis and supervision, I tried to open my way of thinking about being with Paula in order to be more at-one with her picture of the world. I realized that Paula seemed to believe that I was a willfully misunderstanding object trying to force my illness into her.

With many patients, I often experience a greater or lesser degree of what I regard as reverie. By reverie I mean an openness and freedom to listen to myself while listening to my patient (Grotstein, personal communication, 2003). In any given session, the emotional experience of being with a patient may evoke sensations, images, memories, reflections, or sudden intuitive hunches that can become part of the material that eventually forms an interpretation. The capacity to be in reverie sponsors a kind of inquiry into and spontaneous description of the emotional field arising between patient and analyst in the moment. With Paula, I felt little freedom to speak, much less to dream of the session, or to let my mind relax, wander, or play. Instead, I often felt "on the edge of my seat" (sometimes literally) because of the tension in the room. I expected Paula to explode, and sometimes she did.

The question, I think, that faced me in working with Paula was how to be in two places simultaneously. Paula seemed to regard me as the embodiment of a willfully misunderstanding object, amplifying her distress with my apparently cruel and stupid interpretations. I had to find some way to accept this reality during the transference. At the same time, I began to ask myself how I could become the opposite of an obstructive object, a projective identification welcoming object. How could I do this in a way that would feel real to Paula? How could I find a place in myself where I could tolerate the distress aroused in me by being with her? I had to try to find my way toward my own projective identification, welcoming objects to tolerate, contain, and transform my own significant distress so that a space of reverie might become tenuously possible. I think the key point here is the idea that working through the countertransference involves repeatedly reestablishing and contacting the vitality of one's own projective identification, welcoming objects rather than giving into the temptation to slam the door on the potential of living through and transforming both the analyst's and the patient's distress. Each of us has to find our own ways, through experience, to make this kind of opening up to pain possible. The personal obstacles to allowing this kind of development can be significant.

The Welcoming Object and the Transformation of Pain

How does an infant realize a mother's reverie? I suggest that the mother, in reverie, helps to facilitate a transformation that, in its most primitive form, is subjectively registered by the infant as moving from bodily distress to bodily comfort. In the actual beginning of the infant's life, the transformation from beta elements to alpha elements involves a feeling of somatic relief. Before the infant has the capacity to represent this transformation in organized images, I suggest that the infant experience the *shape* of this transformation in bodily experiences of *calming and relaxation*. The capacity of the infant to become calm after a state of anxious arousal is, I suggest, one of the earliest and most important transformations repeatedly facilitated by a mother in reverie. It may be that this first transformation is already developing in fetal life. Whenever it occurs, I name this transformation, descriptively, a transformation from distress to comfort.

An infant able to receive and use a mother's reverie can gradually experience psychical qualities, whereas an infant for some reason deprived of the benefit of reverie may remain trapped within the intensity and concreteness of distress. A projective identification welcoming object promotes the recognition of psychical experience and the presence of a space for thinking, while a projective identification rejecting object leads to a denial or even hatred of psychic reality. A projective identification welcoming object is the basis for the establishment of the evolving relationship between container and contained that promotes the transformation of distress into comfort.

The mother's capacity for reverie and her ability to lend her alpha function to her infant's state of distress are comforts that strengthen her infant's developing mind through the creation of alpha elements that eventually make the comprehension of meaningful emotional experiences possible. The provision of alpha function brings not only relief but also the possibility of a new experience, a novel and evolving relationship to distress that, over the process of maturation, becomes represented in increasingly sophisticated ways. Also at stake is the fate of attention. The infant trapped in distress dissociates its attention from more and more experience, while an infant capable of the transformation from distress to comfort establishes a curious link to other objects and is free to explore experience.

My challenge was to find a way to make real for Paula the experience of this earliest transformation from distress to comfort in order to help her mind to grow freer to learn from emotional experience. Somehow, as I have said, I had to free my own mind to allow more room for observation, reverie, play, and exploration. So, what did I do? First, I began to slow down, to say less, and try to be at-one with Paula's experience rather than trying to describe something about the transference between us. This seemed to help. Gradually, the atmosphere of the sessions began to change. Paula's complaints came nearer to home and focused on her parents and siblings. Why should this be so? It seems to me that I was literally making space for Paula's distress to exist – in her, within me, and between us. Before it could be transformed, spaces had to be discovered where her distress could be tolerated. During this time, Paula began to describe the way she could feel that her distress was really registered by me and that this felt like a disorienting new experience.

Over time, Paula began to bring more dreams. Some of her dreams were horrific. Her dreams began to picture intensely shaming objects, both male and female. These objects were not only willfully misunderstood but also cruel and annihilating. My sense is that our work allowed the obstructive object to begin to take shape in her dream life so that we could begin to face it together. For reasons of confidentiality, I am not reporting Paula's dreams. However, I will share the dream of another patient because it so beautifully pictures the movement from the domination of the obstructive object to the tentative discovery of a projective identification welcoming object:

> A small figure approaches a larger figure. The small figure carries in her arms a large red-hot burning coal. The coal has burned away the hands and arms of the small figure up to the elbows. The small figure desperately wants to pass the coal to the larger figure but is afraid of injuring the larger figure and of how the larger figure will react.

This dream poignantly illustrates the awakening of a search for a projective identification welcoming object and beautifully portrays the experience of raw emotional distress. The red-hot coal represents emotional intensity that is too searing to bear. A passage from John Lampen (1987), a Quaker essayist, gives imaginative voice to the small figure of this dream. This is the sort of thing I think a patient can begin to put into words when they feel in touch with a projective identification welcoming object:

> I need you to take this great lump of pain which I feel . . . . I want you to look at it, and feel it, and think about it. Perhaps you can blunt some of its edges, soften it a little with your tears, or throw it up in the air and catch it to show me it is not so heavy as I thought. Perhaps you can take a measure and show me its proper size. Perhaps you could just hold it a little, while I get back on my feet again. But then you should give it back to me, because it is my load and my task. You may carry away a little of the poison, but the real task of making it safe can only be done by me. (p. 29)

The discovery of a projective identification welcoming object sponsors the yearning to live, experience, and learn despite intense suffering. Paula has begun to express a tentative but powerful sense of being in love with love. This love is so fragile and so painful that it hurts to acknowledge it. She describes being terrified not only of an objectively dangerous and brutal world outside but, even more to the point, of a loss of the sense of emerging preciousness of experience when the old persecutory relationship within herself reappears. All of Paula's critiques of "the real world" apparently serve as screens to deflect our attention from her terrible anxiety of being someone who hates and fears her own emotional experience while at the same time desperately yearning to be more open to experience.

Paula's sense of humor has been of immense help to us both. She has a kind of gallows humor that gives her space to face the immense pain of her life. She has begun to be interested in spiritual questions and has even started to wonder about the meaning of her life in ways that she had never engaged before. Analysis seems to be helping Paula to begin to symbolize her experience, particularly the presence of the cruel, obstructive object. Recognizing and facing this cruel, obstructive object seems sometimes unbearably intimidating. What has been especially important to us both has been the growing capacity for compassion that seems to arise as space is made to observe and describe the ways that her psychic reality is structured around approaching and withdrawing from the violent internal projective identification rejecting object. The more I can clearly and emotionally describe this situation, the more I gradually earn Paula's tentative trust. We have both begun to experience a kind of *living through hell* together. It seems that I *must* experience the feelings of rage, frustration, hopelessness, and helplessness that emerge while trying to think and experience in the presence of an obstructive object. Being more at-one with Paula's experience is necessary in order to really begin to find words that feel truthful to her and that can hold her attention and reorient her to a new kind of relationship.

Concluding Thoughts

This paper has suggested that one of the most painful situations in analytic work involves the obstructive object relationship first described by Bion. The practical task of psychoanalysis is to identify, describe, and, over time, transform the unconscious modes of coping with pain that were learned very early in life and that can be observed in transferences into the present. Our task is to learn to describe – and in doing so, contain and bring awareness to – the shifting levels of pain and anxiety that the patient experiences, moment to moment and session to session. Over time, the mindful reverie that we demonstrate for our patient is internalized and becomes part of the patient's own projective identification welcoming object world. These more creative internal object relationships can be increasingly relied upon to sponsor learning from experience over the course of a lifetime.

There are intimidating challenges in working with obstructive object scenarios. Patients block introjection of the therapist's alpha function because of their own pervasive projective identification. They anticipate rejection and attack because they are identified with an ego-destructive internal object. The analyst has the large challenge of bearing the strain of the Sphinx-like encounter with terror and dread that the patient experiences upon emerging into an obstructive object transference that often has been deeply split off and denied. By avoiding the trap of concretely enacting a projective identification-rejecting object, the analyst, through his actual reverie and presence with the patient, gives the patient an experience that stimulates her own alpha function, and in the best situations allows mourning and the working through of depressive anxieties to take place. This in turn sponsors the reclamation of attention and thwarted life instincts, which may now revive and expand by relying upon the new experience of a projective identification welcoming object and a sense of relationship to one's own internal world. Through successful analytic work, one can observe how the patient withdraws her projections from external objects back into herself and her internal objects. This process happens as she begins to discover the analyst as a containing object, one who welcomes projective identifications rather than rejecting them as anticipated.

References

Beebe, B., & Lachmann, F. (2002) *Infant Research and Adult Treatment: Co-Constructing Interactions*. Hillsdale, NJ: Analytic Press.

Bion, W. R. (1961) *Experiences in Groups*. London: Tavistock Publications.

Bion, W. R. (1962) *Learning from Experience*. London: Heimann.

Bion, W. R. (1977) *Seven Servants: Four Works by W. R. Bion*. New York, NY: Jason Aronson.

Bion, W. R. (1985) *The Long Weekend: Part of a Life and All My Sins Remembered*. Strath Tay Perthshire: Clunie Press.

Bion, W. R. (1993) *Second Thoughts*. Northvale, NJ: Jason Aronson.

Buckingham, L. (2002) "The Hazards of Curiosity: A Kleinian Perspective on Learning"(p. 106–135) in Barford, D. (ed) *The Ship of Thought: Essays on Psychoanalysis and Learning*. London: Karnac.

Lampen, J. (1987) *Mending Hurt: Swarthmore Lecture*. London: Quaker Home Services.

Chapter 2

A Fish in the Stream

Life in Creativity with Virginia Woolf

Meg Harris Williams

This paper is a review of Virginia Woolf's own analysis of creative turbulence, drawing on passages in her diaries, essays, and autobiographical writings that illuminate her own philosophy of creativity. The trials and tribulations of the creative writer speak for everyone but have a heightened sensitivity and "transparency" as she calls it, vividness and color. As is often quoted, Woolf saw her vocation as a writer as founded on what she called the "shock-receiving capacity" ('Sketch of the Past' 85), something equivalent to Bion's (1970) idea of psychic turbulence and its demarcation of points of psychic (catastrophic) change, an idea that characterizes the work and teaching of Mike Eigen with its emphasis on the hidden yet continuous traumas of everyday existence and the search for mitigation and transformation, but not for cure or expurgation. Psychic pain is not to be smoothed away but "suffered," as in Bion's sense of how curiosity (the K-link) is fueled by contrary emotions in the search for meaning, the "thing-in-itself." The core conflict of love and hate gives shape to existence if it can be brought to light, its beauty apparent. But experiencing the conflict involves more pain, not less, in the sense of greater intensity of feeling – "intensity" being, for Woolf as for Keats, a measure of poetic temperature.

The Sustaining Object

How can the self survive such intensity of turbulence? Woolf says she sees herself as a fish in a stream: "deflected; held in place" although she "cannot describe the stream" (*Sketch* 92). This is a statement of the complexity of her task as she saw it. In fact, she is always describing the stream – not just stream of consciousness, or rather of unconsciousness (the submerged truths), but all the little shocks and currents that help to shape the fish-mind (as she calls it). She sees herself as by nature "thinking against the current," meaning, society's pressures, flicking the fish-body this way and that ('Thoughts on peace in an air raid,' *Essays* 486). Often, by contrast, she speaks of "the machine" – not always the same machine, but being, in general terms, an environment or set of values that is set against the "stream" of organic life (*ibid.* 488; *Sketch* 155; *Diary* 144). Her concept of "machine" is equivalent to Bion's "basic assumption grouping": there are a variety of machines

DOI: 10.4324/9781003322986-2

just as there are a variety of basic assumption groups, but they are identical in their claustrum-like constriction of the mind that is trying to absorb shocks, both pleasurable and painful, in its journey down the river.

Woolf described herself as "uneducated" because she did not go to school, yet at the same time, she saw educational institutions as vacuous (as in *The Waves*) and probably saw the new psychoanalytic institutions in the same light, although she was always interested in psychology and imbibed the ideas circulating among her friends. In addition to her own reading, she gained her education via persons or minds whom she respected/valued: mother, father, brother Thoby and his Cambridge friends who comprised the Bloomsbury group, in particular the "violent trembling misanthropic Jew" Leonard Woolf ('Old Bloomsbury' 49), whom she married and who was always her first reader. Melanie Klein was talking about the psychoanalysis of children in the next-door home of her brother Adrian while Woolf was writing her child-centered *To the Lighthouse.* As an adolescent, Virginia also had private tutors, especially Janet Case, who taught her Greek and opened the world of classical drama. Her education came via meaningful relationships rather than institutional frameworks, which she regarded as one type of "machine."

The pressures, or currents, that both hold and deflect the fish are not merely societal, cultural, or educational. They are also "invisible presences" from within (*Sketch* 92). The internal invisible presences, known to psychoanalysis as objects, are in a continuous process of transformation, nudging against the influencing elements (called by Bion "wild thoughts") that fly around in the jetstream like Plato's souls seeking bodies (the topic of an essay Woolf wrote as a child). These are potential ideas if they can find "psyche-lodgement" (as Bion calls it). "It is in our idleness, in our dreams, that the submerged truth sometimes comes to the top" (*Room of One's Own* 24). The author is both fish and fisherman, always "casting a line to make my book the right shape" (*Diary* 1930, 150). The hunt is always to enable the invisible unconscious to become visible, in the form of a "thought" that is captured in an image, a symbol:

> Thought ... had let its line down into the stream. It swayed, minute after minute, hither and thither among the reflections and the weeds, letting the water lift it and sink it until – you know the little tug – the sudden conglomeration of an idea at the end of one's line: and then the cautious hauling of it in, and the careful laying of it out? Alas, laid on the grass how small, how insignificant this thought of mine looked; the sort of fish that a good fisherman puts back into the water so that it may grow fatter and be one day worth cooking and eating. (*Room* 2)

The good fisherman will put the nascent thought back till it is ready, till it can take shape in a novel, having been developed through a further "wash and tumult of ideas." "Will another novel ever swim up?" (*Diary* 1937, 275). Is the pen – that long-refined hunting instrument of the middle classes – "on the scent" (*Sketch* 103)? Has her piece "speared the eel" of its topic (as she once put it, *Diary* 1930, 156)? Sometimes the net comes up with only seaweed, she writes in *Orlando*; sometimes a minimal scattering of small word-fish; but "never the great fish who lives in the coral groves" – the truth that is always elusive (*Orlando* 313). But the great sea of the unconscious is known to nurture all its fish, great and small.

The theme of transformation of psychic turbulence, by means of the pursuit of beauty, characterizes the vocational statements of all poets, writers, and artists in so far as they have "theories" of creativity. They are descriptive theories of course, not prescriptive ones, which all creative writers loathe, hence their suspicion of psychoanalysis, or at least of its explanatory frameworks. (In Woolf, these societal frameworks are associated with patriarchy, academicism, and tyranny – all of which imprison superego-ish structures and obstructive objects rather than fluid, facilitating, organic ones.) She was well aware, of course, of Freud's distinction between mourning and melancholy and was not averse to calling herself (intermittently) a melancholic, but was probably more aware than many psychoanalysts that "working through" never comes to an end, nor should do; it enriches the fund of feelings to be continuously tapped and transmuted; and this is as true of life as of art. Entering a book to write it, she described it as "pitching into [her] great lake of melancholy, what a born melancholic I am!" (*Diary* 1929, 140). But she knows that this is how she "keeps afloat": "if I stop I sink down down". Writing the stream, she is "doing for herself what psychoanalysts do for their patients" (*Sketch* 93).

The creative "shock," she elaborates, brings the realization that it is itself "a token of some real thing behind appearances":

> and I make it real by putting it into words. It is only by putting it into words that I make it whole; this wholeness means that it has lost its power to hurt me; it gives me, perhaps because by doing so I take away the pain, a great delight to put the severed parts together. (*Sketch* 85)

This word-building, seen in terms of reparation (as in Klein) and accessed through pleasure-pain, is a response to something beyond the appearances. Woolf says her "philosophy" is the "constant idea…that behind the cotton wool is hidden a pattern; that we, I mean all human beings, are connected with this; that the whole world is a work of art" (*Sketch* 85).

Woolf wrote in "scenes," the way images typically appeared to her, building them up into a narrative: "we are sealed vessels afloat on what is called reality" (*Sketch* 145). Early on, she describes her child's perception, looking at a flower, that part of it lay below ground and was invisible, but that both parts constituted its "whole," and this was a perception she would store away in her mind as it may be "useful later" (*Sketch* 84). Elsewhere she says, "It is not exactly beauty that I mean… the thing is in itself enough: satisfactory, achieved" (*Diary* 1926, 85). She said she strove to keep her child's perspective alongside the inevitable adult or "contemporary" vision – "I now, I then" (*Diary* 1940, 346; *Sketch* 87). Her aesthetics is dominated by the urge to find or make "the whole," by matching complementary qualities such as male-female, light-shadow, present-past identities, etc., all founded on the intuition from childhood that the coming-together of parts is both aesthetically satisfying and psychologically necessary.

The artist's function, not just for themselves but for common humanity, is one of focusing on intuitive "moments of being" that occur in the midst of all the "cottonwool" of everyday existence, with faith in the idea that ultimately these moments will link up in a greater reality – Bion's "underlying pattern" or "O," the Platonic-mystical denotation of ultimate reality. Such moments not only make the individual creative but also, in a wider sense, affect society as well. In Woolf, there is a fine balance between immersion in the creative process and observation of her own immersion (as in Bion's "third person" in the analytic process), the wider perspective on reality.

In her talk on "Old Bloomsbury," Woolf relates how in the early days of awkward abstract debate (nonetheless felt to be electrifying by contrast with the society "machine"), it happened that Vanessa used the word "beauty" and suddenly the desultory silence came to life: "All our ears were pricked. It was as if the bull had at last been turned into the ring... The bull might be 'beauty'; might be 'good'; might be 'reality'." She never deviates from this Platonic ideal. Yet while in all her writings she says much about her mother's beauty, reiterated as a common fact known by everyone, it is increasingly clear that it is "not exactly beauty" in this obvious sense that is the bull in the ring, activating the *duende*; it is something known only to her, her internal object-relationship. When she recounts writing her childhood essay about Plato's souls flying around searching for bodies to migrate into (*Sketch* 105), it takes on the significance of a moment of being, not solely for the topic of the essay but for the associated link with her mother, for whom (unconsciously) she wrote it, and whose praise made her feel like a "violin being played upon" (the welcoming object). Or, as she puts it later, in a TS Eliot-like way (he was a friend): "We are the words, we are the music, we are the thing itself" (*Sketch* 85).

Woolf's is not a dry or abstract Platonism/mysticism, however. It is a continuous search for a reality that is first glimpsed sensuously, through the transparent watery depths or on the horizon, like a "fin far out" at sea (*Diary* 1926, 100), with its dual aura of fascination and danger (aesthetic conflict). The scene for her "philosophy" is set wonderfully in the opening section of her autobiographical *Sketch*, with the infant "colour and sound memories" set in the nursery at the family's seaside home at St. Ives:

> It is of lying half asleep, half awake, in bed in the nursery at St Ives. It is of hearing the waves breaking, one, two, one, two, and sending a splash of water over the beach; and then breaking, one, two, one, two, behind a yellow blind. It is of hearing the blind draw its little acorn across the floor as the wind blew the blind out. It is of lying and hearing this splash and seeing this light, and feeling, it is almost impossible that I should be here; of feeling the purest ecstasy I can conceive. (*Sketch* 78–79)

This is the "bowl," or "base" of all her imaginative life: the umbilical blind-cord whose wavelike rhythm links the nursery via a balcony with her parents' bedroom. The feeling is of "lying in a grape and seeing through a film of semi-transparent yellow." Sounds are "indistinguishable from sights," "showing the light through" but without a clear outline; merging, transparent. She derives her capacity to transmute or transform emotional shocks from this primary sense of wonder, which in itself invites the Conradian "everlasting sea" into the infant mind yet safely moored to its object via a type of fantasy life-buoy (Meltzer's aesthetic reciprocity). From this position of secure containment, it is possible to dive to the depths of the water or scan the ocean waves, even to encounter the sharks, like the fin she observes far out, heralding the approach of the next book.

The fishing metaphor resurges constantly in Woolf's writings, alongside more traditional metaphors for creativity in hunting and riding (especially "galloping" and "taking fences"), sailing, and adventuring ('There are moments when the sail flaps,' *Diary* 1940, 346). Her first serious reading, she says, was of Elizabethan tales of adventure like Hakluyt, and she maintained a fondness for them, as evidenced by *Orlando*. She associated them with the belief that "this curious steed, life, is genuine" (*Diary* 1929, 145), and she too is "goaded" by a sense of adventure, with the prize being "reality" at the end of it – she disliked the popular view of literature as consolation or escapism. Rather she is always conscious of the horse's back, or sailing boat, in which she travels to that abstract goal. In an essay on Wordsworth, who wrote of "spots of time" (of transcendent meaning) much as she envisages "moments of being," she nonetheless jokes at his neglect of practicalities, describing the poet and Dorothy trudging on foot because their horse has thrown the cart over a bank and William has dropped the chicken and bread in the lake; "all they knew was there was a waterfall ahead" (*Essays* 388). Similarly, she joked about Eliot's admiration for James Joyce: "if you are anaemic as Tom there is glory in blood," at the same time contrasting Joyce's multitude of "tiny bullets" with Tolstoy's "deadly wound straight in the face" (*Diary* 1922, 48), the wound being the quarry, reality.

She disliked overt, imposed symbolism and said she "meant *nothing*" by the Lighthouse as a symbol; it was up to the reader to find their own emotional relevance. Her initial idea for *To the Lighthouse* was to be a portrait of her father, focusing on him sitting in the boat, citing Cowper's "We all perished, each alone," while "crushing a dying mackerel" (*Diary* 1925, 75). This is despite the fact that (she wrote in *Sketch* 139) her father disliked watching dying fish on the floor of the boat, while she as a child was thrilled by the "tug on the line" and it became a metaphor for thought-catching. The ambivalent, creative, and destructive forces are (as she knew was recognized in psychoanalysis) intimately/inextricably intertwined. By confronting these forces in the novel, she rewrote her internal portraits of both father and mother and "laid their ghosts" as she put it (*Diary* 1928, 135). By the end of the long mourning process following the mother's death, the lighthouse itself can become a welcoming object as the eye of its lamp draws the family boat towards it.

Thus, it is not the tension between creation and destruction that makes the fish shudder and judder. Rather, it is the dissonance between emotional moments of being and non-emotional self-packaging in cottonwool. In a posthumously published paper "Fishing," she ruminates upon the confessions of a dull, non-descript man who sat in parliament for 30 years (another father-type), but whose real imaginative life consisted in his fishing expeditions. His narration of "moments of intensity" when the world became real echoed her own "moments of being": they were moments after which, he wrote, "I felt receptive to every sight, every colour and every sound, as though I walked through a world from which a veil had been withdrawn" ('Fishing,' *Essays* 563). It sounds remarkably like Woolf herself, describing how she relies on unconsciousness passivity working at top speed while "the upper mind drowses" (like Bion's "lumbering conscious"). Then, after a pause, "the veil lifts and there is the thing – the thing he wants to write about – simplified, composed" ('The leaning tower,' *Essays* 474). Her humorous comment on the enthusiastic fisherman-author is: "Is it possible that to remove veils from trees it is necessary to fish? – our conscious mind must be all body, and the unconscious mind leaps to the top and strips off veils?" Poetry consists of "baring reality." Like human life, each river is different and:

> full of shadowy fish, and each fish different from the other … with its mentality that we can dimly penetrate, movements we can mystically anticipate, for just as, suddenly, Greek and Latin sort themselves in a flash, so we understand the minds of fish? ('Fishing,' 564)

For the stream is not just made of presences, feelings, and memories, but of words, which, for Woolf, had a life of their own and, if used effectively, could fish for the mind. The art of writing, she says, consists in "laying an egg in the reader's mind from which springs the thing itself – whether man or fish" ('Fishing,' 562). Throwing a line and lifting a veil are both done by words; the writer is a medium, both himself and not himself, driven on by the search for reality. We should remember, she said, that "Words are dangerous things… A republic might be brought into being by a poem" ('Royalty,' *Essays* 463). No state of turbulence is a safe one. In a talk called "How should one read a book?" given at a school, she said that readers are as valuable as writers in that their judgements become "part of the atmosphere which writers breathe as they work," and thus contribute to further writings, by whomever (*Essays* 431). Therefore, she advises, judge with "sympathy and severity" (like Bion's "austere criticism"), but only after there has been a personal emotional immersion based on the "intoxication of rhythm" (incantation) that has swept us along in its stream. In that way, we are contributing to the evolution of society. We should never "herd ourselves under the authority" of even the best readers but rely on suggestions "won honestly in the course of our own reading," Never, that is, enroll in the machine, whether it be patriarchy or even feminism (never "subscribe slave" as Milton put it, to even the most advanced propositions).

"To read a novel is a difficult and complex art," she impresses on the schoolgirls (425), but by this she does not mean academic analysis, which in fact she believed "impaired creativity" (*Diary* 1935, 237). Rather, she meant entering into the kind of identifications that lead us onwards and inwards into ourselves: the goal of true reading is to satisfy that curiosity which possesses us when we linger in front of a house and each floor shows us a different section of human life in being; and as we watch, "the house fades and the iron railings vanish and we are out at sea; we are hunting, sailing, fighting" (*Essays* 426) – and through this, our own creativity is refreshed.

In Woolf's special brand of feminism, words are not servitors any more than women or animals are possessions of those who have married or paid money for them. Asked to give a radio talk on "Craftsmanship," she rebelled, saying it was an "incongruous" notion: words are for "telling the truth," not for being "useful" (*Essays* 439). As it happens, she is always talking about the craft of writing and its uses, but not in the sense of a means of control; she once said she never intended to preach and disapproved of it, and she described her friend E. M. Forster as divided between a pure artist and a preacher-teacher (*Essays* 539). Art is "being rid of all preaching" and concentrating on "things in themselves; the sentence in itself beautiful" (*Diary* 1932, 183). In a semi-comic portrait of Coleridge, she portrays him as "Not a man but a swarm, a cloud, a buzz of words, darting this way and that, clustering, quivering and hanging suspended." Yet paradoxically, at the center of this ideological swarm is indeed "a man at the gate," a stolid everyday figure with his opioid constipation persecutions. Is he a master of words or their servant, and which is most useful? The crucial test is that his words evoke not complacency but fertile "explosions" in the minds of others, the kind of writing which has "the secret of perpetual life" (*Room* 82). "How do we combine the old words in new orders so that they survive, so that they create beauty so that they tell the truth? That is the question" ('Craftsmanship,' *Essays* 441). Only when we recognize that they are "democratic" and "live in the mind" rather than in dictionaries, finding freedom in the gaps between conscious employment:

> Our unconsciousness is their privacy; our darkness is their light…. That pause was made… to tempt words to come together in one of those marriages which are perfect images and create everlasting beauty. ('Craftsmanship,' *Essays* 443)

It is not enough to transform, she writes in her notes on Roger Fry's book of formalist art criticism, *Transformation* (predating by a couple of decades Bion's similar title): "But transformation must express not only change but achievement" (*Diary* 1940, 312). The difficulty is the nature of the transformation: "If art is based on thought, what is the transmuting process?" (*Diary* 1926, 94). The theme of "Craftsmanship" doesn't allow for "incantation and mystery"; as to critics' dismissal of purple patches, the problem was not their color but the fact that they were "only patches." The purple lyricism of the unconscious is there all the time; the currents are crafting and shaping the identity of the fish, even when swimming against them. Thought is based on art, not vice versa. The writing process is like "swimming in the highest ether" (*Diary* 1924, 65) and itself leads the writer onward: "everything is running of its own accord into the stream" (*Diary* 1932, 184). Ultimately, though, it was always necessary to go over the word stream and "put the screw on" (*Diary* 1935, 231).

When words become "transparent," they cease to be just words and become so intensified that "one seems to experience them"; words become, or bring to mind, the feelings that have a life of their own beneath the surface; they can be our line to the unconscious (though there are also obstructive uses, of course, when words are not transparent but obfuscatory). This transparency she associates with contact with reality, the thing-in-itself, which she takes to be a function of the "androgynous" mind, a phrase she adopts from Coleridge. It is not enough to preach from a single-sex vertex; the creative writer needs to be "man-womanly" or "woman-manly" and complexify their vision (*Room* 79). The writer requires "fluid gifts" as well as "bony ones," the driving force being a "backbone of fierce attachment to an idea, compelling words to its shape" ('The modern essay,' *Essays* 194). In this way, combinations of words have a chance to tell the truth even though – or rather, because – the meaning is not known beforehand. The androgynous approach (contact with the combined object, in psychoanalytic terms) links the baby-in-the-bowl (the fish) with the parents at the other end of the blind, the line of thought. It is the line to reality, the thing-in-itself.

Sometimes, she says, she finds her own writing power "incredible, as if belonging to someone else"; it is the opposite of controlling and mastering words and brings her close to "nervous breakdown in miniature" – owing to the fact that it is also transforming the writer, outside their own control. In her essay *Street haunting*, she wanders through the streets of London in search of a symbolic lead pencil with which to write, looking for windows to stimulate curiosity and open the life of imagination. The walk evokes a creative illusion (similar to the entering-into type of imagination that Coleridge saw as Shakespearean):

> the illusion that one is not tethered to a single mind but can put on briefly for a few minutes the minds and bodies of others… a washerwoman, publican, street singer… leave straight lines of personality and deviate into those footpaths that lead beneath brambles and thick tree trunks into the heart of the forest where live those wild beasts, our fellow men? ('Street haunting,' *Essays* 243)

Following the scent, led by the pen at the end of the road, is another metaphor for the stream of life, here being a hunt for the "wild beasts" that enliven its depths. The pen is the original acorn of the blind. In her letter to a young poet, she says: "Stand at the window and let your rhythmical sense open and shut… until one thing melts in another, until the taxis are dancing with the daffodils, until a whole has been made from all these separate fragments" (*Essays* 273). All the minute, idiosyncratic observations, or responses to the current, are indications of a greater reality – the whole, the O, the underlying pattern, the river itself.

After Fry's death in 1934, Woolf was occupied for the following years with writing a dutiful biography, as demanded by her friends. She complained of having to incorporate the opinions of all sorts of people who had known him – not her vision of the fish in the stream at all. Biography was not autobiography and was fraught with the dangers of publishing to please others. Probably none were aware of how soul-destroying it was or how anti-creative. It was the kind of tedious, worthy writing done by her father with his *Eminent Victorians*, who once honestly and sadly admitted that he was only a second-rate writer. The biography of Roger put her in the position of feeling she was the kind of writer who had been killed off by her father's example; if he had lived, she said, he would have killed the [true] writer in her, just as she had to "kill the Angel in the House" (the Victorian feminine ideal) in order to become a writer ('Professions for women,' *Essays* 261). Even Leonard, in this context, felt to be a sharp beak pecking at her, demanding a certain type of portrait of Roger Fry, like Mr. Ramsay's "beak of brass" in *Lighthouse* (*Diary* 1940, 316). The beak represented the prescriptive aesthetics proclaimed by Fry, another form of patriarchy whose currents she felt she needed to swim against. "Mental fight" (she is quoting Blake) means "thinking against the current, not with it" (*Essays* 486), and that was when she did her best work, "back braced to the wall," relishing the sense of being an "outsider" (*Diary* 1938, 297). And indeed elsewhere, she compares herself to Prometheus on his rock, pecked by the eagle, although at the same time "She bites!," and through this metaphor asserts her resilience as a writer, albeit at times difficult to live with (*Diary* 1921, 38).

And in this sense, *Roger* served a function by stimulating a contrasting mode of writing that she could undertake simultaneously as a "relief." If Roger was the veil, the *Sketch* lay beneath it. She escaped from the "grind" and "drudgery" of "word filing and fitting" of the factual biography (*Sketch* 108), engendering a new form for her memoir by narrating past and present in juxtaposition. The fish is held in the stream of her two selves past and present – "I now, I then" – which "come out in contrast" (*Sketch* 87). Yet this has its dangers: the deaths of her mother, sister Stella, father, her favorite brother Thoby, and nephew Julian, whom she felt was like Thoby; sexual abuse by her older half-brothers; and general abuse by the patriarchal "machine" of society, from which she had successfully escaped years before, now merge in layers with the devastation of bombed London, "all that completeness ravished and demolished" (*Diary* 1941, 349).

As war gets nearer, the incantation of the river's flow becomes more ominous, as if foreshadowing her suicide: "getting the past to shadow this broken surface. Let me then, like a child advancing with bare feet into a cold river, descend again into that stream" (*Sketch* 108). Nonetheless, at the same time, she is viewing the natural approach of death in a creative sense, as a new and original topic for writing, an unexplored interest: why not treat the coming of age and death as an experience that is different from the others, "which is a tremendous experience and not as unconscious, at least in its approaches, as birth is" (*Diary* 1939, 304). There is never any sense that suicide is inevitable, just that she feels oppressed by the "grind" of Roger: "My grind has left me dazed and depressed. How on earth to bring off this chapter? God knows."

She discovers her *Sketch* notes in the waste paper basket months later, along with the drafts for her life of Roger (now published). "Shall I ever finish? The battle is at its crisis – comes closer to this house daily" (*Sketch* 109). At this point, she consciously resists its pull: "I wish to go on – not settle in that dismal puddle." But the dismal puddle mounts into a breaking wave.

The Overwhelming Object

If "upholding" is perhaps a better word than Bion's "containment" for Woolf's experiments as a fish in the stream, then "overwhelming" describes her ultimate succumbing to drowning in depression in the river by her Sussex home. Her suicide remains a mystery despite appearing with hindsight as both inevitable and – in terms of its manner – psychologically fitting. Her overpowering waves of depression occurred after significant deaths in her life, and the final one comes in the context of the Nazi onslaught and realistic fear of invasion, which shadows all her final writings, especially the diaries and "Sketch of the Past," and of course was the pervading topic of discussion among all her contemporaries, including plans for suicide (Leonard, she notes, has petrol in the garage for the purpose). Yet this co-exists with continuing work and hopefulness, still hoping to "swim into quiet water" (*Diary* 1941, 332); and she was fully aware that her capacity for self-observation made her darker feelings "serviceable." Manic-depressive does not describe the contrast between her different states of mind, mostly phenomenally hard-working and full of enjoyment of life (this is not mania), punctuated by periods of depression that varied from severe to something equivalent to post-partum depression after finishing a book (the 'season of depression,' *Diary* 1936, 258).

Her depression was not primarily of the guilty type (she is aware) but rather associated with the feeling of "hopeless sadness" that she noted and described in *Sketch* in an incident in which, as a child, before any deaths, she was fist-fighting with her brother Thoby and suddenly stopped because the question arose in her mind, why should anybody hurt another person? So "I let him beat me" (*Sketch* 84). This feeling recurred throughout her life and is probably best understood in Kleinian terms of the world-as-mother and the mindless destruction of the world-babies. The beauty of the world is desecrated. It results at times in what she calls "dumb horror," such as the other childhood episodes recounted in the *Sketch* of being unable to step across a puddle (like Rhoda in *The Waves*), magnifying its claustral threat, or coming face to face with an "idiot boy" and pouring all her toffees into his hands, accompanied by "that hopeless sadness; that collapse… exposed to a whole avalanche of meaning… discharged, unprotected" (*Sketch* 90). The world's deprivation is not containable or tolerable; hence, it is not usually confronted. The fish sinks into its murky depths, and, like Rachel's fantasy in *The Voyage Out*, the body rolls on the ocean floor, turned over by nightmare currents. Is this a state of sea-change, like Shakespeare's pearl-eyes (invoked in her imagery), or of dissolution?

There are "curious intervals" in life, she mused, in which the creative constitution is re-jigged. Before beginning *The Waves*, she imagined that six weeks in bed would make it a masterpiece, essentially owing to throwing off the omnipotence of the technical master: "Who thinks it? And I am outside the thinker? One wants some device which is not a trick" (*Diary* 1929, 143).

In illness, she had suggested, the mind can re-route its habitual tracks. With "the police off duty"; words acquire a "mystic quality". The paper *On illness* is imbued with quotations from poetry, and perhaps echoing Ariel leading Caliban, she suggests: "We grasp what is beyond their surface meaning... The words give out their scent and distil their flavor," meaning "comes sensually first, by way of palate and the nostrils" (*Essays* 249). Illness has its potentialities for creativity and may not necessarily be divorced from the object, but at times, in greater unconscious contact. It is a familiar theme in poetry that it is necessary to somehow deflect existing knowledge, itself obstructive, in order to see "things invisible" (for knowledge can be "too thick," as Bion says). It is "intolerable to be always understood," Woolf says, given that "we don't know our own souls never mind others" (246). We need to exit the machine and enter the stream of our fishy existence in order to pursue the unknown. Entering a horizontal state of not-understanding that to the everyday mind could be called "illness" may strip off the cotton wool of our surface vision and remind us of the art of our necessities. The ordinary currents of life are stilled along with the reclining body, and we can look up at the clouds, "that snowfield of the mind where man has not trodden" (247) – a fish-eye view.

Admittedly the context here is flu, not mental illness, but it constitutes Woolf's own version of a traditional view of creativity, rarely plumbed by psychoanalysis, and for which ordinary combinations of words have not yet knitted a fishing net. Who knows what your pain is trying to tell you? "Take your pain in one hand and a lump of pure sound in the other" as they did with Babel, she says (245), reversing the moral of the myth. In *Professions for Women*, she advises becoming "as unconscious as possible" since then there is the greatest chance of connecting not only with the sensuous origins of meaning but with the great tradition of previous poets (*Essays* 263). It is not primarily the discursive meaning but rather the sensuous properties of language that connect the modern poet with the time when he (or she) was Chaucer or Shakespeare: "You were Byron, remember... You were Crabbe," etc., through "that most profound and primitive of instincts, rhythm," she writes in "Letter to a young poet" (*Essays* 272): "Be a poet in whom live all the poets of the past, from whom all poets in time to come will spring." She gives similar advice to the young women whose voices were not recorded in the past but nonetheless existed potentially if they could "think back through their mothers" but at the same time should consider themselves "Shakespeare's sister." We identify with our objects not through what we are told, but through our feelings – those invisible presences that guide the fish along the currents.

We remember that *The Waves* was originally to be called *The Moths* (in some ways a more fitting title for its group of souls, but she wanted a "sea" background). Moth and fish are thus closely related, and there is a posthumously published essay describing the death of a moth on her windowsill. The moth, like the butterfly, is a traditional symbol for the soul, *psyche.* In Woolf's personal imagery, where it also, of course, suggests moth-er, it represents the feminine "evanescent" part of the personality (the male being imaged by tree-roots, or the pen itself), the imaginative capacity to metamorphose from one state to another. She wrote of a thinking mind having "islands in the stream" and "two different currents": one like "moths flying along," the other, a flower upright in the center, yet not fixed but "perpetually crumbling and renewing" (*Diary* 1929, 140). In illness, the mind can "become a chrysalis," working in idleness (a Keatsian concept); then doors open and "this is I believe the moth shaking its wings in me" (*Diary* 1930, 151). There is a "whirr of wings in the head." In a short essay on *The death of the moth*, the moth represents the energy of the human brain, both marvelous and pathetic, a "tiny bead of pure life" designed to show us life's true nature (*Essays* 508). When the moth slips down on the windowsill, Woolf is about to help support it with her pencil, but she withdraws the pencil when she realizes that the "insignificant little creature now knew death," folding its wings. The pen respects its new state of being and does not interfere with it lying "decently and uncomplainingly composed" (509).

In the context of the oncoming war, Woolf naturally asked herself whether continuing to write was a form of self-indulgence. It was not a new question, but she decided even more emphatically that for her, writing was more valuable and "necessary" than learning "something useful if war comes" (*Sketch* 86). In *The Artist and Politics* (posthumously published), she explained that far from being cloistered, the artist is "besieged by voices, all disturbing" (*Essays* 566), and that the practice of art increased awareness of "needs of mankind in the mass" and of their very survival. The danger lay in instinctual group psychology (Bion's basic assumptions), a natural inheritance: the young airman is propelled not just by loud-speakers but by "ancient voices in himself" (*Essays* 488) – the excitement of the chase. These voices need to be heard, captured by the artist, and transmuted, setting out the process by which the man could be "freed from the machine" and "compensated for the loss of glory and gun by access to the creative feelings" (489).

At the time of her suicide, Woolf was nearly 60 and observed that James Joyce had died two weeks younger than she was. Already, she felt, she had been "useful" enough to the world through her writing. In her diary, she justifies her life (but also her death), refusing to "take on the guilt of selfishness feeling" since:

> I have done my share, with pen and talk, for the human race... I deserve a spring – I owe nobody nothing. Not a letter I need write ... others can do that, this spring. Now being drowned by the flow of running water, I will read. (*Diary* 1940, 318)

By now she was sure her writing had a life of its own, independent of her: for some time she had felt assured of her vision of "reality... in which I shall rest and continue to exist" (*Diary* 1928, 129–130).

In her almost-last book, *The Years*, she asks repeatedly how we may "improve ourselves... live adventurously, wholly, not like cripples in a cave" (*Years* 296), and how to be happy "in a world bursting with misery... death, tyranny, brutality, torture, the fall of civilisation, the end of freedom" (388). Yet she had always known that the more intense the inner life, the greater the futility of death. In a "world bursting with misery," "loneliness means seeing to the bottom of the vessel... Reality I call it" (*Diary* 1928, 129). She had always seen herself as a fighter, "fighting something alone... goaded on by reality" (*Diary* 1929, 144) and upheld in the stream by her own capacity for observation, which made her "despondency serviceable." Only weeks before drowning herself in the river, she determined that "this trough of despair shall not, I swear, engulf me." Or, if she were to sink, "I will go down with my colours flying" (*Diary* 1941, 351). For as she said earlier in "On being ill," "With the hook of life still in us still we must wriggle" (*Essays* 248), and – her final diary entry – there was sausage and haddock to be prepared for dinner.

References

Bion, W. R. (1970). *Attention and Interpretation.* London: Tavistock.

Woolf, V. (1954). *A Writer's Diary*, ed. L. Woolf. New York, NY: Harcourt.

Woolf, V. (1964 [1927]). *To the Lighthouse.* London: Penguin.

Woolf, V. (1998 [1928]). *Orlando.* London: Penguin.

Woolf, V. (2002a). Sketch of the Past. In: *Moments of Being*, ed. J. Schulkind and H. Lee. London: Pimlico, pp. 78–160, pp. 43–61.

Woolf, V. (2002b). Old Bloomsbury. In: *Moments of Being*, ed. J. Schulkind and H. Lee. London: Pimlico. pp. 43–61.

Woolf, V. (2013). *A Room of One's Own.* Prague: e-artnow.

Woolf, V. (2016 [1937]). *The Years.* London: Penguin.

Woolf, V. (2021). *Collected Essays.* Bristol: Read & Co.

Chapter 3

Occlusions, Metabolic Excess, and Other Risks to Subject Formation in the Child

Michael O'Loughlin and Mila Kirstie C. Kulsa

Apart from its erudite and accessible style, one of the great strengths of Michael Eigen's work is its phenomenological groundedness. Eigen's goal is not to build well-fortified theoretical edifices that withstand critique. His is a much humbler and more grounded approach: He seeks to build an understanding of the human psyche phenomenologically using the experiences of his patients and his own unconscious responses to those patients in order to understand where the stuckness in human thinking comes from and how easily we perpetuate our own suffering. Steeped in the literature of psychoanalysis – and indeed, literatures well beyond psychoanalysis that address the human struggle – Eigen writes in an associative style reminiscent of D. W. Winnicott. He invites us to bear witness to human suffering at its most challenging and allows us to sit with him as this master clinician brings his attuned understanding into conversation with each patient's dilemma. Sometimes, this meeting of minds produces remarkable insight, and sometimes little progress appears to occur. As experienced clinicians well know, success in therapy is not indicated by simplistic metrics but is evident, rather, in our capacity as clinicians to sustain ourselves and be usefully present with another human being's suffering. The richness of Eigen's phenomenological and allusive approach to clinical description is that, in a type of parallel process to the patient experience, it allows clinician readers to expand their own associative and metaphoric capacities as they engage with the material.

In this chapter, we wish to focus on one particular concept from Eigen's *oeuvre*, the notion of toxic nourishment. While Eigen works exclusively with adults, and all of the case material in his *Toxic Nourishment* (1999) centers on adult experiences, the work has extraordinary implications for our understanding of the origins of human subjectivity and the hazards of misattunements and misrecognitions in the critical early relational experiences of the infant and young child. We will begin by exploring the richness and complexity of Eigen's concept of toxic nourishment, and then, drawing on themes from British and French psychoanalytic understandings of child subject formation, we will illustrate how prescient Eigen's writings on this topic are to our understanding of what gets subjectivity off to a good start and how early occlusions can limit a patient's aliveness and thereby impair their capacity to live life fully.

DOI: 10.4324/9781003322986-3

Eigen is not so much interested in those clearly recognizable abusive experiences that cause well-documented psychic annihilation. His interest here is much more subtle: He explores the ways in which some parents, however well-intentioned, create unconscious psychic burdens for their offspring. As Eigen notes, "All that is in the parent floods into the child" (p. xv), and a parent, burdened by their own metabolic difficulties, will necessarily communicate "anxious control, worry, death, dread, ambition, self-hate" (p. xv) into their child, intertwined all the while with their best efforts to communicate love to that child. A child may develop complex somatic responses and may become so accustomed to deadness that any potential for aliveness is resisted as pathological. Speaking of one patient, Penny, Eigen describes the oddly paradoxical way she protected herself, having "learned from her mother that deadness can be life-preserving" (p. xviii). Describing another patient, Alice, Eigen illustrates how, having been raised by a self-absorbed, self-hating, and punishing mother, Alice became "overdosed on indifference and disparagement" (p. 3), and any time she was exposed to non-toxic living, she immediately retreated to the familiar: She sought out relationship experiences that were fundamentally toxic, lacking, as Eigen notes, "the equipment to sustain less toxic living" (p. 3). The root cause, in Alice's case, Eigen states, was her mother's imperviousness to Alice's pain. Lacking a receptive Other who could validate her feelings, soothe her, and thereby allow her to develop self-soothing capacities and validation of her own subjective experience through a mirroring process, the child was unmoored, left to sit with her own isolation and despair. The closing scene of "Cupboard," David Firth's (2004) flash video, in which the main character, lacking any means for managing his mental distress, crawls into the safety cupboard to weep in desolation, beautifully captures this melancholic outcome.[1] The imperative yet intrinsically difficult task of introducing aliveness in the transference is readily evident in Eigen's summary of Alice's dilemma:

> Having a one-to-one relationship with a man provoked too many fears, too many dangers. It mobilized all the old terrors of family life: suffocation, loss of will and autonomy, a horrifying mixture of annihilation, longing, deprivation, and the sickening nourishment one takes from the other's ego-centric love. She was too damaged for love. Toxic love had damaged her. (pp. 10–11)

Speaking of Doris, who survived a serious suicide attempt, Eigen explains that she began life by responding to parental expectations for accomplishment with prodigious levels of success. Later, however, when she encountered adversity, she experienced internal collapse. Her well-intentioned but anxious parents had sowed a deep anxiety in their daughter:

> Doris's parents loved her and invested great interest in her. Doris felt cared for. Yet Doris's parents had a way of making her feel anxious about herself. Much emphasis was placed on skills, training, learning to do things...She did not have

much time for herself or time to do nothing or whatever she might feel like doing. If she seemed to be quiet or moping, one or the other parent would ask her how she was doing in one or another of her activities. If she was not busy making progress in something, her parents wondered what was wrong. She was the opposite of a latchkey child. Nearly all her time was planned and productive, with a parent interested in nearly everything she did...What complicates matters is that they loved her but their love seemed to fuel anxiety. (pp. 22–23)

Throughout a lengthy analysis, Doris realized that her mother lived in perpetual disappointment at the lack of accomplishment in her own life. Further, Doris gained insight that, as Eigen puts it, her mother "had been in no shape to take on a real, live baby" (p. 25). Faced with her new baby's need for contact, she came up against her own lack, and, failing to face her own internal difficulties, she transmuted her care for her child into perfectionistic demands for external success – the kind of success that she bitterly believed she, herself, had been denied. As Doris poignantly explained:

But in the heart of that love is a knot of self-hate, a congealed knot. It sickens what I do, what I am. I see now that it was there before I was born, before I was conceived, waiting for me. (p. 27)

The end result was that Doris thrived "in a world ruled by achievement" (p. 31), but this drive was a fragile reed upon which to build a self since continuous success was not guaranteed and since her desire to achieve was fatally tempered by a desire for love that held her back:

My mother made me into a person who needs to work and be the best but also to be loved for what I do. That's what held me back, the need to be loved. I achieved to be appreciated. My boss saw through that. He knew I was a wimp. (p. 31)

When Eigen first meets Doris shortly after her suicide attempt, he confesses that his first impulse was to reassure her. However, he had the wisdom to understand that reassurance would merely be "a drop in the bucket" that would dissolve immediately because Doris "was speaking of inner damage, and unless that was addressed, surface compliments would go to waste" (p. 21). Instead, as Eigen repeatedly notes throughout the book, what is called for is a capacity for containment that allows the patient to learn to stay with feelings and to come to aliveness through feeling feelings. Ultimately, as devotees of Eigen's work understand, the possibility of healing comes from connection and a basic faith in goodness. With respect to his work with Lucia, a patient who finally became pregnant after a series of miscarriages, he noted:

A primacy of faith in the basic goodness of our time together provided a background context for everything that we went through...The concrete clinical effects of basic goodness were many. It provided a tone and atmosphere

("spirit") that could absorb psychic toxins and a wide range of impacts...good-
ness provided a frame for poisonous and stagnant rage and for all feeling states
that had no useful place to go and miscarried. All inadequacies, incapacities,
disabilities—goodness bathed them all. (p. 54)

Eigen's notion of *creative listening* (p. 60) is a far cry from the caricature of the
neutral analyst, and in its aliveness and mutuality, it calls to mind the humanity
and dialogicality of the work of, for example, Christopher Bollas (2012), Sándor
Ferenczi (1988), and Harry Stack Sullivan (see Wake, 2006).

Speaking of the common occurrence of parents being so busy that they cannot
devote time to "being with" their children, Eigen introduces the case of Larry, who
grew up with just such a preoccupied mother: "She was most at ease when working
on her own with her chores, a model for life Larry unwittingly absorbed" (p. 74).
Eigen catalogs how Larry systematically dampened his own aliveness; he muted
himself emotionally because he had learned that that was how things are meant to
be. On one occasion when Larry allowed his aliveness to bubble up, the results were
catastrophic, further convincing him of the need to live a life of constrained spontaneity and restricted affect. As Eigen notes, drawing on Bion, "the very 'urge to exist'
may be experienced as foreign, threatening, and invasive" (p. 79). This, in turn, can
produce the free-floating anxiety – Bion's (1994) *nameless dread* – that can be so
debilitating to the possibility of living freely. Eigen summarizes: "[Bion] depicts a
state of mind (or mindlessness) in which tolerance for frustration is so limited that
mental space cannot function as a container, nor even be represented at all" (p. 148).

Eigen also draws a specific link between early relational ruptures and the potential for psychosis. Drawing particularly on Winnicott's (1974) notion of *fear of
breakdown*, he suggests that a "faulty environmental functioning allowed an external factor to impinge on the infant before the infant could manage it" (p. 172), and
this can ultimately be seen in presentations of "disintegration, unreality feelings,
lack of relatedness, depersonalization, lack of psychosomatic cohesion, split-off
intellectual functioning, falling forever" (pp. 172–173) in the face of life's vicissitudes. A therapist, therefore, faced with such symptoms of breakdown, would be
wise to be alert to the possibility that these unbearable agonies had been previously
experienced but that the primal infant or child psyche was unable to register them
at the time of origin due to the risk of a free fall into psychosis as the boundaries
of subjectivity risked collapse. Freud's (1895/1950) notion of *nacträglichkeit* and
Lacan's (1994) and Laplanche's (2017) articulation of *après coup* offer similar
understandings of this last-resort defensive mechanism.

The Emergence of the Speaking Subject and the Psychic Consequences of Occlusions and Foreclosures[2]

Entering the symbolic is a fraught process, as Jean Laplanche (1999) has noted,
because of the primacy of alterity in subject formation. "I" can only become "I"
through experiences with an Other. An infant, possessing at best a rudimentary or

primal processing system, will, even with the best of mothers, experience meta-bolic excess due to the inherent asymmetry of the infant–mother relationship, in which the mother has desires, the child does not have an apparatus to receive. As Jean Wyatt noted, "the internalized trace of the parental other is never fully assimilated" (2006, p. 191). The child's unconscious is constituted through the absorption of such metabolic excess. Precarity enters, however, if a mother has significant unmetabolized trauma. This will constitute an unmanageable excess in the emerging unconscious of the child. In addition, such a mother, trapped with her own trauma, will lack the capacity to offer metabolizing and containing functions to the child and fail to contain or alleviate the child's unformulated anxiety. This misrecognition will thereby leave the child desolate. This is why, in "Note on the child," Jacques Lacan (2018) articulates the core idea that "the child's symptom is located in the position of a response to what is symptomatic in the family structure" (np). The symptom, therefore, represents a form of *truth* that must be understood. In the case of a mother whose desire is untrammeled, Lacan suggests, the child risks phantasmic capture and will incorporate the mother's desire in the form of a symptom.

In *The Violence of Interpretation*, Piera Aulagnier (2001) suggests that prior to the development of primary process, an infant in the pre-verbal period learns to represent emotions pictographically. In so doing, the infant constructs a prelimi-nary foundational representation of self. Typically, Aulagnier suggests, a mother invites her child into a performative "speaking space" (p. 71) and creates an in-vitation for the child to take up his or her "genealogical destiny" (p. 2) within the family. The discursive demand, Aulagnier notes, "is that the child conform to an image of the child that occupied the cradle long before this body was placed in it" (p. 53). Right from the start, Aulagnier suggests, the child can experience pleasure and what Eigen would call "goodness" from the tone, content, and sym-biotic properties of the mother's performative invitation. Freud (1900), no doubt, witnessed such pleasure as he observed the joy his grandson, Ernst, derived from the reciprocity and aliveness of the *fort/da* game that Ernst had invented. Russell Grigg notes that Lacanian child analysis is all about "the subject's emergence, as what Lacan calls a *parlêtre,* speaking being" (1994, p. x). Difficulty arises, however, if the mother's emotional communication is occluded, for example, by a discrepancy between the goodness of the words offered and the discordant tone, flow, or elements of foreclosure of the possibility of reciprocity in which the mes-sage is embedded. Aulagnier calls such a maternal response violent and says that such an act of violence will shatter the representational capacities of the child and lead to a refusal of meaning-making. Aulagnier explains the construction of the pictographic representation this way:

> The mother's flow of words is the bearer and creator of meaning, but that meaning only anticipates the infant's capacity to understand it and act on it. The mother offers herself as a "speaking I" or an "I speak" who places the infant in the situation of receiver of a discourse, whereas it is beyond his [sic]

capacity to appropriate the meaning of the statement and what is heard can only be metabolized into a homogeneous material with a pictographic structure. (pp. 10–11)

She underlines the inherent power of the mother's discourse in shaping subjective possibilities for the infant:

As long as we remain within our cultural system, the mother has the privilege of being for the infant the speaker and privileged mediator of an ambient discourse whose injunctions and prohibitions she transmits to him, in a form pre-digested and pre-shaped by his own psyche, by which she indicates to him the limits of the possible and the allowable. That is why, in this text, she will be called the word-bearer (*porte-parole*), a term that denotes what is at the basis of her relation with the child. (p. 11)

In extreme cases, foreclosure of the infant's capacity for thought, reciprocity, and meaning construction leads to a flight into madness: "Insanity is the extreme form of the only refusal accessible to the I" (p. 91). Aulagnier states that should a child be left with no alternative but to incorporate alien, negating, or unpleasurable speech, at minimum, it will lead to "amputation of the subject's own psychical space" (p. 52) and leave the child bereft of possibility.

The foregoing description is quite consistent with Eigen's theorization of toxic nourishment, though Aulagnier's detailed theory of the mechanism of occlusion is provocative. There is one respect, however, in which Aulagnier breaks new ground. Although Lacanian theory is clear on how culture and language are constitutive of subjectivity, Aulagnier is unambiguous in explaining how entry into culture – mediated, in the first instance, by parents – must be profoundly violent for the child. Every society, she notes, values the status quo and will use any violent force necessary to inculcate the infant and child into societal conformity, taking care, however, to cast such imperatives as in the best interests of the child. A child, of course, necessarily needs what Marina Wikinski (2021) describes as "filiation, belonging, or social continuity" (p. xvi), but, as Stefania Pandolfo notes, the narcissistic pact by which this is brought about comes at a very high price:

The "narcissistic pact" permits the subject to project herself or himself into an ideal community, to have a place and title through which she or he can articulate a singular voice within a chorus of other voices. But there are situations in which the pact is "falsified at the outset" by the dynamics within the family or by the group, which refuses to grant what Aulagnier calls a "*droite de cité*" (a right to belong)—or proposes an exploitative, slavish, or unacceptable contract. The subject is thus arbitrarily dispossessed of the place that would have been her own, through a history of exclusions within the family, a history that is often enough mirrored in the social world. (2018, p. 49)

More so than any of the authors cited here, and more so than Eigen in *Toxic Nourishment*, Aulagnier pushes toward a social psychoanalytic understanding of the unconscious, documenting societal and sociohistorical occlusions that can manifest in the kind of constrictions we see in the clinic. Karima Lazali's (2021) research on the effects of colonialism, neocolonialism, and neoliberalism in the unconscious of indigenous Algerians is certainly suggestive of this residue, as is O'Loughlin's (under review) study of the long-term psychic consequences of the Great Hunger in Ireland. Recall, too, Deleuze and Guattari's critique of what they called *familialism*. Oedipal theorizing, they argue, represents a "bourgeois moralism" at the heart of Freudian and Lacanian thought:

> By defining psychosis as resistance to the Oedipus complex (in the case of Freud) or as the foreclosure of the signifier and the absence of the name-of-the-father (in the case of Lacan), psychosis "cloaks insanity in the mantle of a 'parental complex.' (2009, p. 9)

Forbidden to Be: The Dead Mother Complex

Picking one particular clinical instance, namely the situation where a child is bound to a mother who experiences severe depression, André Green (1972) poses the question as to what happens to a child's subjectivity in the presence of a psychically dead mother, a mother who, following maternal depression, was transformed from a "living object, a source of vitality, for the child, into a distant figure, toneless, practically inanimate, deeply impregnating the cathexes of certain patients whom we have in analysis" (p. 142). Green suggests that after rising anxiety and attempts at contact have failed to rouse the mother, the infant or child will resort to "decathexis of the maternal primary object" (p. 146). This leaves the child with blank spaces or holes in the psyche because the melancholy preoccupation of the mother ends the symbiotic symmetry so necessary to subject formation:

> …the mother's bereavement modifies the fundamental attitude with regard to the child, whom she feels incapable of loving, but whom she continues to love just as she continues to take care of him [sic]. However, as one says, 'her heart is not in it'. (p. 151)

This, indeed, is the tragedy of the toxic nourishment described by Eigen. Such a child, Green notes, again consistent with Eigen, will experience a loss of meaning-making capacity, and, attributing the failure to him or herself, the child will feel, as Green starkly states it, "forbidden to be" (p. 152). Again, consistent with Eigen, Green notes that a likely response from the child is a descent into workaholism or intellectualization to mask the constriction and emptiness, or, in the worst case, a free fall into psychosis. However, such a patient will have profound difficulties experiencing love because, as Green notes, "his love is still mortgaged to the dead mother" (p. 156). In contrast to Edward Emery (2002), who, discussing a similar phenomenon, argues for abstinence on the analyst's part, Green concurs with Eigen in arguing for a *revivifying* experience for the patient:

> The second, which I prefer, is that which by using the setting as a transitional space, makes an ever-living object the analyst, who is interested, awakened by his analyst, giving proof of his vitality by the associative links he communicates to him, without ever leaving his neutrality. (p. 163)

At its heart, healing, as Green suggests, calls for a process of mourning:

> The lesson of the dead mother is that she too must die one day so that another may be loved. But this death must be slow and gentle so that the memory of her love does not perish, but may nourish the love that she will generously offer to her who takes her place. (p. 172)

Influences from Winnicott

A pioneer in his own right, D. W. Winnicott explored the earliest infantile mind and emphasized the facilitating environment for a child. Winnicott (1959/1989) famously asserted that "there is no such thing as an infant" (p. 54), underscoring that human beings are inherently relational and function through a symbiotic, mirroring process. He continued by stating, "when we see an infant at this early stage we know that we will find infant-care with the infant as part of that infant-care" (Winnicott, 1959/1989, p. 54). Winnicott's background informed the development of his theories; familial deprivation and longing in his own formative years (Kahr, 1996/2018) led to Winnicott's conceptualization of psychiatric suffering as a complex manifestation of developmental difficulties as a function of consistently inadequate relational attunement from childhood. "Winnicott's experience as a pediatrician," Gabbard (1994) noted, "undoubtedly influenced him to focus his attention on a detailed explication of the early mother-infant relationship" (p. 348). Winnicott (ca. 1950/1989) went on to examine specific connections between "not some kind of perfection of mothering, but a good enough adaptation" (p. 44) that fostered adaptive functioning within a child. Winnicott broadened and deepened the psychoanalytic understanding of environmental limitations and how parental failures during a child's critical formative years, in particular, can result in psychiatric disturbances which may surface later in life.

Winnicott (1961/1989) recognized that, in general, people do not resent "*their very own difficulties*" – difficulties which are inherent to life itself and to being in relation to others "because they are their own, that is, are not the result of environmental failures or of neglect" (p. 66, italics in original). Through psychoanalytic work, patients benefit from being attuned to and received through a curative, relational matrix that Winnicott (1960) identified as "a holding environment" (p. 590) and from a therapeutic frame, which collectively allows patients to work through emergent, traumatic material in their own ways, in their own time; however, infancy does not afford that kind of omnipotence. "In infancy," Winnicott (1960) wrote, "good and bad things happen to the infant that are quite outside the infant's range" (p. 585) – the predominant factor being the capacity and readiness for the parent or caregiver to engage in "a living partnership" (Winnicott, ca. 1950/1989, p. 44) with the infant.

Again, even in the best of circumstances, the infant or child may experience a developmental misalignment in some way between themselves and their parent or caregiver because of the complexity of the psyche, fears, and concerns of the parent due to their lived experience, and potentially due to ancestral trauma as well. Bion and Winnicott, for example, held analogous ideas that seeds for later emotional, psychological, and interpersonal problems are sown if a parent fails to sufficiently provide a holding and containing function for their child. While a disturbance may not originally be in the child and may come from others, the child becomes the bearer of others' illness and suffering (Mannoni, 1970/1987). However, if there is timely recognition of a misalliance between child and caregiver and intervention is sought for the child's developing difficulty in life, therapeutic consultation can serve as a primary way to "'unhitch' a developmental catch" (Winnicott, 1965, p. 81) and reactivate a developmental arrest in the child.

The Necessity of Creativity and "Potential Space"

Mannoni (1999) focused on the importance of the child's *play space*, which inherently corresponds with the *space of analysis*. She wrote that, for Freud, "artistic creation was another path toward knowledge of the unconscious, since the artist reveals to the analyst a truth of the unconscious that eludes him" (Mannoni, 1999, p. 157). Freud's (1926/1955) conceptualization of creativity was grounded in instinctual vicissitudes, and he posited that the phenomenon of creative catharsis was characterized by a need "to transpose the disturbing event onto an Other stage, one that welcomes fantasy and dreaming" (Mannoni, 1999, p. 17).

In contrast, Winnicott (1971) argued that creative experience is "a basic form of living" (p. 86), particularly for a child, and that inner or psychic reality, external reality, and a third realm, which he called *potential space*, were integral to search for the self. Winnicott (1959/1989) noted that "these phenomena mark the origin in the life of the infant and child" (p. 57). The last realm of potential space, he noted, is where transitional phenomena develop, meaning that the child plays out how his or her internalization of the parent "might turn out to be the cultural life of the [child]" (Winnicott, 1959/1989, p. 57). He also discussed the creative impulse as characterized by intersubjectivity, situated between the child's creativity and the observer (Winnicott, 1971). Mannoni (1999) wrote that Winnicott was concerned about "the connection between creative life and life itself, and the reasons why this creative life may be lost" (p. 22). According to Winnicott (1971), creativity could blossom during a crucial period in life when a child's creation and imagination could produce the capacity for symbolization, depending on whether or not they feel safe enough to do so. O'Loughlin (2020) discussed the importance of the symbolization phenomenon that Winnicott mentioned in his own writing. O'Loughlin (2020) stated,

> Without what psychoanalysts refer to as active symbolization, a process that seeks to render such losses speakable or representable so that working through is possible, there can be no mourning and the inevitable outcome is absence, silence, flight or dissolution. (p. 6)

Therefore, similar to how life experiences culminate in human beings' varying capacities to manage through major life ruptures (O'Loughlin et al., 2019), "the capacity for creativity is acquired or lost" (Mannoni, 1999, p. 4) based on whether or not the child and their creative expression are actively received and facilitated by an Other.

As discussed earlier, this capacity is undoubtedly impacted by individual differences and is influenced by ancestral memory and intergenerational trauma. Mannoni (1999) spoke of this kind of intrapsychic haunting and wrote, "What remains unspoken is a wound that is handed down from generation to generation, a wound of memory the effect of which is to rob the victim of pleasure in life" (p. 31). There is so much familial trauma, often beyond our knowledge, that reverberates as personal and sociological catastrophes over time. Inner reality, lived trauma, and how both relate to these psychic cascades across generations can be unpacked through psychoanalytic work. This kind of psychoanalytic understanding, Mannoni (1999) wrote, is "aimed at re-establishing a psychic and physical container within which each victim could, through play and fantasy, transform and even overcome the distress of the event" (p. 30). Lacan (1978/1988) argued that what falls away by the end of an analysis is "the accidental, the trauma, the hitches of history. *And it is being which then comes to be constituted*" (p. 232, italics in original).

Cases of Traumatized and Traumatizing Parental Impingements

Similar to Mannoni's (1970/1987) discussion about child psychoanalysis, Angela Joyce (2009) explored an infant's psychosomatic disturbances as a function of a "mother's traumatised and traumatisizing mental states" (p. 62). Analyzing her parent–infant psychotherapy work with the "nursing couple" (Middlemore, 1941) of refugee mother Nazneem and her baby Rozie, Joyce (2009) emphasized the predicament of the infant whose parent was unable to regulate emotion and trauma, which threatened to overwhelm. Joyce discussed the connection between the "paradoxical dyadic potential space" (p. 65), which Winnicott noted, and the striking psychical and bodily connections that can emerge from parental impingements and failures in a child's development – experiences that may contribute to "holes in the fabric of the emergent self" (p. 70). A delicate balance exists between parent and infant during the earliest years of an infant's life: of oneness and twoness, or separateness and merger, which is a paradox, as Joyce (2009) argued, that is best held and not resolved. If the paradox is "resolved" (Winnicott, 1971) in the event that the parent fails to adapt to their infant, the infant can be prematurely faced with separateness and may resort to surviving "by means of the mind" (Winnicott, 1965/1989, p. 156), as Rozie did. "The baby's mind," Joyce (2009) noted, "takes over the mother's functions of thinking and adaptation (one could say this is the origin of a child becoming 'parentified', reversing the looking-after role)" (p. 63). Without an adapting, regulating parental Other either due to an absence and/or an incapacity on behalf of the parent, an infant will show bodily communications of their emotional distress, and if these calls for help go unnoticed and unaddressed, the infant, as in Rozie's case, may find refuge in dissociative states or in psychosis. This understanding is also echoed in Eigen's work; using a metaphor for the call for help a patient like Rozie embodied, he wrote in his book:

A primal response to too much pain or horror is to scream and lose conscious-ness. [...] Screaming may bring a loved one or care-taker, someone who tries to help. But sometimes it fails to do so. If it chronically fails to do so, screaming becomes empty. It does not meet with confirmation. It is a scream in the void. (Eigen, 1999, p. 166)

Joyce notes:

[I]n circumstances where the parents are struggling with their own damaged histories or in current situations perhaps of disturbed states of mind for various reasons, their capacities to put the baby at the forefront of their concerns is often severely compromised. (Joyce, 2009, p. 64)

Unfortunately, Nazneem, with her post-traumatic stress experiences from rela-tional, sexual, and cumulative trauma, was among those parents whose accumulated sociocultural and mental catastrophes disrupted the potential for a good-enough parent–infant environment. Abandoned and persecuted by her family for her sexual trauma, Nazneem was consistently flooded with shame, rejection, and recrimina-tion. The necessary paradox of separateness and merger collapsed as Nazneem believed that she and her baby were both raped and as Rozie could not bear to continue precociously adapting to her mother's emotional instability. Rozie, too, was dangerously engulfed by her mother's unpredictable states. At the age of five months, Rozie developed epilepsy, which Joyce (2009) argued was "*petit mal*-type seizures [that] arose in the context of [her] mother's mental states being over-whelmed" (p. 65). Joyce cites the argument from Winnicott (1986) that, without an active and adequate parent–infant partnership, a breakdown in psychosomatic existence like Rozie's "stem[s] from uncertainty in personality structure" (p. 12) since there was a deleterious lack of "holding and handling the baby" (p. 12). For-tunately, it was through Joyce providing supportive modeling and employing Win-nicott's (1960) idea of therapeutic holding that Rozie no longer had "to collapse into the dissociative defence of an epileptic state" (Joyce, 2009, p. 69).

Conclusion: The Clinical Wisdom of Eigen's Construction of Toxic Nourishment

Ruptures and failures involving unmitigated transferences of toxicity into a child directly relate to early and long-lasting difficulties in the child's construction of subjectivity and, subsequently, their capacity to sufficiently be in the external world. The key here is that Eigen's concept of toxic nourishment is grounded in a Winnicottian framework for the parent-child process. Eigen notes that the "cure" for failures involving toxic nourishment in infancy is the kind of ethically attuned, sensitive, and clinically tactful therapeutic fearlessness for which Winnicott argued. Such breakdown or semi-breakdown experiences rooted in infancy – original madness, or what Winnicott referred to as "X" – can be recaptured, relived, and reclaimed in manageable doses through psychotherapy. Winnicott, Eigen (1999) wrote, allowed for this kind of work through his belief that "reaching towards X is part of what makes one feel more alive and real" (p. 176). Eigen's *Toxic Nourishment* complements a grand and continuing tradition in psychoanalysis that shows the beautiful complementarity between acutely attuned adult psychoanalysis that places emphasis on the genetic origins of adult capacity in early experience and that values the work of those theorists who have devoted their lives to understanding the origins of human subjectivity, and the complex difficulties some children have in experiencing unfettered filiation and belonging.

Notes

1 David Firth (2004), *Cupboard*. https://www.youtube.com/watch?v=oykmawhKWhc.
2 For more detailed discussion of the material in this section, including, in addition, discussion of clinical child work by Laurent Danon-Boileau, Rosine Lefort, and Catherine Mathelin, not explored here due to space constraints, please see O'Loughlin (2006, 2017, 2023) and O'Loughlin and Merchant (2012).

References

Aulagnier, P. (2001). *The violence of interpretation: From pictogram to statement.* A. Sheridan (Trans.). Brunner-Routledge.
Bion, W. R. (1994). *Clinical seminars and other works.* Karnac.
Bollas, C. (2012). *Catch them before they fall: The psychoanalysis of breakdown.* Routledge.
Deleuze, G., & Guattari, F. (2009). *Anti-Oedipus: Capitalism and schizophrenia.* Penguin.
Eigen, M. (1999). *Toxic nourishment.* Karnac.
Emery, E. (2002). The ghost in the mother: Strange attractors and impossible mourning. *Psychoanalytic Review, 89*(2), 169–194.
Ferenczi, S. (1988). *The clinical diary of Sándor Ferenczi.* J. Dupont (Ed.), M. Balint & N. Zaraday (Trans.). Harvard University Press.
Freud, S. (1895/1950). Project for a scientific psychology. In J. Strachey (Ed. & Trans.), *Standard edition of the complete psychological works of Sigmund Freud: Vol. I* (pp. 283–397). The Hogarth Press. (Original work published in 1895.)
Freud, S. (1900). The interpretation of dreams. Part I, *SE,* 4: 1–338; Part II, *SE,* 5: 339–625.

Freud, S. (1926/1955). Inhibitions, symptoms and anxiety. In J. Strachley (Ed. & Trans.), *The standard edition of the complete psychological works of Sigmund Freud: Vol. 20* (pp. 87–172). The Hogarth Press. (Original work published in 1926.)

Firth, D. (2004). [davidfirth]. (2009, October 19). Salad fingers 8: Cupboard [Video]. YouTube. https://www.youtube.com/watch?v=oykmawhKWhc

Gabbard, G. O. (1994). Classic article. *Journal of Psychotherapy Practice and Research*, *3*(4), 348–349.

Green, A. (1972). The dead mother. In *On private madness* (pp. 142–173). International Universities Press.

Grigg, R. (1994). Foreword. In R. Lefort (Ed.), M. Du Ry, L. Watson, & L. Rodriguez (Trans.), *Birth of the other* (pp. vii–xi). University of Illinois Press.

Joyce, A. (2009). Infantile psychosomatic integrity and maternal trauma. In T. Baradon (Ed.), *Relational trauma in infancy: Psychoanalytic, attachment and neuropsychological contributions to parent-infant psychotherapy* (pp. 82–94). Routledge.

Kahr, B. (1996/2018). *D.W. Winnicott: A biographical portrait*. Taylor & Francis. (Original work published in 1996.)

Lacan, J. (1978/1988). *The seminar of Jacques Lacan: Book I: Freud's papers on technique, 1953–1954*. J.-A. Miller (Ed.). W. W. Norton & Company. (Original work published in 1978.)

Lacan, J. (1994). *The four fundamental concepts of psychoanalysis*. J.-A. Miller (Ed.), A. Sheridan (Trans.). Routledge.

Lacan, J. (2018). Note on the child. R. Grigg (Trans.). *The Lacanian Review*, *4*, 13–14.

Laplanche, J. (1999). *Essays on otherness*. J. Fletcher (Trans). Routledge.

Laplanche, J. (2017). *Après coup*. J. House & L. Thurston (Trans.). Unconscious in Translation.

Lazali, K. (2021). *Colonial trauma: A study of the psychic consequences of colonial oppression in Algeria*. Polity.

Mannoni, M. (1970/1987). *The child, his 'illness', and the others*. Karnac Books. (Original work published in 1970.)

Mannoni, M. (1999). *Separation and creativity: Refinding the lost language of childhood*. S. Fairfield (Trans.). Other Press.

Middlemore, M. (1941). *The nursing couple*. Hamish Hamilton.

O'Loughlin, M. (2017). The emergence of the speaking subject: Child therapy and the subject of desire. In B. Seitler (Ed.), *From Cradle to Couch: In honor of the developmental psychology of Sylvia Brody* (pp. 359–384). International Psychoanalytic Books.

O'Loughlin, M. (2006). On knowing and desiring children: The significance of the unthought known. In Boldt, G., & Salvio, P. (Eds.). *Love's return: Psychoanalytic essays on childhood teaching and learning*, (pp. 185–202). Routledge.

O'Loughlin, M. (2020). Ethical loneliness in the psychiatric clinic: The manufacture of non-belonging. *Ethics, Medicine and Public Health*, *14*. https://doi.org/10.1016/j.jemep.2020.100518 2352-5525/

O'Loughlin, M. (2023). Negotiating agency in the formation of subjectivity: The child, the parental Other and the sovereign Other. In M. O'Loughlin, C. Owens, & L. Rothschild (Eds.), *Precarities of 21st century childhoods: Critical explorations of time(s), place(s), and* identities (pp. 241–260). Lexington Books.

O'Loughlin, M. (under review). Cultural ruptures and their consequences for mental health across generations: The case of Ireland. In I. Lambrecht & A. Lavis (Eds.), *Culture and psychosis*. Routledge.

O'Loughlin, M., Arac-Orhun, S., & Queler, M. (2019). *Lives interrupted: Psychiatric narratives of struggles and resilience*. Lexington Books.

O'Loughlin, M., & Merchant, A. (2012). Working obliquely with children. *Journal of Infant, Child, & Adolescent Psychotherapy, 11*, 149–159.

Pandolfo, S. (2018). *Knot of the soul: Madness, psychoanalysis, Islam*. University of Chicago Press.

Wake, N. (2006). "The full story by no means all told": Harry Stack Sullivan at Sheppard-Pratt, 1922–1930. *History of Psychology, 9*(4), 325–358.

Wikinski, M. (2021). Foreword. In K. Lazali (Ed.), M. W. Smith (Trans.), *Colonial trauma* (pp. viii–xviii). Polity Press.

Winnicott, D. W. (1950/1989). Ideas and definitions. In C. Winnicott, R. Shepherd, & M. Davis (Eds.), *Psycho-analytic explorations* (pp. 43–44). Harvard University Press. (Original work estimated to be dated in early 1950s.)

Winnicott, D. W. (1959/1989). The fate of the transitional object. In C. Winnicott, R. Shepherd, & M. Davis (Eds.), *Psycho-analytic explorations* (pp. 53–58). Harvard University Press. (Original work presented in 1959.)

Winnicott, D. W. (1960). The theory of the parent-infant relationship. *International Journal of Psycho-Analysis, 41*, 585–595.

Winnicott, D. W. (1961/1989). Psycho-neurosis in childhood. In C. Winnicott, R. Shepherd, & M. Davis (Eds.), *Psycho-analytic explorations* (pp. 64–72). Harvard University Press. (Original work presented in 1961.)

Winnicott, D. W. (1965). A clinical study of the effect of a failure of the average expectable environment on a child's mental functioning. *International Journal of Psycho-Analysis, 46*, 81–87.

Winnicott, D. W. (1965/1989). New light on children's thinking. In C. Winnicott, R. Shepherd, & M. Davis (Eds.), *Psycho-analytic explorations* (pp. 152–157). Harvard University Press. (Original work presented in 1965.)

Winnicott, D. W. (1971). *Playing and reality*. Basic Books.

Winnicott, D. W. (1974). Fear of breakdown. *International Review of Psychoanalysis, 1*, 103–107.

Winnicott, D. W. (1986). The ordinary devoted mother. In T. B. Brazelton, S. I. Greenspan, & B. Spock (Eds.), *Babies and their mothers* (pp. 11–18). Addison-Wesley.

Wyatt, J. (2006). Laplanche's reconstruction of Freud's other-centered subject: The enigmatic signifier and its political uses. *Psychoanalysis, Culture & Society, 11*, 190–198.

Chapter 4

Abraham's and Isaac's Fear and Silence

Louis Rothschild

A childhood friend who has business that keeps him on the road in the rural southern United States likes to send occasional photographs via text message, showing me what I am missing as a result of having chosen indoor work. One photograph has stayed with me for the manner in which it affords psychoanalytic traction in the warp of living history held by popular culture. The photograph depicts the front of a restaurant named Abe's Bar-B-Q. Abe's is located in Mississippi at the intersection of Highways 49 and 61. As the restaurant's website (www.abesbbq.com) reports, folklore suggests that this is the location where bluesman Robert Johnson sold his soul to the devil. However, that sacrificial transaction is not the point of this chapter's introduction. More germane is that the creator of this business founded in 1924, Abraham Davis, started a barbecue eatery at these crossroads that fittingly bears a condensation of the name Abraham. Possession of working knowledge in western religions affords kindling to consider that a man named Abraham serving a burnt offering of meat is in itself an overdetermined idea.

Thanks to Bob Dylan's (1965/2004) reworking of Genesis 22, the binding of Isaac, there is more. In a manner harmonically consistent with Franz Kafka's (1977) playful conception that Abraham worried he would turn into Don Quixote following the sacrifice of Isaac, Dylan moves the site of the binding of Isaac from Mount Moriah to Highway 61. Abe's eatery is literally on Highway 61. Sadly, I have received no photographs of windmills at the crossroads near this restaurant to further verify and complicate my thoughts. Still, the confluence of name and geographic location found in the day-residue of the photo that I did receive leaves me wondering about the manner in which life and art influence each other and how that dialectic impacts our so-called common sense and fantasy lives.

Before I knew of Abe having set up shop on Highway 61, I'd written a paper on breakdown and recovery in the work of Michael Eigen (Rothschild, 2015), in which I quoted Bob Dylan's writing about Abraham balking against commands to sacrifice Isaac on this highway. The eatery does, in fact, predate the song, but I am not certain if Dylan knew of it or ate there before writing. Conceptualizing memory traces is a tricky business, and I tend to be suspicious of the desire for essentialist origin stories. As the highway itself begins in Minnesota, the state where Dylan was born, it is equally possible that he began dreaming of this ancient recurrence

DOI: 10.4324/9781003322986-4

in the modern world as a child without any knowledge of the restaurant. Origins aside, the translator of Søren Kierkegaard's (1985/2003) *Fear and Trembling*, Alastair Hannay, also quotes Bob Dylan's song in his introduction to that work. Hannay considers that whereas for Kierkegaard, faith begins where thinking fails, for a modern reader, Abraham's faith appears as a disease that, as Dylan considers, implicates a punishing god. Influenced by Wilfred Bion (1991), Eigen makes a distinction between faith as diseased certainty and faith as a willingness to enter into uncertainty.

Distinctions in faith revolve around the simplifying function of a singular certainty. Eigen (1999) observes that Jacques Lacan's (2005/2013) focus on ruptured unions that have driven our myths shows that it is the Symbolic that attempts to represent the complexity of wounded unions while the Imaginary perpetuates endless seamless misreadings. Through a disavowal of what is wounded, misreadings afford a defensive purview that, in denial, asserts singularity. In this chapter, a narrative that human culture developed in a linear and seamless fashion, moving from child sacrifice to animal sacrifice and finally to prayer, is considered a misreading that functions to disavow or turn a blind eye toward the realities of present-day violence and aggression that threaten children's lives in cycles of breakdown and recovery. The persistence of contemporary dislocation and violence implicates scandalous neoliberal promises of harmony and prosperity that seek to deny physical violence and the accompanying experiences of psychic alienation and fragmentation (cf., Derrida, 1999; Yates, 2015). The binding of Isaac, hereafter referred to by the Hebrew word for binding, *Akedah*, is more than a simple story of transformation of aggression into compassion. The *Akedah* is read here as a complicated story depicting an indigestible incorporation (Abraham & Torok, 2005; Emery, 2002) or traumatic intromission (Amir, 2019; Laplanche, 1999) between a father and son that represents a chronic and multicultural wounded union or trauma. Through a focus on what is damaged, indigestible, or symptomatic in the *Akedah*, there is a motivational emphasis toward avowal that labors to break the polarized representations and introjects of the Imaginary.

On the Grill

Aided by the apparent simplicity of its narrative structure, the *Akedah* leaves significant gaps in which a reader may imagine what is found between and inside the edgy space comprising Abraham's and Isaac's relationship. The *Akedah* is then considered to be a fragmented narrative or graft (Derrida, 1981) in need of digestive aid in order to situate readings that place Abraham as a mad knight against other readings that exalt him as a knight of faith. In its simplicity, Abraham and Isaac set out for Mount Moriah following the commandment of Elohim (a generic form of God) with servants and Isaac's brother from another mother, Ishmael (who in *The Qur'an* [Abdel Haleem, 2014/2015] switches places with Isaac). In Genesis, for the last part of the journey, Abraham and Isaac separate from the rest of their party. As they approach the site of the sacrifice, we may hope that Abraham is aware that the name Isaac, translated as "to laugh," is indeed a covenant in laughter, not tears, and hopefully not maniacal laughter but a laughter that is joyful. Abraham tells Ishmael and his servants that he will return. It is Isaac who does not know, and is the one who asks, where is the sheep for the sacrifice? Abraham tells him that God will provide one.

Does Abraham hope or have faith? Does Isaac trust that he is safe? According to the story, after being bound, Abraham holds a knife to Isaac, and only due to Adonai's (a particular or personal form of God) last-minute intervention is a ram provided to take the place of Isaac, allowing him to live. One interpretation of the linguistic relational movement from generic Elohim to the particular Adonai is that this story of different Gods or aspects of God marks a movement from a detached conceptualization to a compassionate and engaged conceptualization of the Godhead (Plaut, 1981). The *Akedah*, then, may be one of the oldest illustrations of the difference between the compassion that is necessary for mutuality and the damage wrought by the detachment that is endemic to hegemonic masculinity. To that end, the aforementioned crossroads housing Abe's, while substantially different, are not far from the crossroads where, in a case of mistaken identity, Oedipus kills his father.

Writing in the middle of the 20th century, psychoanalyst Erich Wellisch (1954) considered that the *Akedah* illustrates the first crime of humanity, infanticide, in a better fashion than the emphasis on patricide found in the Oedipus myth. Stories of child sacrifice exist across cultures in which sacrifice is reframed not as murder but as a virtuous act (Rothschild, 2023a; Wellisch, 1954). Wellisch maintains that the *Akedah* serves the psychoanalytic enterprise in a more favorable fashion because of the emphasis on child precarity and because Abraham moves from aggression to love, as depicted through his sacrifice of a ram instead of his son.

Indeed, a contemporary of Wellisch's writing a review of his book in the *International Journal of Psychoanalysis* (Rosenfeld, 1955) agreed with Wellisch that the psychological move from identifying with the aggressor to identifying with the victim constitutes a new era in civilization. While I like the idea of focusing on a story that emphasizes child precarity, survival, empathy, and a new and loving god, I am suspicious regarding the extent to which the strong hypothesis of a paradigm shift (cf., Kuhn, 1962) holds in regard to a new era in civilization. The assumption of a new era presents as though the threat of dysregulated aggression disintegrates like an atom bomb in reverse through a linear developmental progression to a managerial ego fitting the cold war culture in which Wellisch wrote. This idealistic, if not dissociated, narrative is rife and therefore in need of critique. To the extent that aggressive identification and murder remain threats in daily life, the promise of the *Akedah* has yet to be realized.

We need to ask: After seeing the same knife held to him used to murder a ram, how likely is it that Isaac truly feels safe enough to be candid with Abraham, much less laugh or cry with him as they descend the mountain? Additionally, Abraham's mental status becomes curious. How does such an edgy sensibility in silence typify contemporary masculinity? Can either Abraham or Isaac cry tears of relief? That these questions serve a modern, if not postmodern, individualist psychology is apparent. However, it bears to reason that even outside of a modern and individualist cultural frame, Abraham and Isaac might well have felt significant duress, and that if they did not, their processing had become disassociated.

Principle Beyond Pleasure

Abraham's willingness to prepare Isaac for sacrifice is a traumatic and contemporary representation of fathering and hegemonic masculinity. With an attitude of humility, Jacques Derrida (1999) considers it ordinary to find ourselves preoccupied in a manner akin to holding a knife over or radically neglecting relationships through mis-recognition of what we love. Examining himself, Derrida considers that by writing philosophy, he fails to engage other responsibilities and relationships in a manner that is consistent with Abraham's singular obedience to Elohim. He considers this ironic, and he also believes that Isaac experiences the uncanny in witnessing the narcissistic enactment of Abraham's attempted fidelity to singularity. To that end, Derrida focuses on Kierkegaard's (1985/2003) depiction of Abraham asking God for forgiveness for having listened to and loved him faithfully in a manner that betrays Isaac.

Simply put, for Derrida, progress is found in recognizing that singularity cannot be ethically justified and in working with the conflicting desires for singularity and the failure of singularity that psychoanalysis has much to offer. Similarly, John Updike considers that Kafka's perceived helplessness in relation to his father was based in a limited singularity of shame (Updike, 1971 in Kilborne, 2002). A demand to maintain singularity necessitates an inhibitory function that has been compared to repression (Arbuthnott et al., 2006). In the failure of singularity, rapprochement becomes a possible site for renewal.

With multiplicity comes complexity, and rapprochement entails a repeating that seeks a difference aimed toward improved reality-relating. In his appraisal of repetition, Freud (1920) informs us of a dichotomy in which some repetition aims toward pleasure while other repetition is preoccupied with mastery. *In Beyond the Pleasure Principle* (Freud, 1920), Freud focuses on preoccupation and writes of his grandson, whose play with a spool of thread is concerned with mastering anxiety found in his mother's absence. In this example, there is an admixture of engaging detrimental tension creatively and quite possibly finding pleasure in the relief of mastery. Freud describes this same child as also using the same spool in play regarding his repeating the leave-taking of not only his mother but also an absent father who is fighting in World War I. Evidently, the boy had overheard that his father was at the front and was exclaiming in play with the spool of thread that he was in fact sending his father away and that his father was not needed. Favoring an oedipal interpretation, Freud considers that the boy wanted his father gone so that he could have his mother to himself. There, Freud misses the father hunger (Herzog, 2001) that is apparent to a contemporary reader.

Following Lacan (2005/2013), we may consider intromissions of absence related to father hunger, who in fact is speaking as the boy orders his father fetish spool of thread to the front, and in this regard, what sort of trauma clot (Eigen, 1999) is this boy attempting to digest? Lacan adds that to take speech, such as the father not being needed, literally, as opposed to wondering about what is taking place intrapsychically, is a perversion. In this regard, Freud's interpretation may be considered a forced misreading, and Freud would have benefited from Bion's insight that good analytic listening entails making oneself artificially blind in order to see what is dark (Bion, 1970).

Freud (1920) helpfully offers the idea that in passively experiencing absence, this boy was overpowered, but by becoming active in pained play, the boy changes his experience. Like this boy, Isaac is also passively acted upon in the *Akedah*. Following his passivity and the sacrifice of a ram, Freud's grandson may serve to illustrate some aspects of Isaac's state of mind. Following Isaac's internalization of the uncanny in potential sacrifice, it is possible to imagine a silent scream of "I don't need you" as a reversal of "I need you." Like Freud's grandson, will Isaac create an *Akedah* playset in an attempt to master what happened? The question appears Kafkaesque and implicates repetition within the respective liturgies of the fertile crescent religions. Although a three-dimensional and liturgical *Akedah* playset may be relegated to fantasy life, a video game called *The Binding of Isaac* in which a crying boy must fight his way out of a locked basement is enjoying some 21st-century popularity (Bentley, 2020) while supporting a Freudian sense of a quest for mastery in repetition through manipulation of a child symbol as opposed to control of a Symbolic adult.

In regard to traumatic reactivity, Freud considers that in addition to being passive, surprise is indeed significant, and adds to this that being physically wounded works *against* (italics original) the development of psychological symptoms. Given Isaac's questioning his father about a missing ram, it appears reasonable to consider that Isaac was not expecting to be bound and that he was also passive in being bound. Following Freud, the absence of a concrete wound may also increase the felt, uncanny sense that the binding was possibly not experienced. Certainly, the algorithm of passive surprise and lack of physical wound applies to Isaac, and by this formula, we may say that he and possibly Abraham as well were traumatized.

Such a reading of the *Akedah* suggests the presence of disavowal (Bass, 2000) in [mis] readings that treat as nihilist any who are concerned with the manner in which the existence of trauma implicates what Derrida calls a "good conscience" (Derrida, 1999, p. 85) or a singular assertion that everything is alright. Questions regarding the interpretation of knives and scars (symbolic circumcision or lack thereof) that avow working with the invisible scars marking contemporary transmissions of traumatic or radioactive material between well-intentioned fathers and sons in precarious positions become central.

Transmission of Tradition in Bloody History

A willingness to kill suggests a hardening that brings to mind the erotically charged idea of masculinity as a chronically strong and steady singularity that disavows vulnerability within the self (cf., Kupers, 1993; Rothschild, 2003). In contrast to God's movement toward a soft heart, hardening the heart as a path to a mature manhood haunts patriarchal culture, as case studies not only biblical but also psychoanalytic reveal. For example, reflections on talk therapy with men (Corbett, 2009) show poignant grief due to breaking with personal creative interests felt to be illegitimate in order to become successful but often impersonal professionals.

A patient in session with me says, "Just what does 'A man's gotta do' even mean?" Breaking with the detachment of Elohim, I do not perversely tell him that the threat of death is an initiation ritual that facilitates growth. Due to our alliance, he knew that I might answer his possibly rhetorical question along the lines that compassion for one's self and another is needed for Abraham to lay down his knife (cf., Germer, 2009), and that embodying such an attitude is akin to the Buddhist conception that a warrior is one who lovingly occupies a raw space without skin (Trungpa, 2009). However, my patient additionally worries that his elementary school age son is being prepared for sacrifice by learning to duck walk with his young classmates in a fashion that is part and parcel of a sacrificial school-to-prison pipeline. I could analyze his concern as a projective fantasy that is not culturally relevant or tell him that psychic alienation resulting from depersonalization often appears in the demand for successful development, but those responses would be cold. Instead, we surf feelings of pain and vulnerability. What is a man to do?

In these associations, I have in mind appreciating Wilfred Bion's writing that he died in World War I (Bion, 2015) as a soft-hearted rupture challenging cultural tendencies to cyclically deny traumatic histories (Davoine & Gaudilliere, 2004). To consider the *Akedah* along traumatic lines is to shatter the unified ethic of the father as a protector (cf., Seidman & Frank, 2019). Witnessing psychological death in ethical shattering is consistent with comparisons made between Abraham's binding Isaac and the hardening of Pharaoh's heart leading to the killing of the first-born sons by the Angel of Death in the Passover story depicted in Exodus (Levenson, 1993). While the Bible does not quibble about Pharaoh's hubris, Abraham is typically viewed as a loving father due to his transformation. My point is not to deny the significance of a ram instead of a son, but to underscore that reworking a relationship following a threat of murder is not a simple binary matter.

Judaic historical scholar Jon Levenson (1993) considers the tenth and final plague of the Passover story, in which rams' blood applied to doorposts serves a prophylactic function. Protecting first-born sons from death does much to explain the substitution of a sheep or a ram in the place of Isaac. Heartshakes, a word I encountered from Michael Eigen over email, are common to each story. Levenson emphasizes child precarity in the hard-hearted choice to sacrifice a human or the soft-hearted affirmation of substitution in spilling the blood of a ram. Levenson considers that the culture that produced the Torah was not individualistic and therefore allowed substitutions, such as an animal for a son.

Presenting an additional challenge to a hypothesis of the linear development of a new era in civilization due to moving from sacrifice to prayer, all four gospels agree that Jesus was sacrificed during Passover (Levenson, 1993). In the letters of the New Testament attributed to Paul, there is the idea that the willingness of God the father to sacrifice his own son supersedes the *Akedah* in a manner that renders practitioners of the Jewish religion separatists for not recognizing Jesus (Levenson, 1993). Within either religion, a loving god with a hard heart is a confusing double image of an impersonal Elohim coexisting with a personal Adonai. In this manner, traumatic intromissions form a helix with loving identifications.

As a bloodied site of sacrifice, Mount Moriah lives in divergent social representations. Narratives such as Solomon building the inner sanctum of the first temple in Jerusalem on the ashes left behind in Abraham's offering of a ram co-exist with the idea that this same location is the hilltop on which Jesus was sacrificed (Wellisch, 1954). Links to the *Akedah* are apparent, and it is through a reactively hardened heart that one favors sacrifice and also favors one group over another. Abraham blesses only one of his sons. In the Torah, Isaac follows this by not blessing each of his sons. Even earlier in biblical history, Cain was unable to bear God's suggestion that Cain's resentment regarding his brother being favored need not prove fatal (Eigen, 2021; Levenson, 1993). The final Passover plague, or sacrifice, is but another example among many in which one escapes while another loses. This doer and done-to (Benjamin, 2018) tradition created in blood sacrifice appears as a fixed singularity or centuries-old repetition compulsion (Freud, 1920).

Philosopher Richard Bernstein (1998) considers that the problem of tradition (its origins and transmission) takes us to the core of psychoanalysis. Bernstein focuses on Freud's (1939) examination of *Moses and Monotheism*, and the retelling of the Passover story for its explicit request that each generation must feel this traumatic aspect of being human in order to situate civilized life and ego function as a tradition worthy of our collective attention. Such conscious relation to transmission requires an engagement whereby choosing relationality affords a limit to pathological narcissism so that an other may live.

In his focus on sacrifice within biblical tradition and psychoanalysis, Bernstein is in the company of fellow philosopher Derrida (1996) and cultural historian Yosef Hayim Yerushalmi (1993), who also find that tradition is at the heart of Freud's treatment of Moses. Like Derrida, Bernstein breaks with Yerushalmi's concern that Freud's evolutionary thinking on transmission is untenable in finding that through a focus on unconscious conflict, anger, and trauma, Freud's theoretical dreaming remains significant for its inquiry into cultural transmission.

Conceptions of transmission need include child sacrifice as a part of human history that became equated with sin through the civilizing foundations of humanity laid in China, India, Persia, Palestine, and Greece between 800 and 200 BCE (Jaspers, 2003). In this narrative, child sacrifice is a problem, while for Freud, patricide is the original guilt-inducing sin that the sacrifice of a son attempts to resolve (cf.,

Zaretsky, 2015 who contrasts Freud's critical project with Jasper's generalizing philosophy).

Although patricide as an original sin may be considered a fairy tale or a misreading, concern over 'which came first' may be misplaced. Simply put, dysregulated affect leading to murder can well be considered the superordinate or original sin. I do like Freud's emphasis on patricide in that it suggests that children have strong feelings, thoughts, and conflicts that need to be taken seriously. It also identifies toxic masculinity in that patricide occurred in response to abuse. Through thought on patricide, I begin to wonder if Isaac wanted to wield his father's knife or, in traumatic activation, to swim, fly, or run away. As I think all exposed children or wise babies know, child sacrifice warrants attention simply for illuminating the relational asymmetry of vulnerability in childhood, whereby a parent is needed as a container. Freud does not miss the problem of child sacrifice but instead labors to explain why something as bizarre would exist in the human record.

In the book of Isaiah, the anthropomorphized, stone-hearted, idol with the head of a bull that the Israelites are forbidden to sacrifice to is called Molech (Levenson, 1993). The name Molech is a combination of the Hebrew words for king and shame, which suggests an awareness that something was indeed wrong or upside down with sacrificial idolatry. In Exodus and the *Akedah*, something leading a king to become ashamed is shown to be child sacrifice to the godhead. The book of Leviticus contains the idea that, led by Moses, the Jews left Egypt, as depicted in the Passover story, and that four decades of wandering resulted in a new recognition that idolatry and child sacrifice were not simply foreign but sins.

Freud (1939) theorizes that Moses demanded that the people who left Egypt with him adopt a monotheism that had failed to take hold in Egypt, and that resentment regarding the demand to worship an abstract god resulted in Moses being killed. Freud states that his ideas about Moses and monotheism comprise a narrative that arcs toward a consistent view of patricide in conjunction with ambivalence toward the abstract and singular demands of monotheism. Support for ambivalence toward strict monotheism is found in Jewish mysticism, known as Kabbalah. Prior to the Roman's destruction of the second temple in 70 CE, evidence of cherubs or graven images was recorded by Philo (Patai, 1967). Consistent with the plurality of cherubs, Kabbalah reveals tensions within monotheism whereby old (Molech) and new (loving God of monotheism) aspects of the godhead remain in conflict (Scholem, 1946).

The *Akedah* is considered to have existed in a time of Molech, as Abraham is allowed but not commanded to make a substitution (Levenson, 1993). In support of his argument that these practices co-occurred, Levenson turns to ancient Phoenician colonies of North Africa. Cross-cultural and archeological data suggest that in the city of Carthage, Molech was worshiped, and it appears that, while not mandated, an animal could be substituted for a sacrifice. That evidence suggests that the tradition of Molech overlaps temporally with the traditions of Abraham and those of ancient Greece. Therein, Levenson suggests that the cultural practices of sacrifice and substitution appear to have migrated. Congruent with a theory of cultural migration, Freud (1901), in a letter to Fliess, considers Molech, as he writes that Zeus and the first Jewish god were each originally worshipped as bulls.

To Freud's credit, religious narratives seeking a tidy break from Molech appear idealistic. Furthermore, Freud's (1914) consideration of dissociation, forgetting, and repetition offers some help in regard to an explanation of this idealism. Freud suggests that subsequent interpretation impacts a particular memory and that repetition does as well in that, when devoted to mastery, repetition may aid in the repression of a feeling of helplessness. These conceptions of plasticity in and function of memory support the theory that one may repeat or enact a telling of ritual sacrifice to deny or alter a memory of an earlier trauma or murder (Freud, 1912–1913). It appears that placing Isaac in the Imaginary suggests that he is fine, while reading the *Akedah* in a Symbolic register reveals trauma. Psychoanalyst Donald Moss (2012) pursues a similar idea in consideration of the mind being blown apart due to an inability to distinguish pleasure from harm as war trauma migrates through perseveration and silence across three generations of his family history. It is remarkable that Freud dared to suggest that such trauma could be transmitted across centuries.

In *Totem and Taboo* (Freud, 1912–1913) and *Group Psychology and the Analysis of the Ego* (Freud, 1921), Freud offers what he refers to as a scientific fairy tale in which cultural formation plays a role in shaping attitudes toward murder. There, an original, or barbaric, and incestuous primal father violently rules a horde of people. A subgroup of brothers exiled by this father/ruler come together to kill and eat him. Freud adds that this father becomes stronger in death due to a sense of guilt felt by the murderous brothers, which led to subsequent prohibitions regarding murder and incest. The insight that social relations facilitate guilt and that guilt helps increase sensitivity to and bind social relations (cf., Eigen, 2001, 2009; Zaretsky, 2015) is a brilliant one, and Freud links this guilt to the movement from polytheism to monotheism as he considers that monotheism signifies a return to the unlimited dominion of this early, murderous father. Abraham's willingness to bind Isaac is indeed suggestive of orders from a barbaric god with unlimited dominion. For Freud, sacrifice is a cross-cultural occurrence also found in the feast in which a sacred totem animal is eaten and in the sublimated act of consuming a communion wafer. The blowing of a ram's horn (*shofar*) on the Jewish holidays of Rosh Hashanah and Yom Kippur to signify Isaac's survival may be added to this list for its symbolic import. For his part, Lacan (2005/2013) adds that, in consideration of a traumatic past, Freud clarifies a gap that Kierkegaard reveals in the *Akedah*.

Although not a totem animal, it is worth considering that the idol Molech the bull also functions as a sacred animal that demands a hard heart motivated to avoid critical thought. Thinking of fathers and fetishes like communion wafers, shofars, and totem animals, Lacan (2005/2013) states that it is a fetish that transposes the Imaginary into a symbol and that it is a loving work to conjoin reality and symbols in order to represent partiality (cf., Eigen, 1999). Lacan considers symbolic movement from the Imaginary akin to the care required for a capacity for awe (cf., Bion, 1981), as through symbolic movement, the misreadings that deny the narcissistic cannibalism in sacrifice can be transcended. With similar intent, Adorno

(1951/1982) writes that idealization accompanies devouring. Such thinking links to the singularity of a rationalist engulfment, as idealization fuels a prejudiced hostility toward introspection. Through introspection, critical or pluralistic thought threatens narcissism in a manner that leads Adorno to tie the singularity of violent nationalism to narcissistic identifications.

The Freudian clarification that Lacan points to in the *Akedah* is greater than the killing of the father in that, like Derrida (1999), Lacan is pointing to the uncanny in which part of what is frightening is not simply death, but the trauma of a threatening surprise, or the anxious knowledge that another has the power to conceal and effect one negatively (Freud, 1919). In consideration of this power, Lacan (2005/2013) writes that a subject becomes anxious upon finding themselves in the other. In regard to anxiety, if not confusion in identification, I think Isaac would agree with Lacan. To the degree that trauma is present, Abraham's eventual restraint may represent no more than a small step in moral progress. Yet, the small step is significant, as through associating with what is painful (cf., Stern, 2010), it becomes possible to break with singularity and to work with an enigmatic awareness that some of what we do is unavoidable and inexcusable (cf., Fackenheim, 1968).

Issues of excess and of the uncanny in identification appear as thorny as the *Akedah* itself, and Lacan (2005/2013) argues that psychoanalysis has stalled because of shying away from the question of whose voice the subject assumes when he speaks. Although Lacan appears to have been a casualty for this thinking about identification and voice (Miller, 2005/2013), a rejuvenation of psychoanalytic thinking has expanded conceptions of identification and transmission through scholarship regarding incorporation (Abraham & Torok, 2005) and intromission (Laplanche, 1999), whereby what is internalized may exist in a multifaceted register that includes not only positive identifications but also what is negative or radioactive (Harris, 2019). The extent that such transmission remains unconscious is the extent to which reunion is limited by alienation.

Tracks of Dissociated Tears

Despite his focus on traumatic memory traces revealing patriarchal murder, Freud fails to consider father hunger during a world war. Could Abraham have been as blind? Freud's grandson exclaims that his father is not needed. Freud hears the denial of need for father as a triadic problem of rivalry and fails to consider love. In this, Freud himself appears to suffer from a hard heart, and I think that this is exactly what Lacan (1966/2002) has in mind when he writes that: "No doubt a corpse is a signifier, but Moses' tomb is as empty for Freud as Christ's was for Hegel. Abraham revealed his mystery to neither of them" (p. 304). I am interpreting the Abrahamic mystery that Lacan writes of as an awareness of movement from a disembodied hardness into embodied tenderness in love through an intersubjective space between a father and a son. Avowing hospitality in a father's love shifts conceptions of identity through its shattering of a siloed and sexist portrayal of tenderness within psychoanalytic theory.

Through a study of Freud's relationship to pediatrics, Carlo Bonomi (2015) maintains that the fantasy of rescuing a child from sacrifice gave psychoanalysis a mission statement. Yet, an audit of tenderness in Freud's writing reveals that within a gynophobic focus (Gentile, 2016), for Freud, tears are reserved for women and children (Rozmarin, 2020). The failure of Freud to mentalize a soft heart as an essential component of adult masculinity that is needed in the relational space between a father and son emanates from Freud's own family history. In regard to his own son's serving in World War I, Freud appears indifferent (Freud, 1915 in Rozmarin, 2020). To the extent to which vulnerability and tenderness are denied as legitimate components of a masculine identity, Freud's work is considered to center around identifications with aggression (Rozmarin, 2020), and Sándor Ferenczi's treatment of aggression addressed in the previous chapter has been considered a deconstruction of the disembodied or dissociated aspects of Freud's system (Bonomi, 2018).

Like Isaac, Freud knew something about trauma with a father that left no physical scars, as Freud's (1900) self-analysis reveals evidence of trauma disrupting the intersubjective space between father and son. Oft-cited examples include the dysregulated words from Freud's father, Jakob, that Sigmund would amount to nothing following his childhood offense of urinating in his parent's bedroom (Shengold, 1993). That utterance haunted Freud's mind, functioning as part of a life-long self-reproach (cf., Bonomi, 2015). Yet father Jakob's identification with an aggressor (cf., Ferenczi, 1933/1980) is only one defensive side of this traumatized matrix. Another is a withdrawal illustrated when Jakob informs his son that an anti-Jewish man had knocked his new fur hat off in the street during the Sabbath and that he had done nothing to defend himself (Freud, 1900). That quiet response stands in sharp contrast to a declaration Sigmund made years later when he remarked that he was ready to kill a man who made an anti-Jewish remark on a train (Freud, 1961 in Gilman, 1993).

A binary algorithm that says that being passive and vulnerable amounts to nothing while something may be gained through aggression haunts this traumatized dyad, revealing self-reproach to be a central component of toxic masculinity. Freud's conception of gender as a hard assembly (cf., Harris, 2005) equates passivity and vulnerability with traumatic loss in a manner that neglects the importance of fluctuations between Elohim and Adonai. In this regard, Freud's assertion that he saw his father as weak (Shengold, 1993) may contain his denial (Gilman, 1993) or conscious hiding (Bakan, 1990) of a Jewish heritage linked to Abraham choosing a ram in which masculinity is imagined to be softer (cf., Salberg, 2010) than the surrogate and harder or impersonal identifications from Moses to Hannibal's father that Freud sought in keeping with a life-long relationship to power felt by most of his inner circle (Shengold, 1993).

However, assumptions of Abraham as soft-hearted are problematic. For example, Holocaust survivor turned philosopher Emil Fackenheim's (1968) considers that in the mid-19th century, European Jews were similar to Abraham simply by choosing to have children and raise them as Jews while living in an overtly anti-Jewish environment. Recent psychoanalytic scholarship (Gerhardt, 2020) has labored to illustrate that it is psychic devastation akin to bearing witness to a hostile or indifferent environment that impedes the capacity to cry. In this regard, Eigen recommends cultivating a soft heart, as a therapist needs to be prepared to sit with a terrifying and terrified scream of *Akedah*-like moments, providing a background, possibly for decades, so that something may grow over time (Eigen, 2010, 2012).

Recent popular writing by two fathers (Black, 2020; Coates, 2015) has produced public letters to their respective sons. These works each focus on the threat of violence in the United States. Each letter seeks to deconstruct the reification and naturalization of both the physical threat of gun violence and the psychic devastation encountered in the wake of shootings. In regard to the concern of children being victims of gun violence, the writings of Coates and Black implicate a fault line within the masculine idealizations of hard-heartedness. Harmonizing with contemporary feminist psychoanalytic scholarship (e.g., Benjamin, 1988; Gilligan & Snider, 2017), these two letters from fathers to sons aim beyond Freud's avowed indifference by setting sights on embodied feeling within the fabric of normalized cultural violence that is congruent with the social violence that aided and abetted Freud's own reactivity. Of contemporary concern is how a father moves from indifference to feeling and how an alienated and counter-dependent individuation may be amplified or reduced by a father's psychology. In this manner, indifference is understood as part of an overdetermined and traumatic relational representation of fathers and sons found first in a father's mind, which in this case is haunted by the nightmare that a son may amount to nothing.

Molech on Highway 61

In concern for his own son, Ta-Nehishi Coates (2015) seems to know that, at least for Black boys in the United States, the God speaking to Abraham about sacrificing Isaac on Highway 61 is none other than Molech. Following the structure of James Baldwin's (1963/1992) civil rights era letter to his 15-year-old nephew concerning the traumatic effects of racism, Coates (2015, p. 82) writes in a letter to his own son: "You are all we have, and you come to us endangered. I think we would like to kill you ourselves before seeing you killed by the streets that America made." Coates' intergenerational concern resonates as a terrorized and terrified witnessing of the insidious danger of violent disembodiment (cf., Grand, 2000). Coates shares a literal fear of being a target of violence with Jakob and Sigmund Freud that marks a specific location whose coordinates implicate history and prejudice. Situating a historicity in which Black men face risk factors unknown to Whites due to centuries of disavowal reaching back to slavery and the failures of reconstruction (Vaughans, 2014), Coates states that he writes to his son because people of color are beaten and killed by uniformed officers.

In his letter, Coates uses the trope of *dreamers* to describe those affluent enough to live in a manner often referred to as the American Dream, thus having the privilege to maintain denial of their own flaws and vulnerability in a manner consistent with an identification with an aggressive position that becomes a "habit and addiction" (p. 150). The ability to stay with fear as opposed to disavowing risk is felt by a reader as Coates wonders to his son how to "erect a democracy independent of cannibalism" (p. 105) whereby those who have "'safety' [quotes original] in schools, portfolios, and skyscrapers" (p. 85) might like Abraham awaken from the detached singularity of the Imaginary.

As long as misreadings in the Imaginary persist, safety remains tentative, as at any moment a skyscraper or school may, like Highway 61, become a site of sacrifice. Years have passed since child sacrifice was marked as a crime in Greek and Biblical systems. Evoking Molech in the present century, historian and journalist Gary Wills (2012) writes of child sacrifice as a failure to contain writ large following the massacre at Sandy Hook Elementary School in Newtown, Connecticut. Wills' sentiment is maintained in comedian and journalist Michael Ian Black's (2020) letter to his own son, who, as a young boy, attended school a few miles away from Sandy Hook on the day of the mass shooting. Black writes to his now-older son that words like lockdown did not exist when previous generations considered schooling. He adds in comedic style that he does not know how to explain mass murder to a child who has only known the death of a hamster.

In concert with the idea of traumatic transmission in the *Akedah* and the critique of Freud's disavowal, Black considers that the unspoken truth of masculinity is that fear is not confined to women. Black writes: "We raise boys to go to war; we go to war because of the way we raise boys" (p. 135). In his letter, Black expresses concern over seeing that his daughter continues to foster an integrated relationship with her feelings while his son has become detached. His writing makes a plea for emotional integration and hopes that his son's generation might shatter traditional masculinity while finding the good in being playful, competitive, and in a willingness to test limits. Similarly, Coates writes of learning to love differently through encounters with diversity and adds that while wishing he could be even softer with his son, his son will also continue to grow through nurturing encounters so as to be able to ethically respect every human being as singular yet wounded. Still, many, like Abraham holding a knife to Isaac, remain anesthetized in a dissociative dream.

This dream favors an impersonal, technocratic supremacy that harmonizes with Erich Fromm's (1964) expansion of necrophilia to be a love of the mechanical over the organic. In light of Fromm, I consider avowing the traumatic experience of perceiving that one is dwelling in a perverse age in which terror appears endless and the lines between the organic and mechanical are blurred (cf., Knafo & Lo Bosco, 2017) to include feeling and thinking in a context of *necrophobia* (Rothschild, 2023b). Illustrating necrophobia is the terror that Black and Coates seek to contain through writing against violence. Their work may be read as an extension of the Lacanian mystery of Abraham. This plea for cultivating emotional embodiment intentionally follows the spirit of Jewish philosopher Emmanuel Levinas (1968/1990), who considers that all humans who have achieved compassionate self-consciousness in breaking with singularity are descendants of Abraham and, like Isaac sparred, warrant being received within an ethical obligation of hospitality.

With an eye to sacrificial problems outside of the United States, Derrida reso-nates with Levinas, Coates, and Black in considering that Isaac's sacrifice remains pending and that his sacrifice also occurs daily as warring groups compete on Mount Moriah to claim Abraham as their own (Derrida, 1992 in Ofrat, 2001). To the extent that the *Akedah* affords sacred touchstones in Islam, Christianity, and Judaism, Isaac is evoked when a child of any of these lineages is killed due to so-cial violence. Therein, a futuristically oriented and novel humanism of soft-hearted hospitality requires a sophisticated multicultural cosmopolitanism to contain the trauma of a hard-hearted history. Such a hospitality seeks Jerusalem as a men-tal representation of peaceful hospitality stripped of nationalist violence, thereby standing against the alienating present-day walls of occupied territories and the Nakbas or catastrophes that prevent contemporary versions of Isaac from break-ing bread with present-day versions of Ishmael (cf., Ofrat, 2001; Sheehi & Sheehi, 2016; Zerubavel, 2008).

Placing Moriah and the *Akedah* in a symbolic frame of mind allows for the ap-prehension of Molech as a complicated cultural inheritance.

References

Abdel Haleem, M. A. S. (Trans.). (2014/2015). *The Qur'an*, 37: 103–107. Oxford Univer-sity Press.

Abraham, N., & Torok, M. (2005). *The Wolf Man's magic word: A cryptonymy*. University of Minnesota Press.

Adorno, T. (1951/1982). Freudian theory and the pattern of fascist propaganda. In: A. Arato & E. Gebhardt (Eds.): *The essential Frankfurt school reader*, 118–137. Continuum.

Amir, D. (2019). The malignant ambiguity of incestuous language. *Contemporary Psychoa-nalysis*, 55:3, 252–274.

Arbuthnott, K. D., Arbuthnott, D. W., & Thompson, V. A. (2006). *The mind in therapy: Cognitive science for practice*. Lawrence Erlbaum.

Bakan, D. (1990). *Sigmund Freud and the Jewish mystical tradition*. Free Association Books.

Baldwin, J. (1963/1992). *The fire next time*. Vintage Books.

Bass, A. (2000). *Difference and disavowal: The trauma of eros*. Stanford University Press.

Benjamin, J. (1988). *The bonds of love: Psychoanalysis, feminism, and the problem of domi-nation*. Pantheon Books.

Benjamin, J. (2018). *Beyond doer and done to: Recognition theory, intersubjectivity and the third*. Routledge.

Bentley, J. (September 24, 2020). Best Roguelikes to Keep You Saying "Just One More Round". Gamesradar+. https://www.gamesradar.com/best-roguelikes-roguelites/3/

Bernstein, R. J. (1998). *Freud and the legacy of Moses*. Cambridge University Press.

Bion, F. (1981). Memorial meeting for Dr. Wilfred Bion. *International Review of Psycho-Analysis*, 8, 3–14.

Bion, W. R. (1970). *Attention and interpretation: A scientific approach to insight in psycho-analysis and groups*. Tavistock.

Bion, W. R. (1991). *A memoir of the future*. Karnac.

Bion, W. R. (2015). *War memoirs: 1917–1919*, second edition (F. Bion, Ed.). Karnac.

Black, M. I. (2020). *A better man: A (mostly serious) letter to my son.* Algonquin Books of Chapel Hill.

Bonomi, C. (2015). *The cut and the building of psychoanalysis, volume 1: Sigmund Freud and Emma Eckstein.* Routledge.

Bonomi, C. (2018). *The cut and the building of psychoanalysis, volume II: Sigmund Freud and Sandor Ferenczi.* Routledge.

Coates, T.-N. (2015). *Between the world and me.* Spiegel & Grau.

Corbett, K. (2009). *Boyhoods: Rethinking masculinities.* Yale University Press.

Davoine, F., & Gaudilliere, J. M. (2004). *History beyond trauma.* S. Fairfield (Trans.). Other Press.

Derrida, J. (1981). *Dissemination.* B. Johnson (Trans.). The University of Chicago Press.

Derrida, J. (1992). Donner la mort. In: J.-M. Rabate & M. Wetzel (Eds.), *L'ethique du don (Colloque),* 1–79 Metairie-Transition.

Derrida, J. (1996). *Archive fever: A Freudian impression.* E. Prenowitz (Trans.). University of Chicago Press.

Derrida, J. (1999). *The gift of death and literature in secret.* D. Wills (Trans.). The University of Chicago Press.

Dylan, B. (1965/2004). *Highway 61 revisited. Lyrics, 1962–2001.* Simon and Schuster.

Eigen, M. (1999). *Toxic nourishment.* Karnac.

Eigen, M. (2001). *Damaged bonds.* Karnac.

Eigen, M. (2009). *Flames from the unconscious: Trauma, madness, and faith.* Karnac.

Eigen, M. (2010). *Eigen in Seoul, volume 1: Madness and murder.* Karnac.

Eigen, M. (2012). *Kabbalah and psychoanalysis.* Karnac.

Eigen, M. (2021). Rebirth: Its been around a long time. In: K. Fuchsman & K. S. Cohen (Eds.): *Healing, rebirth, and the work of Michael Eigen: Collected essays on a pioneer in psychoanalysis,* 3–16. Routledge.

Emery, E. (2002). The ghost in the mother: Strange attractions and impossible mourning. *The Psychoanalytic Review,* 89:2, 169–194.

Fackenheim, E. L. (1968). *Quest for past and future: Essays in Jewish theology.* Beacon Press.

Ferenczi, S. (1933/1980). Confusion of tongues between adults and the child. In: M. Balint (Ed.), E. Mosbacher (Trans.): *Final contributions to the problems and methods of psycho-analysis,* 156–174. Brunner/Mazel.

Freud, S. (1900). *The interpretation of dreams. S. E.,* 4: ix–627. Hogarth.

Freud, S. (1901). Letter from Freud to Fliess, July 4, 1901. *The Complete Letters of Sigmund Freud to Wilhelm Fliess, 1887–1904* 42, 443–446.

Freud, S. (1912–1913). *Totem and taboo. S. E.,* 13: vii–162. Hogarth.

Freud, S. (1914). *Remembering, repeating and working-through. S. E.,* 12: 145–156. Hogarth.

Freud, S. (1915). *Thoughts for the times on war and death. S. E.,* 14: 273–300. Hogarth.

Freud, S. (1919). *The "uncanny". S. E.,* 17: 217–256. Hogarth.

Freud, S. (1920). *Beyond the pleasure principle. S. E.,* 18: 1–64. Hogarth.

Freud, S. (1921). *Group psychology and the analysis of the ego. S. E.,* 18: 65–144. Hogarth.

Freud, S. (1939). *Moses and monotheism: Three essays. S. E.,* 23: 1–138. Hogarth.

Freud, S. (1961). Letter from Sigmund Freud to Martha Bernays. In: E. Freud (Ed.), T. Stern & J. Stern (Trans.): *Letters of Sigmund Freud 1873–1939,* 51: 7–217. Hogarth.

Fromm, E. (1964). *The heart of man: Its genius for good and evil.* Harper & Row.

Gentile, J. (2016). *Feminine law: Freud, free speech, and the voice of desire*. M. Macron (Contributor). Karnac.

Gerhardt, J. (2020). The traumatic no man's land of psychic devastation: Beyond mourning and melancholia. *Psychoanalytic Perspectives*, 17:1, 84–106.

Germer, C. K. (2009). *The mindful path to self-compassion: Freeing yourself from destructive thoughts and emotions*. The Guilford Press.

Gilligan, C., & Snider, N. (2017). The loss of pleasure, or why we are still talking about Oedipus. *Contemporary Psychoanalysis*, 53:2, 173–195.

Gilman, S. (1993). *Freud, race, and gender*. Princeton University Press.

Grand, S. (2000). *The reproduction of evil: A clinical and cultural perspective*. The Analytic Press.

Harris, A. (2005). *Gender as a soft assembly*. The Analytic Press.

Harris, A. (2019). Melancholic fathers: Tantalizing and dangerous objects. *Psychoanalytic Perspectives*, 16:3, 340–352.

Herzog, J. M. (2001). *Father Hunger: Explorations with adults and children*. The Analytic Press.

Jaspers, K. (2003). *The way to wisdom: An introduction to philosophy*. Yale University Press.

Kafka, F. (1977). Letter to Robert Klopstock, Matliary, June 1921. In: R. Winston & C. Winston (Trans.): *Letters to friends, family and editors*, 284–286. Schocken Books.

Kierkegaard, S. (1985/2003). *Fear and trembling: Dialectical lyric by Johannes de silentio*. A. Hannay (Trans.). Penguin Books.

Kilborne, B. (2002). *Disappearing persons: Shame and appearance*. State University of New York.

Knafo, D., & Lo Bosco, R. (2017). *The age of perversion: Desire and technology in psychoanalysis and culture*. Routledge.

Kuhn, T. (1962). *The structure of scientific revolutions*. University of Chicago Press.

Kupers, T. A. (1993). *Revisioning men's lives: Gender, intimacy, and power*. The Guilford Press.

Lacan, J. (1966/2002). *Ecrits: A selection*. B. Fink (Trans.). WW Norton & Co.

Lacan, J. (2005/2013). *On the names of the father*. B. Fink (Trans.). Polity Press.

Laplanche, J. (1999). *Essays on otherness*. Routledge.

Levenson, J. D. (1993). *The death and resurrection of the beloved son: Transformation of child sacrifice in judaism and christianity*. Yale University Press.

Levinas, E. (1968/1990). *Nine talmudic readings*. A. Aronowicz (Trans.). Indiana University Press.

Miller, J.-A. (2005/2013). *Introduction to: J. Lacan: On the names of the father*. B. Fink (Trans.). Polity Press.

Moss, D. (2012). *Thirteen way of looking at a man: Psychoanalysis and masculinity*. Routledge.

Ofrat, G. (2001). *The Jewish Derrida*. P. Kidron (Trans.). Syracuse University Press.

Patai, R. (1967). *The Hebrew Goddess*. K'tav Publishing House.

Plaut, G. (1981). *The Torah: A modern commentary*. Union of American Hebrew Congregations.

Rosenfeld, E. M. (1955). Isaac and Oedipus: A study in biblical psychology of the sacrifice of Isaac, the Akedah: By Erich Wellisch. *International Journal of Psychoanalysis*, 36, 410.

Rothschild, L. (2003). Penis. In: M. Kimmel & A. Aronson (Eds.): *Men and masculinities: A social, cultural, and historical encyclopedia*, 597–600. ABC-Clio.

Rothschild, L. (2015). Sensing the mustard seed: Defense, awakening, and fragmentation. In: S. Bloch & L. Daws (Eds.): *Living moments: On the work of Michael Eigen*, 307–322. Karnac.

Rothschild, L. (2023a). *Rapprochement between fathers and sons: Breakdowns, reunions, potentialities*. Phoenix Publishing House.

Rothschild, L. (2023b). Necrophobia as a nihilistic preoccupation in paternal fantasies of maturation gone awry. In: M. O'Loughlin, C. Owens, & L. Rothschild (Eds.): *Precarities of 21st century childhoods critical explorations of time(s), place(s), and identities*, 193–208. Lexington Books.

Rozmarin, E. (2020). Fathers don't cry: On gender, kinship, and the death drive. *Studies in Gender and Sexuality*, 21:1, 38–47.

Salberg, J. (2010). Hidden in plain sight: Freud's Jewish identity revisited. In: A. D. Richards (Ed.): *The Jewish world of Sigmund Freud: Essays on cultural roots and the problem of religious identity*, 5–21. McFarland and Company.

Scholem, G. (1946). *Major trends in Jewish mysticism.* Schocken Books.

Seidman, S., & Frank, A. (2019). *Psychoanalysis and contemporary American men: Gender identity in a time of uncertainty.* Routledge.

Sheehi, L., & Sheehi, S. (2016). Enactments of otherness and the searching for a third space in the Plaestine-Israel matrix. *Psychoanalysis, Culture & Society*, 21:1, 81–99.

Shengold, L. (1993). *The boy will come to nothing: Freud's ego ideal and Freud as ego ideal.* Yale University Press.

Stern, D. B. (2010). *Partners in thought: Working with unformulated experience, dissociation, and enactment.* Routledge.

Trungpa, C. (2009). *Smile at fear: Awakening the true heart of bravery.* C. R. Gimian (Ed.). Shambhala.

Updike, J. (1971). *Forward to Franz Kafka: The complete stories.* Schoken.

Vaughans, K. C. (2014). Disavowed fragments of the intergenerational transmission of trauma from slavery among African Americans. In: K. C. Vaughans & W. Speilberg (Eds.): *The psychology of Black boys and adolescents, volume 2*, 563–575. Praeger.

Wellisch, E. (1954). *Isaac and Oedipus: A study in biblical psychology of the sacrifice of Isaac the Akedah.* Routledge & Kegan Paul.

Wills, G. (December 15, 2012). Our Moloch. The New York Review of Books NYR Blog. http://www.nybooks.com/blogs/nyrblog/2012/dec/15/our-moloch/?utm_medium= email&utm_campaign=December+18+2012&utm_content=December+18+2012+ CID_2a376c0d1d593739082addeff7aadfdc&utm_source=Email%20marketing%20 software&utm_term=Our%20Moloch

Yates, C. (2015). *The play of political culture, emotion and identity.* Palgrave Macmillan.

Yerushalmi, Y. H. (1993). *Freud's Moses: Judaism terminable and interminable.* Yale University Press.

Zaretsky, E. (2015). *Political Freud: A history.* Columbia University Press.

Zerubavel, Y. (2008). Memory, the rebirth of the native, and the "Hebrew Bedouin" identity. *Social Research*, 75:1, 315–352.

Chapter 5

Grappling with the Obstructive Object in the Neapolitan Novels of Elena Ferrante

A Reflection Based on the Works of Michael Eigen

Marlene Goldsmith

> *"The wound that never heals meets*
> *the fire that never goes out...."* (Eigen, 2001, p. 165)

Introduction

All female protagonists in Elena Ferrante's Neapolitan Novels bear deep wounds, having lived through periods, if not lifetimes, grappling with severe psychological breakdown and paralysis. For Ferrante, the "biggest worry...is to...reach the true story of the wound" (Ferrante, 2016, p. 308). This wound centers around conflicts with obstructive objects as well as related difficulties with projective identification and toxic nourishment. Michael Eigen's elaboration of these interrelated concepts, especially as implicitly and explicitly described in his books, *Toxic Nourishment and Damaged Bonds*, provides a unique perspective from which to comprehend their suffering. The obstructive object manifests itself in numerous dynamic forms in the characters' lives. It comes into play in relationships with parents, friends, spouses, and even the city and neighborhood (*rione*). The first section below will concentrate on Eigen's work. The following four sections will adumbrate each one of the relational areas in dialogue with that work, focusing upon two protagonists from Ferrante's Novels: Elena Greco and Rafaela (Lila) Cerullo. It will be shown that the obstructive object is not only an idiosyncratic phenomenon but also one that is interfused within a wider psychosomatic and sociocultural matrix passed down from generation to generation.

The Obstructive Object, Projective Identification, and Toxic Nourishment

According to Eigen, we are "object seeking" personalities with a "drive for psychophysical nourishment" (Eigen, 2001, p. 35). Our personalities need help with murderous, parasitic, and creative urges, or "tropisms," which are fused. It seeks a welcoming object that can tolerate projective identification of these urges (Eaton, 2015, pp. 131–148). The introjecting object modifies and transforms aggressive urges and is critical in developing self-acceptance and contact with reality. It makes possible human contact as well as hope and creativity (Eigen, 2001, pp. 35–37).

DOI: 10.4324/9781003322986-5

Encountering an obstructive object in this search leads to significant psychic impairment. The damage done can disrupt processes essential to feelings of aliveness, creativity, thinking, dreaming, etc. Eigen writes that the "Damage inflicted when personality is forming can reach unconscious substructures necessary to support psychic life" (Eigen, 2001, p. 2). Eaton (2005) states that the obstructive object "perpetuates…intense mental pain, violence, and self-attack." It is "ego-destructive" and operates like a *"projective identification rejecting object* [PIRO]…." It is lived through "as someone or something actively hostile toward emotional experience, creating an emotional experience of escalating pressure and violence" (p. 355, author's italics).

Another essential function of projective identification is to assist in the realization of what Winnicott describes as "personalization" or "self-feeling, me-ness" (Eigen, 1999, pp. 90–91). Eigen writes that personal feeling is "co-extensive neither with consciousness nor with body. It needs to establish toeholds in both." It does so through finding objects that welcome projective identifications. Eigen writes that for Winnicott, "self and psyche are warmed by the warmth of other embodied percipient psyches. Cold psyches depersonalize body and existence" (p. 90).

Toxic nourishment is a phenomenon related to the development and inner flavor of personalization. The individual experiences toxic nourishment when "Emotional nourishment and poisons…[are] so interwoven that it is difficult, if not impossible, to tell the difference between them" (Eigen, 1999, p. xiii). Many mixed gradations of toxic nourishment are possible. Eigen cautions that "an overload of emotional toxins fused with nourishments can have dire somatic consequences, sour a person's life-feeling, and influence whether one wants to live or die" (p. xvi). I believe that the obstructive object, or PIRO, is powerful in delivering such catastrophic toxins.

The Parental Obstructive Object

> I don't know what the Neapolitan mother is like. I know what some mothers
>   I've known are like, who were born and grew up in that city. They are cheerful and foul-mouthed women, silent victims, desperately in love with males and male children, ready to defend and serve them even though the men crush and torture them; prepared to claim that men have to be men; and incapable of admitting, even to themselves that, with that, they drive them to become even more brutish. To be female children of these mothers wasn't and isn't easy. Their vital, obscene, suffering subjugation, full of plans for insurrection that end in nothing, makes both empathy and disaffected rejection difficult. (Ferrante, 2016, pp. 219–220)

Elena Greco, the protagonist and fictional author of the Neapolitan Novels, is a young girl growing up in an impoverished, crime-ridden, and squalid *rione* (neighborhood) of Naples. For the most part, Elena is an obedient, even submissive, daughter with an outstanding, curious intellect; her mother, Immacolata, finds nothing of value in her gift or in her presence. When Elena was only six years old, her mother "did her best to make me understand that I was superfluous in her life" (Ferrante, 2012, p. 44). At times, she admonishes her daughter so "abusively that …[Elena] wanted to hide in a dark corner and hope that she wouldn't find me" (p. 45). Immocolata resents Elena's enrollment in middle school and high school, both of which are optional and incur costs for this impoverished family. When Elena needs eyeglasses to rectify her vision during middle school, Immocolata becomes angry over the cost. She reprimands Elena harshly by telling her school has caused the problem. Reading too many books has weakened Elena's eyes.

Interactions with her mother do not change during adolescence. As Elena's body transforms into that of a woman, Immacolata shames her for having large breasts, which she finds "indecent." Taking her to buy a bra, the mother seems "more abrupt than usual. She seemed ashamed that I had a bosom, that I got my period. The crude instructions she gave me were rapid and insufficient and barely muttered." Before Elena could ask any questions, her mother had walked away (Ferrante, 2012, p. 102).

This trip to buy a bra with her mother is an example of what Eigen calls "toxic nourishment" (Eigen, 1999, p. 1). The nourishment exists in Immacolata's tacit acknowledgment that her daughter's body is growing into womanhood and has transformed needs. She herself will help Elena fulfill them. However, her poisonous statements and innuendos about the indecency of Elena's breasts, as well as her refusal to take the time to answer questions, constitute the projection of psychic toxins. Elena suffers a deep narcissistic injury.

Although scarce, there are moments when her mother is supportive. For example, Elena fails her first year of middle school and must take the entrance exam again. Elena despairs, believing she will never pass without a tutor, which her parents cannot afford. Surprisingly, her mother encourages her. She tells Elena that, despite not having a tutor, she can study on her own. When Elena looks at her quizzically, wondering if this is truly her mother speaking, the mother who so adamantly complains about her daughter's school, Immocolata adds, "Nowhere is it written that you can't do it" (Ferrante, 2012, pp. 104–105). This moment is one of the rare instances when Elena finds herself in her mother, nourished emotionally, recognized for her intellectual gift, and mirrored back positively. She begins to study more actively (p. 105).

Elena's mother suffers jealousy and resentment toward her adult daughter's achievements, especially her intelligence. On the cusp of Elena's marriage to a bourgeois professor and her move out of the *rione*, Immacolata becomes enraged. She insists that Elena has given too short notice of her fiancé's upcoming visit to ask for her hand. She attacks Elena in low but scathing tones.

> We are nothing to you. You tell us nothing until the last minute. The young lady thinks she's somebody because she has an education, because she writes books, because she's marrying a professor, but my dear you came out of this belly and you are made of this substance, so don't act superior and don't ever forget that if you are intelligent, I who carried you in here are just as intelligent, if not more,

and if I had had the chance I would have done the same as you, understand? (Ferrante, 2014, p. 47)

In this exchange over their mutual intelligence, Elena's mother tacitly underscores a valued, shared quality and, in so doing, recognizes and mirrors Elena's intelligence. However, the positive attribution survives by a sliver. One can feel it drowning in Immacolata's torrential outpour of toxic words. In a rage, she turns her daughter's hard-earned achievements – education, publication, social advancement – into acts of familial abandonment, selfishness, and arrogance. Without her mother, Elena would be nothing. Her intelligence is not her own. It belongs to Immacolata. It passed from her to Elena through the "substance" of her mother's womb. The two of them have merged at the deepest level of enfolded flesh. They will never separate (2014, p. 47).

Implicit in Immacolata's diatribe are jealousy, narcissistic injury, competition, and the stubborn refusal to reflect back on her daughter's considerable talent. Immacolata herself appears to be narcissistically starved for the mirroring, achievement, and praise she refuses her daughter. Only when Elena's talent radiates back onto her will she acknowledge its existence. She gloats while boasting with neighbors about her daughter's accomplishments, seeing herself reflected back admiringly in her friends' eyes. When Elena eventually leaves her husband, Immacolata's fury reaches murderous depths. She physically assaults her daughter, tries to pull her hair, and calls her a "bitch" and a "whore" in front of Pietro and her grandchildren. "Come here, I gave birth to you, and I'll kill you" (Ferrante, 2015, pp. 65–66). Eventually, as Elena holds on to her decision, her mother collapses into tears and announces she wants to die. Elena's differentiation is an annihilating, narcissistic wound. One of them must surely die. Among her many losses from the eventual divorce is the fact that she will no longer be able to brag about her daughter's marriage. Rather, she will feel a staggering shame.

From childhood on, Elena responds with hatred to her mother's hostile, enmeshing force (Ferrante, 2012, p. 69). Not only is Immacolata's psychological presence deformed and deforming, but her body is as well. She has a pronounced limp and a wandering eye. These bodily defects repulse Elena. The emotional abuse and physical deformities fuse in Elena's mind, creating an especially severe, unforgiving hatred. This fusion, in turn, creates an intensely anxiety-ridden puberty. Elena fears and fights any identification with her mother. Terrified, she feels like the victim of unknown forces beyond her control. The enfolded flesh holds a seed from which her mother's defective body will be reborn through her daughter's.

…I locked myself in the bathroom and looked in the mirror, naked. I no longer knew who I was. I began to suspect that I would keep changing, until from me my mother would emerge, lame, with a crossed eye, and no one would love me anymore. I cried then, without warning. My chest, meanwhile, became large and soft. I felt at the mercy of obscure forces active inside my body. I was always agitated. (2012, p. 96)

Elena finds respite from her mother's abuse in elementary school, where her first-grade teacher, Maestra Oliviera, sees her as a prized and precious student, compliments her often, and recommends that she go on to middle school. Elena's maestra provides a maternal warmth for Elena, frequently having the girl sit next to her while she teaches. With few exceptions, Elena will continue throughout high school and college to find warm positive mirroring, acceptance, and recognition from instructors for her academic work. She is her father's favorite, although he is not averse to using violent language while disciplining her; he often threatens to "break both…[her] legs" if she does not obey (2012, p. 126). Although these two relationships bring some warmth and balance to Elena's emotional needs, for the rest of her life, she will struggle with feelings of shame, inadequacy, self-hatred, and low self-esteem as dimensions of a recurrent depression. Accolades and the warm compliments of others will be necessary in motivating her to work when she suffers withdrawal and paralysis. She will actively pursue those friends and professors who are most likely to compliment her.

Based on the above extracts from the Neapolitan Novels, Immacolata can be seen as a pervasive obstructive object, force-feeding her daughter an "overload of emotional toxins" embedded in rejecting projective identifications. At the same time, she keeps alive a cold, hostile dependency. The embodied warmth Winnicott writes of is absent. Immacolata forcibly projects a poisonous, interfused braiding of her body and Elena's. In this braiding, it is the maternal body that has primacy and control. Immacolata fantasizes that Elena's intelligence comes from her all-powerful maternal "substance." It wields the omnipotent ability to plant the mother's superior intelligence in the daughter.

The Obstructive Object in Friendship

As a young child, Elena cannot alter her mother's disparaging presence, but neither does she suffer that presence passively. She acts on her own agency and seeks out a friendship with another young girl in the *rione*. Together, they become enlivening, welcoming objects for one another, creating an imaginative world all their own (for more on the welcoming object, see Eaton, 2015, pp. 131–148).

That child is Rafaela (Lila) Cerullo, whose circumstances with her family are also emotionally destructive. Lila's father frequently responds to familial conflict with physical abuse. Lila fervently desires to attend middle school, but her father refuses to send her. She argues relentlessly with him on several occasions. During one of the quarrels, his rage over her incessant badgering becomes blinding. He throws Lila out of the window of their first-floor apartment. She suffers a broken arm but does not cry or complain. Lila hardens herself and will give no one the satisfaction of seeing her pain. She denies its existence. Despite his murderous behavior, she insists that she loves him and takes the blame for his actions upon herself. Later in life, Lila's father will call her a "whore," as well as disown her in front of her young son because of a marital affair. Even this disparaging rupture does not keep Lila from valuing her father. Later in life, when she is affluent, Lila financially supports him and her immediate family.

In this example, one sees the father as an obstructive object so profound that his actions are murderous. His toxic nourishment is violently prominent. We see Lila splitting her father into the good and the bad object, so desperate is her need for his love. Nonetheless, the emotional damage he has inflicted has become permanent. Throughout her life, Lila will repress and deny her actual feelings, forming a hardened false self to protect her from the outside world and her inner fragility.

Despite the morbidity of her situation, Lila is dynamic, electric, and brilliant. Elena describes her "quickness of mind" as like "a hiss, a dart, a lethal bite" (Ferrante, 2012, p. 48). She reminds Elena of "birds of prey" (p. 105). Starting at age three, Lila teaches herself to read. In elementary school, she solves complex mathematical problems in her mind and writes a story, *The Blue Fairy*, that, in adulthood, Elena will use, unconsciously, as a model for her first published novel (p. 455). As an adult, Lila shows artistic talent and teaches herself, along with her eventual partner, to be a computer specialist.

Elena pursues Lila's friendship, believing that her brilliant mind and quick body will suppress the abject mother from appearing.

> Something convinced me…that if I kept up with her, at her pace, my mother's limp, which had entered into my brain, wouldn't come out, would stop threatening me. I decided that I had to model myself on that girl, never let her out of my sight, even if she got annoyed and chased me away. (2012, p. 46)

Elena identifies with Lila, creating a psychic space for her to inhabit. "I had made a place for her in me" (p. 97). Elena finds herself acting more daring and savvy in middle school and then realizes it is the result of Lila acting on her "like a demanding ghost" (p. 97). When Lila realizes that Elena needs to repeat her entrance test for middle school, she takes the initiative to help her friend study Latin (pp. 110–112). As a result, Elena passes the test (p. 119).

In these examples, Lila projects psychological nourishment into her friend, which the latter incorporates into her psyche, or, as she phrases it, takes into "the place" she had made for Lila inside her. Lila projects care, interest, concern, and a loving valuation of Elena as well as a desire for her to succeed. Elena is able to digest Lila's nourishment and use it to act in the world. Her sense of aliveness and self-confidence grow.

This nourishment in their friendship is reciprocal. Both girls live in a terrifying, crime- and camorrista-infested neighborhood. Violence erupts frequently in the streets. Elena writes that the most frightening event of her childhood was seeing a friend's father arrested for murder by the carabinieri. He, his wife, and four children wept vociferously as he was dragged away, swearing his innocence and holding onto furniture he had made so that the carabinieri had to drag him. In response to desperate events such as this one, the two girls take up creative play.

> There was something unbearable in the things, the people, in the buildings, in the streets that, only if you reinvented it all, as in a game, became acceptable.

> The essential, however, was to know how to play, and she and I, only she and I, knew how to do it. (Ferrante, 2012, pp. 106–107)

What Elena describes here is the girls' ability to create a healing, transformative inner and outer space. In this space, they suffer the terrifying impact of obstructive objects, deconstruct these objects internally, metabolize them, and finally transform them into new imaginative worlds. They open to one another, allowing a rich exchange of both creative nourishment and projective identifications. The girls show a gift for symbolic thinking, a capacity the more concrete thinking of the *rione's* inhabitants do not possess. Through this transformative process, the girls are unconsciously creating what Eigen calls "the rhythm of faith" (Eigen, 2007, pp. 109–110). Although his context is therapy, I believe this phenomenon applies here as well.

> Eigen frequently approaches different moments of experience as part of a larger evolving pattern. The "rhythm of faith" incorporates moments of crucifixion and resurrection; "the rhythm of recovery" consists of periods of traumatization and reconstitution. The decentering terms of each cycle unfold into restitution during an overarching evolution in which both participate. (Goldsmith, 2015, pp. 46–47)

The friendship between the two girls lasts a lifetime, but it is not without conflict, envy, mutual hatred, competitiveness, and deep hurt. An abrupt change comes when Lila cannot go on to middle school and Elena can. She becomes envious of her friend. Surreptitiously, Lila creates an incident she hopes will cause Elena's parents to withdraw their daughter from middle school. She convinces her friend to skip a day of elementary school and walk with her to the sea. Lila cannot go through with the plan, and midway through their walk, to Elerna's utter surprise, she turns back. Nonetheless, Elena is caught by her mother. Forced by Immacolata, Elena's father beats her but does not take middle school away.

   This event is the first appearance of toxic nourishment in their relationship. Another occurrence is when Lila, as a married woman, begins an affair with Nino, a character whom Elena has loved since elementary school. Elena surreptitiously convinces Lila to vacation on Ischia, where Nino will be staying for the summer. Elena has unshared plans to win Nino's love. Instead, when her friend and Nino become lovers, she is devastated. Lila's loving and eroticized confidences torment her. She suffers in silence, becoming an active accomplice in the lovers' trysts. Her relationship with Lila swells with agony and rage.

> I felt chained to an intolerable pact of friendship....I was covering for her adultery. I was preparing it. I was helping her take Nino, take him in my place, be fucked....give him blow jobs....My temples began to throb. I kicked the sand with my heel once twice, three times...I wished that they would drown, and that death would take from them the joys of the next day. (Ferrante, 2013, p. 277)

Lila emerges vividly as an obstructive object, projecting into Elena the toxins of her betrayal. These manifest as roiling and pressure-laden emotions, seeking for an outlet and finding it, although pathologically so, in Elena's murderous, self-suffocating rage.

Although long periods of estrangement occur after such events, their friendship never dies. The two share an impassioned, even fierce, love of words and literature that is primal in its intensity and sometimes leads to ecstatic experiences. Elena writes that "the exchanges I had had with Lila…ignited my brain….in the course of which we tore words from each other's mouth, creating an excitement that seemed like a storm of electrical charges" (Ferrante, 2013, p. 195). As described here, there is a psychosomatic field of fierce communion in which projective and introjective identifications flare, with two participants striking against one another like elements engaged in creation. Unlike the contaminated braiding Immacolata projects, the one experienced here is a "dual union" of creative fires à la Eigen.

Marriage and the Obstructive Object

Both Elena and Lila go into their marriages having illusions about who they are marrying.

Lila's fiancé, Stefano Caracci, is an affluent, much-admired young man who owns a thriving grocery store in the *rione*. He appears quiet and gentle, caters to her every whim, and buys her designer clothing. Walking the streets of the *rione*, Lila arouses considerable jealousy and gossip. Lila's father is a shoemaker, and she has taken it upon herself to design a pair of men's leisure shoes, which she then constructs with her brother, Rino. She and Rino hope to become rich by making and selling Lila's designs in the shop. This first pair, however, is so expensive that no one in the neighborhood can afford them. Stefano buys them. When reconciling after a quarrel about their wedding, Lila makes him promise the shoes will never fall into the hands of the Solara family, camorristas whom she despises, especially one of the sons, Marcello. The shoes symbolize both their fealty and their loving promise.

Lila's illusions become quickly dispelled when Marcello Solara comes into the wedding celebration wearing her shoes and a victorious smile. Stefano has broken his promise because of a business deal with the Solara family that he believes will make him rich. Lila's face pales, and Elena understands, as she watches events unfold, that the marriage is over. In the car on the way to their honeymoon in Amalfi, Lila rages. She will accept no excuses about the shoes, and she hits Stefano over and over again on his shoulder with her fists. He reveals to Lila that it was her brother and father who agreed to give Marcello the shoes, hoping that this awareness would calm her. Lila remains enraged that her husband did nothing to stop the exchange. She calls them all "shit men…*uomen' e mmerd*" and wants to be taken home (Ferrante, 2013, p. 33, author's italics). Provoked by the phrase, Stefano slaps her violently. "She winced, startled by the painful burning of her cheek." Stefano blames her for his violence. "See what you made me do? See how you go too far?" For Lila, it is a slap of truth (pp. 33–34). Stefano is just as violent as the men of the *rione*.

Lila's perceptual world changes dramatically with these traumatic events. Stefano transforms physically and emotionally before her eyes. The "youth" she married that morning is gone. She is with "a stranger. Was Stefano really so broad, his legs short and fat, his arms long, his knuckles white. In whom had she found herself forever? The rage that had overwhelmed her during the journey gave way to anxiety" (2013, p. 35). The altered reality begins to destabilize her, leading to psychic disintegration.

More intense, destabilizing emotions arise as the violence becomes heightened on their wedding night. Lila fights to refuse Stefano's sexual advances. He responds by tearing her nightgown, slapping her over and over, and adding verbal abuse. She perceives Stefano's camorrista, black market father, Don Achille, rising from the blood of Stefano's body.

> He was never Stefano…he was always the oldest son of Don Achille. And that thought immediately brought to the young face of her husband, like a revival, features that until that moment had remained prudently hidden in his blood but that had always been there, waiting for their moment….Lila was seized by a childish terror. Don Achille was rising from the muck of the neighborhood, feeding on the living matter of his son. The father was cracking his skin, changing the gaze, exploding out of his body. (2013, p. 41)

Stefano taunts her with words charged by a pathological narcissism and grandiosity. He

> kept telling her see how big it is, eh, say yes, say yes, say yes until he took out of his pajamas his stubby sex that extended over her, seemed like a puppet without arms or legs, congested by mute stirrings….Now I'll make you feel it…look how nice it is, nobody's got one like this…. (Ferrante, 2013, p. 42)

Fearing that he would kill her if she resisted further, Lila "emptied herself of all rebellion, yielding to a soundless terror…every sensation was absorbed in a single feeling: she hates Stefano Carracci…." (2013, p. 42). Over the course of their marriage, she will be beaten and raped many times. Lila has lost almost all control over her life and safety to Stefano.

Elena's disillusionment is more gradual. She believes that Pietro Airota is a progressive, educated man. At his young age, he already has a book he will publish after graduation from college. He and Elena both study Latin literature at Pisa, and she is impressed with his command of refined quotes and his careful and sober thinking. He has an accomplished and professional family renowned for their liberal views. Rather than a church wedding, Pietro insists on a civil ceremony. Elena harbors no doubt that he will support her professional needs and agree to her going on the pill until after she has written her second novel.

Elena's disillusionment begins to develop just before their marriage. She becomes increasingly aware that, despite her husband's education and progressive parents, he remains as stubbornly backward regarding the role of a wife as the men of the *rione*. His attitudes indicate that control, domination, and power belong to men. Elena's first surprise comes when, the day before their marriage, she finds he is opposed to her taking the pill. He cites health, illegality, as well as arguments over love, sex, and reproduction as reasons not to take it. He argues that if one must write, expecting a child will not hinder the process (Ferrante, 2014, p. 228). They quarrel and remain angry with one another on the day of the wedding.

Love-making becomes problematic for Elena starting with their honeymoon. Pietro is a laborious lover. "His thrusting was deliberate, violent, so that the initial pleasure slowly diminished, overwhelmed by the monotonous insistence and the hurt I felt in my stomach." He becomes sweaty, which ends Elena's desire altogether. After they finish and Elena drifts off to sleep, Pietro goes back to his study to work. To her astonishment, Elena finds her groom working there when she awakens in the middle of the night (2014, pp. 230–231).

When their first child is born, Pietro does nothing to help. Their baby's crying, feeding, changing, holding, and soothing are all Elena's responsibility, as are the cooking, cleaning, laundry, and shopping. Only once does he agree to watch the baby so that Elena can nap. However, she is awakened by hearing desperate wails. She finds Pietro working in his study while the baby cries in its crib next to his desk (p. 239).

Pietro abhors having a professional wife. He refuses to read whatever his wife writes. She leaves an article on his desk only to find it later under a pile of papers (2014, p. 267). He never reads her first novel. Eventually Elena realizes that "he wasn't happy about not only the success of my first book, but its very publication. As for the second, he never asked me what had happened to the transcript....Pietro every day revealed himself to be worse than I had expected" (p. 278).

When alone in the house with the baby, Elena "...let out terrible cries, not words, only breath, spilling out along with despair. But that difficult time would not end. It was a grueling tormented time" (2014, pp. 241–242). Elena and her mother-in-law confront Pietro with the need for hired help, but he resists even this remedy. He proclaims that he does not want "slaves" in his home. When Elena questions whether she herself is not a slave, he replies, "You're a mother not a slave" (p. 244).

Elena slips into a deep depression. She begins to ignore the baby. She no longer takes care of herself. On different occasions, both her mother and mother-in-law come to help out, but both stay up in quarrels with their respective offspring. Elena begins to question why she ever went to school. "I was always holding a book a journal, even though I hardly managed to read anything....I tried to write for the newspaper. But I no longer had time—and certainly not the desire...." (Ferrante, 2014, p. 242). She begins quarreling more and more with Pietro, accusing him of abandoning her during a horrible period in her life. She believes that he no longer values her as "capable of having a serious discussion." During one argument, he shouts at her to "*shut up, you speak in clichés*" (pp. 249–250, author's italics).

Both Lila and Elena have married men who become obstructive objects for their wives, both internally and externally. Stefano and Pietro have a need for dominance and control. Through their words and actions, they exercise an omnipotent, denigrating, ponderous power that, through projective identifications, annihilates their wives' agency and subjectivity. The women are dehumanized, their self-identifications smothered. Creative and emotional growth devolves into severe depression and outer compliance for Elena, who introjects her husband's toxins. She describes herself as empty, helpless, and alone; her outer compliance alternates with marital quarrels. Lila has repeated episodes of destabilization and disintegration, especially when raped by her husband.

Stefano's sense of power over Lila masks his own inner fears, insecurities, and helplessness. In part, his brutality demonstrates a need to control the forces of life and death that unconsciously terrorize him. As a child, the "mere presence" of his murderous father, Don Achille, terrorized him. Stefano learned to wear a "half smile," to be "slow" and "tranquil" in movement, and to keep a distance from the world surrounding him. These tactics kept his terror at bay, as did "the desire to tear open his chest with his hands, pulling it apart, rip out the heart." Later, his father will be murdered, resulting in another deep inner anxiety. An all-powerful, superior penis is his defense against harrowing, murderous figures (Ferrante, 2013, p. 352).

Through rape, all of Stefano's unconscious angst is projected into Lila. The terror instantiated throughout his body is gathered and expelled through the act of penetration. Such expulsion provides temporary relief from his inner pressure.

That psychological pressure now explodes in Lila's psychosomatic being, resulting in an experience of "dissolving margins" (Ferrante, 2012, p. 176). This is Lila's term for the disintegration she experiences in such moments. Her diaries reveal that the most frightening aspect of dissolving margins involves people and things losing their "boundaries" and overflowing into

shapelessness…the disintegration of Stefano in the passage from fiancé to husband terrified her….she was afraid of finding him formless on the bed, transformed into excrescences that burst out because of too much fluid, the flesh melted and dripping, and with it everything around…she herself…broken, sucked into that stream polluted by living matter. (Ferrante, 2013, pp. 355–356)

This passage brings to mind Eigen's discussions of an originating catastrophe at the psyche's birth. The catastrophe, which he conceives of in conjunction with the thought of Bion, is akin to the earth's primal birth in the Big Bang. It is a "constitutive psychic shattering." Ironically, "Catastrophe links personality together." In psychosis, this originary linkage explodes. The psyche shatters into "bits and pieces….flotsam and jetsam." These float in the therapy room, much like the broken, amorphous pieces of Lila's dissolving margins become sucked into a toxic, polluted fluid (Eigen, 2012, p. 19).

Pietro's abandonment of all emotional and domestic support erodes the nourishment of Elena's creative capacities, which need loving warmth and acceptance in order to flourish. We have seen how, in the face of Pietro's attitudes, her writing abilities freeze and her self-confidence fades. Throughout her life, Elena's depressive, paralyzing retreats from school and creative work have revived only in the face of warm, positive mirroring and nourishment from those she values. Pietro's toxic, aggressive projective identifications, embodying his own unconscious self-doubts and low self-esteem at work, strongly evoke her identification as someone unworthy of exercising freedom, creativity, and agency. Despite the fact that Pietro's behavior is not physically abusive, he brutalizes her psychic well being with massive attacks against the totality and integrity of her Self. These attacks eradicate compassion for her emotional pain and physical exhaustion. As Elena recognizes, she is a slave in her own home.

Naples as an Obstructive Object

In the Neapolitan Novels, Naples takes on the force of another character, an all-pervasive, engulfing, squalid, and brutalizing protagonist. Naples itself becomes an obstructive object invading going-on-being. It robs life of vitality, imagination, love, and creativity, instilling it with despair, hatred, dread, and anxiety. Its forceful brew ejects a projective identification that violates the mind and body of its victims. Elena describes it as a "pall" that spreads in and through the neighborhood. Assault, crime, drugs, theft, disease, revenge, rape, and a dialect embodying them all constitute daily experience. Children are not spared exposure to its rampant violence. They grow up with fear woven into the texture of their waking and often sleeping lives. Nightmares plague their dreams.

> We grew up in a world where children and adults were often wounded, blood flowed from the wounds, they festered, and sometimes people died....Our world was full of words that killed: croup, tetanus, typhus, gas, war, lathe, rubble, work, bombardment, bomb, tuberculosis, infection. With these words and those years, I bring back the many fears that accompanied me all my life. (Ferrante, 2012, p. 33)

Wife beating is common, even accepted, among men and women. It demonstrates the machismo so valued by the community and passed on from generation to generation. Both Lila and Elena see their mothers beaten. Lila herself, as shown above, is the victim of murderous paternal violence. Children are violent with one another. For example, Lila was beaten as a child by the teenager Stefano because she had defeated his younger brother in a school competition. Children often hurl rocks at one another. On one occasion, young Lila suffers such a severe blow that she is knocked to the ground (2012, pp. 34–35).

Men are not the only perpetrators. Terrified, Elena sees two women from her apartment complex brawling, pulling one another's hair, and tumbling down the inner landing and stairs. Fights break out more often, and rage lasts longer among the women than the men.

As a child I imagined tiny, almost invisible animals that arrive in the neighbor-hood at night, they came from the ponds, from the abandoned train, cars beyond the embankment, from the stinking grasses…from the frogs, the salamanders, the flies, the rocks, the dust, and entered the water and the food and the air, making our mothers, our grandmothers, as angry as starving dogs. (Ferrante, 2012, pp. 37–38)

The very connective tissue of Naples consists of corruption, rage, and revenge, as well as a generationally inherited violence and misogyny. It slips into the bodies of its inhabitants and burrows into their psyches, where it never leaves, even if left. When deeply enraged, Elena finds herself sliding from the use of her educated, formal Italian into the course squalid forms of the *rione's* dialect, or mother tongue. Like a Siren, Naples always calls. Before the four novels end, Elena will move back temporarily because of a writing project. The monstrous obstructive object that dozes in her psyche lies as background to her educated, sophisticated, literary self. It awaits an encounter potent enough to make it arise.

Conclusion

The obstructive object in the Neapolitan Novels embodies an expanding and con-tracting inter- and intrapersonal force. It arises from and feeds back into a greater psychosomatic-sociocultural matrix. This matrix is passed on from generation to generation, spreading inwardly and outwardly through mothers, fathers, friends, children, and Naples itself. Its death-driven energy imparts a deadened and deadly quality to the personalities of its inhabitants and, in turn, absorbs qualities from them in a continuous, dialectical loop. Processes such as love, creativity, dreaming, and imagination succumb to its annihilating power. In their place, a transactional mentality characterized by greed, rage, dehumanization, and violence flourishes. Naples itself is a poisonous wound that never heals. As a wounded and wounding protagonist, she neither shelters nor heals her suffering inhabitants. Their relation-ship to the city and one another is one of continuous grappling with the multi-di-mensional, unrelenting obstructive object running through its veins.

References

Eaton, J.L. (2005). The obstructive object. *Psychoanalytic Review, 92*(3), 355–372.
Eaton, J.L. (2015). Becoming a welcoming object: Personal notes on Michael Eigen's Im-pact. *Psychoanalytic Review, 92*(3), 131–138.
Eigen, M. (1999). *Toxic Nourishment.* London: Karnac.
Eigen, M. (2001). *Damaged Bonds.* London: Karnac.
Eigen, M. (2007). *Feeling Matters.* London: Karnac.
Eigen, M. (2012). *Kabbalah and Psychoanalysis.* London: Karnacs.
Ferrante, E. (2012). *My Brilliant Friend* (A. Goldstein, Trans). New York: Europa Editions. (Original work published 2011).
Ferrante, E. (2013). *The Story of a New Name* (A. Goldstein, Trans.). New York: Europa Editions. (Original work published 2012).

Ferrante, E. (2014). *Those Who Leave and Those Who Stay* (A. Goldstein, Trans.). New York: Europa Editions. (Original work published 2013).

Ferrante, E. (2015). *The Story of the Lost Child* (A. Goldstein, Trans.). New York: Europa Editions. (Original work published 2014).

Ferrante, E. (2016). *Frantumaglia* (A. Goldstein, Trans.). New York: Europa Editions. (Original work Published 2016)

Goldsmith, M. (2015). The work of Michael Eigen: Into the heart of psychoanalysis. In: S. Bloch and L. Daws (Eds.): *Living Moments: On the Work of Michael Eigen*, 33–50. London: Karnac..

Chapter 6

Undreamable Dreams

Françoise Davoine

Introduction

Mike Eigen's profound comments on Bion's work resonate with Jean-Max Gaudillière's seminar at the EHESS (Paris 2001–2014), whom he considered his friend. As a token of our friendship across the ocean, I will speak about "undreamable dreams."

When Bion coined the expression *"thoughts without a thinker"* (Bion 1977, p. 165), he may have borrowed this expression from Laurence Sterne's *Tristram Shandy*: "I believe in my conscience I intercept many a thought which heaven intended for another man" (Sterne 1980, p. 381), as I will probably intercept from Mike, many a thought, drawn from his prodigious experience with persons doomed to be *unanalyzable* for lack of transference, by mainstream psychoanalysis. When they challenge my neutrality by wishing to stop coming, I feel useless, speechless, and lacking imagination and theoretical tools.

Time Stops

At the start, I will give an example that I quote often. Recently, it came to my mind under a new "vertex," as Bion would say, some 40 years after it had visited me initially and helped me make contact with an unreachable so-called schizophrenic analysand. The new vertex came from her recent phone call. Meanwhile, she had resumed her work and the care of her children, which was regularly interrupted before we met by frequent hospitalizations.

Here is the news. Many years after our first encounter, she wished to share with me that a film and a book came out about her mother's professional life that she was vaguely aware of before her assassination at Auschwitz. She had been a creative librarian for children, so a plaque was to be put on the library wall where her mother had worked, in the street not far from my home.

I was stunned. So, an inscription was bringing justice to her mother, whose betrayal had been unmasked, thanks to a strange transference revealed by the dream I will tell. I call it "undreamable" for two reasons. My first reaction was to say to myself: It was not a dream, just a tape recording of our previous and first session. When, after a long while, I could identify the agency speaking in it, I was amazed.

DOI: 10.4324/9781003322986-6

This lady was one of my first patients in private practice some 40 years ago, a very long time for the inscription of her mother's memory. It took Bion 50 years to write down his experience of WWI in two autobiographical books and fictional dialogues entitled *A Memoir of the Future*. The new vertex upon that dream, related to an unspeakable experience that I realize now, was "a premature knowledge," Bion's expression, that pushed me to become an analyst with persons condemned to a psychotic structure, like her.

The most uncanny part of that experience is being confronted with the stoppage of time at critical moments when the past becomes present as well as the future, as says Bion's title, *A Memoir of the Future*. The expression "memory of the future" is repeated in Kurt Vonnegut's bestseller *Slaughter House Five*, published in 1969, a year after Bion's exile to Los Angeles. It stems from the author's incarceration in an underground slaughterhouse in Dresden, which saved his life when the town was destroyed in February 1945. I may say that the premature knowledge in that undreamable dream expressed a memory of my future practice. This was a strange feeling when the worldwide pandemic and the recent war in Europe happened that we could not have imagined a few years ago, actualizing the ancient plagues and world wars in the present. Vonnegut calls it a "*Timequake.*"

Historical Context

The following is the context preceding the timequake that erupted in the short dream. In the seventies, as Jean-Max Gaudillière and I worked in a sociological lab called The *Center for the Study of Social Movements* at the EHESS, we followed Lacan's seminars and joined the École Freudienne (by the way, the two did not like each other). We had decided to research anti-psychiatric movements and landed, for comparison, in a public psychiatric hospital situated on the battlefields of the North of France, where we stayed against all odds, thanks to the medical director, Edmond Sanquer, who was also an analyst. Although we were neither psychiatrists nor psychologists, we turned to become analysts, trained by confined patients, some of them staying there since the last war. Until his retirement, we followed Sanquer to two other hospitals, the last one near Paris.

It took me a very long time to realize that Bion and my grandfathers had fought close to the grounds of the first hospital. But right away, after conversing with a man who told me about his hospitalization just after the war, I was struck by a *dreamable dream* in which that grandfather appeared. I knew he had been a stretcher-bearer, but he never spoke about it. Later on, reading a book published in 1919 about his regiment, I learned he had been on all the fronts of WWI.

In the meantime, we had to lead a mandatory weekly seminar in our institute, which lasted 40 years until Jean-Max's death in 2015. Sitting on the fence between social sciences, mainstream psychoanalysis, and the analytic psychotherapy of psychosis, we considered madness as co-research on erased parts of historical catastrophes for both the patient and the analyst. We entitled our seminar *Madness and the Social Link.* Confidentiality prevents us from discussing clinical cases with an interdisciplinary audience. We read, each year in our turn, an author akin to our seminar topic, such as Bion and many others.

After some years, I started a private practice. I used to see discharged patients for free in the dispensary for outpatients, but some insisted on consulting me in another setting for a few euros. Having a salary, I did not care about the money. In that context, a lady who had escaped from another hospital got my address from a nurse who knew a nurse in the ward where I worked.

Her face was very white. Her stoney eyes were familiar, like those of other patients and my mother's at times. But that occurred to me much later on. In a monotonous tone, she told me about her repetitive confinements when she was caught by a demon and could not go to work nor care for her children. I asked her what triggered that demon each time. When, as a regular Lacanian analyst, I heard the signifier "commune" repeated in every circumstance, I asserted firmly, out of the blue: "Commune is what drives you crazy." Right away, her face became pink, and she told me the following story:

Her parents were communists. Her mother had been arrested in front of her eyes when she was three, and both were separated. Later on, she was deported to Auschwitz. She had not been told that her mother was dead, only that "your mum will not come back," so she waited for her, still looking for her among the living dead in the hospital. Every year, a celebration was held by the party before the plaque, celebrating her mother as a heroine of the communist resistance. As far as she remembers, these memorials unsettled her a great deal. Now she could put words to that infernal sensation.

She was the only one to know that her mother had been arrested by the militiamen as a Jew and not as a resistant. But that truth was impossible to tell anyone. Her father, who remarried a comrade, came from a Jewish family too but considered the matter irrelevant. After delivering that message, she rose up and left. I quickly gave her an appointment for the following week, not expecting she would come back, but she did. She had been discharged from the hospital, and we started meeting once a week, with ups and downs and a re-hospitalization that occurred the following year.

The head of the hospital phoned me, saying that psychoanalysis was contraindicated as it caused her to relapse. Trembling, I asked him to allow her to come for her subsequent session. To my utter surprise, he said yes. I almost regretted having insisted when I saw her mother's ghost enter my office – as she looked indeed like an old woman – and, through her daughter's mouth, shout at me that I was Mengele and that I had done experiments on her. Shaking again, I answered that, as a young analyst, I had probably done experiments *with* her, not *on* her. Anyway, after she slammed the door, I was lost in space and time. She returned, discharged from the hospital, and in great shape after we had faced together the "attack on linking" performed by the ruthless agency that had murdered all otherness, including her mother.

I said "together," and I will trace now how our link started right away thanks to the "undreamed dream" that occurred the night following our first session.

An Embryo's Dream

I was inside a house where there was an indoor pool, which was very unusual. Inside, my baby son had drowned. I took him and proceeded to do mouth-to-mouth resuscitation, and he turned pink. That was the dream.

This dream upset me since I was, at the time, a young mother. It took me some time to question the strange indoor pool. Much later, I realized that the French word for pool, which is "bassin," also means womb. Another signifier? I had been in my mother's womb when the Nazis caught her, and after being confined in three different jails, she was nearly sent to a concentration camp. She never talked about it except to say, "Had I been Jewish, I would not be here." Me neither.

Believe me, her story seemed normal to me in times of war, which was also normal for me since I saw the light in the middle of it. After her improbable release, I was born in my native alpine region, on the border of Italy, where the war was raging. My father was part of a resistance network that met in our kitchen. Hence, perhaps this explains my familiarity with traumatized people diagnosed with psychosis in hospitals. By then, the word trauma was not in fashion, and my very Lacanian analyst was not interested at all in wartime.

Yet the assertive tone that I eructed in our first session brought us to the present time of the war, evidence-based by the dream.

A young historian, Hervé Mazurel, recently wrote the book *The Unconscious and the Oblivion of History*. I agree with his writing, although among his wealth of references, he does not quote the names of pioneers in the psychoanalysis of psychosis who trained themselves in military hospitals with traumatized soldiers. For example, he does not quote Bion, who wrote, "I died in Cambrai, in Amiens," then being Captain Bion, commander of a tank section, when all the men of his crew were killed. The names of those pioneers, like Frieda Fromm Reichmann in Germany, Sandor Ferenczi in Hungary, William Rivers in England, Harry Stack Sullivan, and Thomas Salmon in the US, had worked in military hospitals during WWI, with Salmon at Ellis Island beforehand. They were totally ignored in our school of psychoanalysis. Jean-Max and I discovered them in the 1980s when we started to visit the Austen Riggs Center regularly and talked with analysts who, contrary to orthodoxy, proved that transference was possible with psychosis. Both Otto Will and Martin Cooperman, psychoanalysts at Riggs, were veterans of the Guadalcanal battle in the Pacific.

The new vertex for my undreamable dream is to consider it as dreamt by a veteran embryo. Of course, we could interpret the drowned baby becoming pink when I reanimate him as a metaphor for the patient. Still, it expressed the real threat of that embryo being drowned if my mother had not escaped. Transference manifested itself the following night as interference between unspeakable elements, called by Bion in his Grid (1977) "beta elements," and by Socrates in the *Thaetetus* (Plato,

1955, 202b) *"stoicheia aloga:* primary elements," without speech, "the intertwining of which," he says, "creates the *logos,* meaning speech and reason," Bion's "alpha function."

My own oblivion of history as presented by the dream struck me belatedly when I read Bion, who had read *Tristram Shandy.* In fact, the opposite is true for me: I read the *Memoir of the Future* only in 2017, when I transcribed, thanks to the Erikson Institute at Austen Riggs Center, my notes of Jean-Max's EHESS seminars (who spoke without any notes!). However, in 2008, I started a seminar on Laurence Sterne's novel, which I continued for two more years since he claims to follow the footsteps of Cervantes, who was my hero in previous seminars. Like him, who calls Don Quixote "his son," whom he sends on the road through the novel, hallucinating his author's unspeakable wars and slavery, Sterne writes down his military father's campaigns, thanks to Captain Shandy's and his Sancho Panza, Caporal Trim's, traumatic revivals.

But I was not prepared to start the novel with the prenatal psychoanalysis of Tristram's embryo, who, at the very beginning, launches a peremptory "I Wish," uttered from his mother's womb, followed by the sentence: "(I wish) either my father or my mother, or indeed both of them, as they were in the duty both equally bound to it, had minded what they were at when they begot me" (Sterne 1980, p. 1). It came to my mind that I could have said the same thing (Davoine 2023).

So, what is undreamable is the "timequake" of my embryo taking the floor and coming to the rescue of a three-year-old girl, left totally alone. Likewise, in the *Memoir of the Future,* Bion gives voices to his embryonic cells called "Somites."

Image Thinking

So I wondered if the words "commune" and *"bassin"* were not at first signifiers, but images of words, Mike, may attribute them to Freud's primary process. They became signifiers only when they were linked by a narrative, that is, when they could be addressed thanks to the transference. In her recent book, Mieke Bal calls "image-thinking" a process dealing not only with visual images but also sounds. It aims to create another from scratch in the absence of all otherness.

In the first session, when I uttered, "It's the commune which drives you crazy," I felt ashamed by my tone of voice, as I was trained to echo signifiers in a less abrupt style. That very tone, often used in my native region, was also discordant with the academic rhetoric, making me fearful of speaking in public or even writing according to the rules.

I realize only now that the rhythm of the accent and the rough humor of people there were still alive when I told stories to my patients, as well as in our seminar, sometimes bursting into an old song that the participants would sing joyfully. I was so far from the analytic jargon *peppered* with Lacanian puns. Visual images and sounds appear on the brink of death zones, *area di morte,* according to Gaetano Benedetti, – an analyst in Basel of psychoses – and in the transference, they give birth to a "transitional subject," which, in the story, I told, is a political subject.

Another essential reference for such an atypical transference is given by Wittgenstein, when he modified the last sentence of his *Tractatus Philosophicus*, written when he was fighting in the Austrian army on the Eastern Front, "Whereof one cannot speak one must be silent." In his *Philosophical Investigations*, written after he returned to Cambridge in 1929, having spent ten years in Vienna in a PTSD state, he contended that whereof one cannot speak, one cannot help showing what cannot be said. To whom? That is the question. It may be, as he writes at the end of his book, "a tone of voice, a glance, a gesture, a facial expression," manifesting an "imponderable evidence that the person is not pretending."

I call my dream undreamable since it is neither a dream of repressed desires nor a traumatic dream. However, it manifests the imponderable evidence of an embryonic therapist at the side of the little girl whom her own people had betrayed – the definition of trauma by Jonathan Shay in his book *Achilles in VietNam*. As a matter of fact, the etymology of the word therapist is a Homeric word, *therapôn*, which has a double meaning: the second in combat, and the ritual double, in charge of funeral duties (Nagy 1999).

That duty was accomplished when the old, lonely little girl saw the name of her mother inscribed in the book *Memorial* listing the names of each convoy toward the concentration camps, published by Serge Klarsfeld. Should I have disclosed that dream? At that time, I did not dare. Later, I was encouraged by Gaetano Benedetti to do so. He said we are not the owners of such dreams; they belong to the space-time of the session, where intense images flock to the border of death areas in the arrested time of the catastrophe.

Time stops when the symbolic chain collapses, as symbolic numbers are no longer available for chronology. Yet, for the sake of survival, Bion notes, a memory remains, registering every detail through hyper-vigilance, in a "timeless time," so that it "cannot forget." The lady's white face and far-away glance when she arrived were probably her expression and also her mother's when she disappeared forever. Much later, I learned that she had been allowed to call the babysitter. I could not forget either what happened during my mother's pregnancy, when now and then she showed a far-away look, which seemed normal to me.

Conversely, I am told by analysts who come for supervision from different backgrounds that they do not dare speak to colleagues about strange dreams, blunders, or uncanny impressions connected to their patients who have gone through extreme experiences. They anticipate the answer: "That is not psychoanalysis; you should go back on the couch."

The question is, what is psychoanalysis in such circumstances? It is better to ask Freud.

Freud's Non-Repressed Unconscious

After he abandoned his "Neurotica," his psychoanalysis of traumas, in a letter to Fliess (September 21, 1897), turning to the Oedipus complex, Freud returned to his Neurotica on several occasions, including in his commentary on Jensen's *Gradiva*, which was published in 1907. The short story features a young delusional archeologist fascinated by the ankle of a Pompeian girl who died in 79 AD under the ashes of the Mount Vesuvius eruption.

The archeologist is particularly shaken by a dream in which he sees her agony as she lies on a bench in front of a temple, so he decides to travel to the archeological site. There, he will be healed from his madness thanks to the chance encounter with a young neighbor whom he did not recognize at first. When he hallucinates that she is his beloved Gradiva, she does not flee nor diagnose him as paranoid, but enters his delusion, playing Gradiva's part in his dream when she faces her death. Then she rises up again, telling him her name: Zoé, life in ancient Greek.

Transference between them is a genuine intertwining of "primitive agony," as per Winnicott (1974, p. 104). Both are orphans. Death struck him at a young age when he lost his two parents. She had also lost her mother, leaving the little girl with an entomologist father who was more interested in his insects than in his daughter.

Two sentences in Freud's essay are closely related to my topic. Freud asks us to pay attention to the expression "repressed memories" applied to the young man's childhood relations with the young girl. He writes: "Everything that is repressed is unconscious, but we cannot assert that everything unconscious is repressed."

This non-repressed unconscious cannot be constituted by the signifiers of the symbolic chain, Freud's secondary process, since the latter collapsed, but by images of words and things of the primary process, recorded by our senses. Aby Warburg calls them "surviving images, *nachleben*," surviving disasters.

At the beginning of his *Gradiva*, Freud ponders the conundrum of "dreams which are not dreamed," such as those "which are imagined by creative writers." And he answers with a beautiful sentence: "Creative writers are our valuable allies, *Bundesgenossen*, and their evidence is to be prized highly, for they are apt to know a whole host of things between heaven and earth of which our philosophy has not let us dream." We can add "neither do our schools of psychoanalysis." Indeed, the kind of dream I mentioned may be credited to an authorship, creating, in between us, "a political subject," who fights against the erasure of traces by hatred and denial.

My friend Jeanne Wolf Bernstein, an analyst in Vienna, gave me another translation for Freud's word *Bundesgenossen*, which also means "fellow travelers." An exceptional creative writer, Mike Eigen is also our precious "fellow traveler" who takes us by the hand all along the perilous journeys of our co-research with people who have gone through extreme experiences. The large culture that he shares with us generously is expressed in a unique rhythm and a style full of wit and storytelling, taking us from negativity toward sources of life and spirituality. As Bion says, "he is an analyst who works with his personality." I thank him for transmitting his indomitable courage to us.

Bibliography

Arendt, H. (1976). *The Origins of Totalitarianism*. Harcourt Brace & Company.
Bal, M. (2022). *Image-Thinking*. Edinburgh University Press.

Benedtti, G. (1980). *Alienazione e Personazione nella Psychoerapia della Malattia Mentale*. Einaudi.

Bion, W.R. (1977). *The Grid and Caesura*. Routledge.

Bion, W.R. (1982). *The Long Weekend*. Karnac.

Bion, W.R. (1985). *All My Sins Remembered*. Karnac.

Bion, W.R. (1993). *Attacks on Linking in Second Thoughts*. Karnac.

Bion, W.R. (2018). *A Memoir of the Future*. Routledge.

Davoine, F.A. (2023). *Shandean Psychoanalysis, Tristram Shandy, Madness and Trauma*. Routledge.

De Cervantes, M. (2015). *Don Quixote*. Baker & Taylor.

Freud, S. (1985). *The Complete Letters of Freud to Wilhelm Fliess, 1887–1904*. Harvard University Press.

Freud, S. (1990). *Jensen's Gradiva* (vol. 14, p. 73). Penguin Books.

Gaudillière, J.M. (2021). *The Birth of a Political Self* (Trans. by F. Davoine). Routledge.

Mazurel, H. (2021). *L'inconscient ou l'oubli de l'histoire*. La Découverte.

Nagy, G. (1999). *The Best of the Acheans*. Johns Hopkins University Press.

Plato (1955). *Thaetetus*. Liberal Arts Press.

Shay, J. (1994). *Achilles in Vietnam*. Touchstone Books.

Sterne, L. (1980). *The Life and Opinions of Tristram Shandy, Gentleman* (vol. XIII, ch. 2, p. 381). Norton.

Vonnegut, K. (1969/1991). *Slaughter House-Five*. Random House.

Vonnegut, K. (1997). *Timequake*. Penguin Books.

Warburg, A. (1923). *A Lecture on Serpent Ritual*. Journal of the Warburg Institute, 2 (4), 277–292. [Trans. by W.F. Mainland]

Winnicott, D.W. (1974). *Fear of Breakdown*. International Review of Psychoanalysis, 1, 103–107.

Wittgenstein, L. (1975). *Tractatus Logico—Philosophicus*. Routledge.

Wittgenstein, L. (1984). *Philosophical Investigations*. Basil Blackwell.

Chapter 7

Impenetrable Obstructive Object

A Poem

Robin Bagai

Epigraphs:

> *I sometimes wonder if wars between parts of personality and wars between groups of people will diminish together.* —Michael Eigen (2018a)
> *As above, so below, as within, so without...* —Hermes Trismegistus

1

Hunting Unconscious Pain

Ever present... always elusive
You pain me but I cannot find you
   Before dawn I awaken cold, frozen

At noon I wear camouflage to elude you
At night you plague me with mares
of despair and fear
   If I could spot you, target you

I would kill you without thinking,
Even if that meant killing myself
   The suffering you bring is

unbearable, a black rainbow:
frozen grief, silent terror,
unrelenting psychic pain
   I cannot tolerate you

I will not suffer you
I refuse to let you in
I refuse to let you win
   Fighting you deadens me

DOI: 10.4324/9781003322986-7

deforms my human,
I fight ghosts with
helpless rage against
your silent palpable pain.

2

Evacuation

I've found you
out there...
I see you
In Others,
enemies I blame
   I'm convinced

Your badness
must be punished
killed...
to save myself
   Destroy the bad ones

and my world
will be saved
   I will do

anything
not to find you
inside myself...
here, where you live
festering
cancerous
invisible and quiet
like a slow poison
   I turn my

insides outward
for relief
from too much
to bear
   It calms me to

identify enemies
responsible

for my pain…
They must be
destroyed.

Epilogue: What the World Is Up Against

The victim is an emblem of the pain of life, all that one endures, the mutilated self. It is as if, for a moment, (the perpetrator) becomes the master of pain, master of the sense of injury. At the same time (the perpetrator) *is* the injured party once removed.… (Eigen, 2018b, p. 14)

To say that we swell with power in response to emotional impotence is to say that we are plagued with widespread emotional indigestion or are psychically suffocating. Psychic reality is a seemingly unlocalizable chronic irritant. The need for food, education, civil rights seem more tangible. Emotional reality may be more elusive but no less real. How we affect each other, respond to each other and use these responses—what can be more important, more difficult? (Eigen, 2005, p. 8)

References

Eigen, M. (2005). *Emotional storm.* Middleton, CT: Wesleyan University Press.
Eigen, M. (2018a). *The challenge of being human.* London and New York, NY: Routledge, p. 61.
Eigen, M. (2018b). *Damaged bonds.* London and New York, NY: Routledge. (Original work published in 2001).

Chapter 8

Dreaming a Long Day with Michael Eigen

Stefanie Teitelbaum

Introduction

The first time I heard Michael Eigen's voice, he said, "Freud understood me better than my mother and father ever did." Understood and stood under sounded like a bedrock of support. This seemed to be an unusual way to begin a course titled *Psychoanalytic Theory and Practice with Psychosis*. Many years later, I heard the voice say, "Bion got underneath me and lifted me up." My thoughts about Michael Eigen are infused with his voice. Can you hear it?

> When I was a little boy, I remember seeing a tree. Half of it was withered and dead and the other half was blooming. Then I realized that one could be dead and very much alive, concurrently. (Eigen, in Kara-Ivanov Kaniel, 2013)
>
> "No" seems not to exist so far as dreams are concerned. They show a particular preference for combining contraries into a unity or for representing them as one and the same thing. (Freud, 1910, pp. 155–161, this quotation: 155; citing 1900a, S.E. 4: 318)

Freud and Eigen's voices blend. Their duet is polytonal and is an expressive "distinction-union structure" (Eigen, 2011). Eigen said, "dead and <u>very much</u> alive concurrently." His life dominance sings out over Freud's neutrality. Eigen's titles, *Toxic Nourishment* (1999) and *Damaged Bonds* (2001a), express such life dominance. Such nourishment and bonds are life nouns, modified yet not destroyed by death adjectives. These bounds, both toxic and nourishing at the same time, abound in both the autobiographical drama of the Tyrone family and Eugene O'Neill's family in external reality The O'Neill/Tyrone family live, die, and are reborn under the assault of envy, greed, poverty, and substance abuse and thrive in love for each other, spiritual love, and love of arts and letters.

The long day of O'Neill's drama and of this essay is the day of mother Mary Tyrone's morphine relapse. I look at this day as a damaged dream. "Dreams try to represent what hurts and weave a wombing effect round it, but the womb keeps breaking apart" (Eigen, 2001a, p. 43).

DOI: 10.4324/9781003322986-8

Breaking Apart

When the dream womb is shattered, the containing womb is neither obstructive, obtrusive, nor destructive. It is *gone*. The pain of the formerly present now absent womb becomes a no-womb, a hallucinatory present albeit persecutory womb filling the empty space of the absent womb (Bion, 1965; Eigen, 1996). *A Long Day's Journey into Night* is filled with survival amid rupture, repair, damaged dreamwork, and substance abuse (Eigen, 2001). Freud taught us that the dream is wholly egoistic. Through an egoistic lens, Eugene O'Neill's creation and all its players are representations of the author's effort to dream himself.

Epistemology and Reversal

Eugene O'Neill's drama of *epistemology and reversal* (Eigen, 1986) represents in creative drama what would be a psychotic process in waking life. Love and hate are now reversed, now fused, now facing one another, vying to overthrow the other's boundary and occupy the entire self; now back-to-back like a Janus head in a negative hallucination of the other, nullifying the entire self, nullifying experience. In the epistemological reversal, O'Neill's characters contain their undreamable selves (Eigen, 1996, 2001a) in morphine, alcohol, accusatory barbs, and other no-breasts while crying out their love for each other. Reversal of material to immaterial means that an immaterial emotional state created by absence takes on the form of an excruciating embodied presence.

O'Neill was a *replacement child*. The playwright's dream thought came to consciousness via that most primitive primary process function, *reversal*. He replaced the name of his elder brother, who died in infancy, with his own name. The dead Edmund O'Neill is represented in the dreamer's play as Eugene Tyrone. The replacement child, Eugene O'Neill, is represented as Edmund Tyrone. In the absence of answers, the binaries continue to reverse. In his epistemological crisis, Edmund/ Eugene asks more than, am I my brother's keeper? He asks, am I my brother? Am I dead or alive? Am I wanted or unwanted?

Wanted and Unwanted, Dead and Alive

The fetus's innate death instinct is stronger than its life instinct (Eigen, 1996; Ferenczi, 1929). The fetus, and/or newborn, depend on the mother's auxiliary life instinct to survive the shock of aliveness. The psychosomatic expression of the death instinct tries to kill the baby, completing the destructive imperative. Edmund Tyrone has consumption, which could be fatal. Mary Tyrone fears that her own conflicts about having a child to replace the dead one and her own nerves and fears when she was pregnant with Edmund are responsible for his illness. The playwright intuits the depletion of libido in the preoccupied, bereft mother, rendering the mother's auxiliary primary processor (Eigen, 1996) inadequate to overcome the baby's death instinct.

Mary Tyrone (Act 2 Scene 2, pp. 90–91):

"I swore after Eugene died; I would never have another baby."

"I shouldn't have let you insist I have another baby to take Eugene's place, because you thought that would make me forget his death."

"I did want him! More than anything in the world! I meant for his sake."

"And now, since he's been so sick … I've been so frightened and guilty."

Stage Direction: Then, catching herself, with an instant change to stubborn denial.

"I know it's foolish to imagine dreadful things when there's no reason for it."

The assault on the truth of emotion (Bion, 2018a; Eigen, 1986, 2001a) leads to loss of reason and loss of feeling.

Moral Violence

The no-thing a psychical illusion of a discernible presence to fill the space of an absence. It can take on a moralistic tone. Each member of the Tyrone family has a familiar litany of grievances and injuries that are called up as the reality of a loss or an emptiness never filled pushes its way into consciousness. A patient whom I did not notice in a coffee shop screamed about my moral shortcomings when I was too good to talk to him unless he was paying me. At the end of the session, I asked which would be worse for him, if I had deliberately ignored him or I really didn't see him. He stopped shouting, and the color drained from his face. There was blood nowhere. "I can't even think about you really not seeing me." Of course not. It is unthinkable. He hallucinated a predatory present me to erase the encounter with the absent me.

"Bion (2018, 1965) characterizes psychic murder as moral violence" (Eigen, 1996, p. 49). Moral violence against self and others takes the place of the potential healing in a dream womb. The causalities of the wounds become no breasts, marking the spot of the absent breast. Rapid fire reversals of cause-and-effect murder emotion and the reality principle. Instead of a dream, psychic death takes place.

Mary Tyrone and Mary O'Neill made decisions to prioritize love for her husband over primary material preoccupations (Eigen, 2012). The play's dialogue clearly dramatizes her touching on the reality principle and retreat. Using this contact with reality required the capacity to tolerate such contact with the concurrency of her own guilty and not guilty verdicts. Without such capacity, Mary's turn to moral violence until it fails to soothe, and then to morphine to numb the shock of too much.

Too Much

Sometimes the light fills you up too much and burns your abilities. Too much light can also be harmful for a person. (Eigen, Kara-Ivanov Kaniel, 2013)

I sought your nearness.

With all my heart I called you.
And in my going out to meet you,
I found you coming toward me. Yehuda Halevi (c.1075–1141)

Eigen (2001, p. 225) writes about Susan Deri's patient, who had a heart attack on his honeymoon following decades of longing for marriage. He talks about people whose lived experience of calling and going out to meet a long-sought absent thing can go into shock at the longed-for thing coming toward them *too quickly*. Humans need to develop the capacity to *suffer happiness*. A recovering anorexic needs tiny bits of food, and a dehydrated shipwreck survivor needs tiny sips of water so as not to traumatize the psychic-soma's central nervous system. The entire Tyrone family seems to experience Mary's return to health after her drug detox rehab treatment without the structures to suffer her health.

Mary's relapse day happens two months after leaving a sanitorium. Twelve-step programs ask newly sober members to attend 90 meetings in 90 days. They know the danger of "the pink cloud," the temporary euphoric state of having gotten clean, which crashes when the pain of reality principle makes itself known. Mary's nervous drumming of her fingertips at the beginning of the play suggests she has already fallen off the pink cloud. She could not survive so much sober aliveness and so much love from her family so quickly.

Too Loud

Noise that is too loud causes deafness. (Eigen, Kara-Ivanov Kaniel, 2013)

Hearing The Voice speak of its love and respect for Mechachem Schneerson, the 7th Lubavitcher Rebbe, created a concurrency crisis for me. The Lubavitchers are an orthodox Jewish community rooted in Eastern European traditions. The Rebbe is more than a Rabbi. My dilemma involves a large truck, known as a Mitzvah tank, with an incredibly effective loudspeaker system. It parks on the street in front of my office around noontime and plays Jewish music so loud that it enters my 11th-floor office's closed windows, sometimes drowning out the sound of a patient's voice. I like Jewish music very much, but this intrusion into my analytic spaces became a pilot light, igniting my moral violence. It created a spiritual impasse, as the loud music is a deliberate intrusion to reach and awaken a Jewish soul (see Notik[1]). The loud music is a mitzvah, a sacred commandment. While working on this essay, I found myself standing by the truck one morning when no music was playing. I was transfixed by a giant portrait of the Rebbe's face on the side of the truck. I imagine the proportion of that face and my body are akin to the size of the mother's face to the baby. I left the truck transformed. Eigen and Phillips (1993, p. 122) said the presence of a face lets us know another personality is present. The portrait, like a photograph, contained the Rebbe's soul. The out-of-control loud music was itself a no-breast for me, filling the void of a human face. The metal, mechanical truck, when I couldn't see the face and feel the personality, took on the role of Tausk's

(1993) "influencing machine in Schizophrenia." The unintegration panic I felt in the absence of a containing presence lifted. The trauma reaction to the music from the tank is gone. Sometimes, a patient joins me listening. Sometimes, there is a new intimacy in the treatment as I move my chair closer to the patient so I can hear.

Schneerson's eyes in the photo portrait on the truck are more alive than Mary Tyrone's drugged eyes. My transformation of the mitzvah music from predatory to the representation of a containing face was the opposite of Mary Tyrone's. Throughout the play, a foghorn in the distance starts as a sound of affection, then irritation, then rage, and finally a "melancholy moan." Mary's devolution, the loss of the affectionate container, reminds me of alpha-function in reverse, leaving only beta debris (Meltzer, 1976). Too much and not enough, as one and the same exploded.

Not Enough (Eigen, Kara-Ivanov Kaniel, 2013)

In response to Dr. Kara-Ivana's question, Eigen responded that the mother's milk given to the crying-out baby is not enough. It's about the quality of the entire feeding environment. I once saw a mother in the playground. Her baby was in a carriage. She held a bottle in one hand, holding it into the carriage and the baby's mouth. She held an open book in her other hand, her eyes fixed on the book. Eigen said that in such a situation, the baby lives, but the quality of life is compromised. Two of Mary Tyrone's sons survived with a compromised quality of life. One son did not survive.

Ears and Sounds

Halevi, in his search for the other, calls and goes forth to find you coming. He does not specify if the sensory finding is an image or a sound. I hope they are each representations of the other, *one* at the same time.

> We take the soul of things into our soul through our eyes. Eyes are a kind of mouth, an incorporative organ par excellence, the more dramatic because they take in at a distance. Distance is bridged by spiritual, emotional, and intellectual ingestion – a greater acrobatic feat than swallowing food. Unlike literal eating, the object remains outside us as we take it in. (Eigen, 2001, pp. 59–60)

I took in Eigen's soul through my ears in a more sensorial form than the soul that entered through my eyes. My ears are a kind of mouth. Van Gogh's ear was a toxic mouth. He cut it off to try to stop his demonized auditory hallucinations. As Mary Tyrone's eyes glazed over in a morphine haze, the men cried out, soul cries trying to reach her through her ears. Their pleas fall on Mary's *dead ears*.

Winnicott (1969, Eigen, 2012) wrote of the baby's last un-screamed scream before giving up the hope of a container. The baby takes in a decathected no-sound trauma that it can only expel but cannot eat for nourishment.

I hear an opera when I read or see this play. I wish I had the talent to write it. There are arias, duets, trios, quartets, and a ghostly quintet. The dead baby, Eugene/Edmund, sings out in the quartet of the drama's protagonists, like the ghost fifth of a perfectly in-tune barbershop quartet. They reverse verbal accusations and remorse, one another for Eugene/Edmund's death, Edmund/Eugene's consumption, James' penury, Jamie's drinking, and Mary's relapse. They are alternately dissonant and in tune, but not at the same time.

In my own journeys to the unconscious, I found musicians have been there before me more often than poets. I think Eigen finds them both and adds to their repertoires.

Dead Ears Rejecting Containers

Sigmund Freud was known to say that wherever he goes he finds a poet has been there before him. Poetics softens the shock of the longed-for other's approach. Bion taught us that we have to develop the capacity to suffer happiness. Poetics serves as a psychical digestive aid. I wonder if Freud felt some shock at the poets coming toward him.

Jamie Tyrone was the elder child whom Mary blamed for Eugene/Edmund's death. It was Jamie, who had measles, who went into the baby's room. Mary thinks he did it on purpose. Throughout the play, he calls out to dramatists, philosophers, and poets along with sarcasm, moral violence, and alcohol for self-wombing. In the final scene, he calls out to Swinburne, an alcoholic poet. The poet comes toward him to help him suffer the loss of his mother's ear.

Jamie (with increased bitterness)

> Let us go hence, my songs; she will not hear.
> Let us go hence together without;
> Keep silence now, for singing-time is over, And over all things and all things
> dear.
> She loves not nor me as all we love her.
> Yea, though we sang as angels in her ear,
> She would not hear. (Swinburne, 1866, pp. 176–178, Act 4)

The poet intercepts Jamie from a place Freud never reached. Freud had an uncomfortable relationship with music. The songs and silence are objects. This silence is a no-song.

> Let us go hence, go hence;
> She will not see.
> Sing all once more together; surely she,
> She too remembering days and words that were, Will turn a little towards us,
> sighing; but we,
> We are hence, we aree gone,

Sd thought we had not been there.
Nay, and though all men
Seeing had pity on me,
She would not see. (Swinburne, 1866, pp. 176–178, Act 4)

Eigen (2012) said we can think of early hate of frustrating reality as a kind of destruction of frustrating reality. In this context, the baby's scream tries to destroy the pain of life. The men in Mary Tyrone's life each try one last scream, trying to get her to turn their gaze toward them and then to destroy the pain of her relapse.

"Mary, for the love of god. You can stop".

Mary screams back, "No!" She destroys the pain of life with a scream of negative hallucination.

Swinburne's poem represents Jamie's last un-screamed scream to try to turn his mother's eyes toward her crying babies. The poet gives up.

Live Ears – Welcoming Containers

Auralism is a word for the love of hearing. It is the counterpart of voyeurism, the love of looking. Eigen (2001, p. 158) wrote about sleeping in his parents' bedroom till he was 6 and listening to the sounds in the night. He said he never stopped listening. I imagine Freud's dislike of being gazed upon for eight hours or more (Freud, 1913) might have been in the service of greater gratification of his auralism. His dislike of music might disguise his auralism. After all, the talking cure's alive mouth needs an alive ear receptor.

The Voice read Bion's (2018) surgical shock metaphor that *there is blood everywhere* to us, his students, on Halloween 2000. He read in a deep, resonant baritone, scary-for-children's voice. Both my parents read to me, but never scary stories. I loved hearing my parents, and Mike read. I memorized what I heard. Digesting Bion, Freud, Green, Grotstein, Kristeva, Meltzer, Winnicott, and, of course, Eigen is cathected with the digestive aid sound of Mike's voice. I can take them in, eat them, and learn from them without choking. I realized much of my psychoanalytic training involved gobbling theory whole through my eyes and ears and expelling it outward. Or, in a reversal of subject and object, the theory became the subject and, like the big bad wolf, gobbled me up whole. I was a living duck quacking inside the wolf's stomach, represented by Prokofiev's oboe in Peter and the Wolf. It is no wonder that I particularly gravitated to Donald Meltzer's *Claustrum* (1992, 2008) with Mike's voice as a tutor. Eigen (2005) wrote about his grandmother serving his pet duck Quickie for Shabbos dinner. Shabbos, with its accent on the first syllabus, is the Eastern European pronunciation of Shabbat, the Sabbath. Rhythm is an element of music. The voice told me about this incident some years before the date of publication. The familiar music of the Eastern European rhythmic trope is another royal road to the unconscious. This music in common made this trauma all the more real in my ear. There was no music to soften the blow to such a young child, yet Mike's love for his grandma survived the mutilation. I searched YouTube for a performance of Peter and the Wolf with a narrator who might sound like Mike. I was delighted to find a performance narrated by Boris Karloff. He didn't sound like Frankenstein, but he also didn't sound like Mike. I had the same shocked reaction to Karloff's English-accent voice as I did the first time I heard a recording of Bion's voice. I had heard Bion in Mike's voice.

No-Self

Self may arise in relation to a void or background Other, the latter supporting self without self s awareness of being supported Might be infant Jesus blessing the world on Mary's lap. (Eigen, 2001, p. 458; Elkin, 1972)

As in a dream's day's residue, Mary's morphine addiction had already attached itself to her psyche before she actually took the drug, before the curtain rose for Act I. She lost her idealized maternal object and retreated from the external world to her days in the convent before love, marriage, death, and morphine deadened her spirituality and her joy in playing the piano. Freud's decathexis of the real world and the body in the dream state unfolds in the Long Day's dream.

Addiction and No-Spirituality

Mary calls on the Blessed Virgin Mary to mark the spot of her absent faith. The Blessed Virgin is a no-breast. Morphine is also a no-breast. At the same time, Mary retains her core decency. Eigen (2016) quoted hearing Hobart talk about psychopathy, wherein people don't have the decency to go crazy, and about her own effort at a winning lie (Eigen, 1996). The vestiges of life sparks are there. Tiny sparks of light shine through the cracked vessels (Eigen, in Kara-Ivanov Kaniel, 2013). Her morphine prevents her from going crazy as she struggles with her own self-hatred.

"If I could only find the faith I lost, so I could pray again!"
   She pauses-then begins to recite the Hail Mary in a flat, empty tone.
   "Hail Mary full of grace."
   Sneering
   "You expect the Blessed Virgin to be fooled by a lying dope fiend reciting words! You can't hide from her!" (p. 99, Act 3)

Mary Tyrone needs the blessed virgin's forgiveness to endure the pain of morphine withdrawal. Like Job needing direct contact with only God (Eigen, 1998, p. 84), she needs to see Mary directly in the foreground. She sings out her vision of "O."

some day when the blessed virgin Mary forgives me, it will be so easy. I will hear myself scream out and, at the same time, I will laugh because I will be so sure of myself. (p. 99, Act 3)

She lacks the capacity to internalize Mother Mary as a background object. She can only internalize morphine. One can ingest morphine, be soothed by it, and even be protected from breakdown and suicide. One cannot learn from up. The drug is a toxic and potentially lethal protector.

As the play ends, Mary has lost the Blessed Virgin in both foreground and background. Her husband and two sons have each swallowed their last un-screamed screams and washed the dead screams down with whiskey. Four protagonists sit in silence, a thing-in-and-of-itself and a representation of a no-song. They can tolerate being together and survive contact with the depths of love and despair at the same time, with the background support of their addictive substances (Eigen, 2011). As the "They" sit in silence, that replaces the cacophony of their love and hate cries. The family survives in a damaged dream-womb. As the curtain falls, "She stares before her in a sad dream. Tyrone stirs in his char. Edmund and Jamie remain motionless." None of the men have touched their drinks.

I offer Eigen's dedication in Toxic Nourishment to the Tyrone Family:

To all who live
Through the unlivable
To the life no poison
can kill. Michael Eigen (1999, vii)

Damaged Dreamwork

A dream within a dream is a fossilized piece of trauma (Eigen, 2001). There is minimal evidence of dreamwork – just enough to create some easily decoded disguise, but not enough to use in the work of transformation. A damaged dream is still a dream. In the work of the transference, the damaged dream can heal. The psychoanalyst's dream womb is an auxiliary primary processor (Eigen, 1996) that has the capacity to bring life feelings into the fossils' rendering them dead and alive concurrently. O'Neill's unresolved drama is like a dream within a dream. It remembers and repeats but does not work through (Freud, 1914).

My first psychoanalyst's mind began to die before his body did. His skin tone was gray, matching his silver hair and the gray suits he usually wore. I had two gray fossil dreams in our termination year. In one, he was a gray, larger-than-life-size cardboard cutout in his undisguised office. I was like one of Harlow's monkeys, trying to hug him. The figure was two-dimensional; there was no interiority around which to wrap my arms. It was a no-container. The wire mother monkey had an interior space, artificial as it was. In the second gray dream, I lay on the analytic couch in the still undisguised office. His face hovered over me on the ceiling; his gray suit fabric was a cloud-blob without a body. Both dreams were dreams within a dream, with long confusional states where I tried to wake up multiple times and was unsure if I was awake or asleep. There was blood nowhere, and in its negative form, blood nowhere represented blood everywhere. At the last session, he said, "See you after Labor Day." He forgot that I was not coming back. I saw him once more at his funeral. He wore his gray suit, gray hair, and gray skin in a shockingly not-Jewish open-casket. I howled out from the depths, like a gray wolf cub crying over its dead mother.

Dreaming an Undreamable Object (Eigen, 2001)

Eigen was Mike and a *replacement analyst concurrently*. Mike welcomed Dr. Other into my treatment with open arms. "I could never replace him. He will always be your analyst." Mike named Dr. Other "your analyst" and immediately foreclosed his role as a placeholder no-analyst. Re-place became place. He was an original for me. I had a dream; Dr. Other was sitting upright – dare I say "erect" – on a horse, wearing a bright red fox-hunting jacket, jodhpurs, boots, and a helmet. There was color in his living cheeks, and his eyes were dead concurrently. There was blood somewhere. Unlike the gray dreams, this was not a dream within a dream. The image in the dream was a snapshot. I love the primary process, especially condensation.

Mike (see Eigen, 2001, pp. 77–92) wrote about the role of photography in psychosis recovery. Mike said that primitive people believed that the photographer had captured the soul of the photographed subject. The Other on horseback was a step toward recovery from a psychotic kind of expulsion dreaming. Dr. Other's living soul was inside me.

> The distinction between foreconscious and unconscious activity is not a primary one but comes to be established after repulsion has sprung up. ... A rough but not inadequate analogy to this supposed relation of conscious to unconscious activity might be drawn from the field of ordinary photography. The first stage of the photograph is the 'negative'; every photographic picture has to pass through the 'negative process,' and some of these negatives which have held good in examination are admitted to the 'positive process' ending in the picture. (Freud, 1912, p. 257)

Mike's dreamwork was my alpha-function and negative developer. I woke up refreshed with a clear head. I reported the dream. He giggled, "I love the creative unconscious. You took an upper west side Jew and turned him into an English aristocrat." He told me that Donald Meltzer, another upper Westside Jew who became an Englishman, rode horses in Central Park. Meltzer was becoming important to me at that time, thanks to Mike's psychosis syllabus. Jewish Mike's office is on the upper West side. I love Upper West Side Story. The session ended when Mike smiled and said, "and you're the fox." I wondered about the role of disgust in the creation of this snapshot. I never had any erotic feelings for Dr. Other, and

I had strong feelings of sanctioned affection for him. The disgust barrier for this mainly Oedipal-level analysis was powerful. Perhaps Mike's signifying himself as not-my-analyst lifted that inhibition in my analysis with Mike; need I say more?

The fox-hunter dream turned into days of residue in this writing and a notation of a memory trace in still-evolving dreamwork. I remember a gray photograph. It is a picture of my mother as a little girl, sitting upright on a pony that an itinerant photographer brought to her neighborhood for children to sit on in a professional picture. My mother's thirteen-months-younger sister stood beside the pony and held the reins. My mother told me that her mother, my grandmother, was horrified at finding herself pregnant when my mother was four months old. I also learned that my mother could not digest the breastfeeding infused with the hormones of early pregnancy. She could neither be nourished by nor learn from the breast. Her weaning was traumatic, and she developed pica symptoms. She ate dirt from the backyard and ate the fuzz of her pink blanket until it was gone. She ate her potential transition object. Family legend has it that my grandmother was practically "jumping off the piano" to try to cause a miscarriage. The baby was born and was beloved by the family. Aunt Selma would die in a drowning accident when she was 24, two years before I was born. I hear the narrative of my grandmother's guilt in Mary Tyrone's voice. In Jewish mystical tradition, I was named after Selma. Such naming invites the soul of the dead to inhabit the living baby's body. All Jewish children in that mystical tradition are replacement children. I carry the soul of the baby whom my grandmother tried to murder and loved the best of all her children. My dead aunt and I have anglicized names. We have the same Jewish name, Sara.

Freud (1905) said that all love relationships are modeled on the baby's relationship with the breast. Therefore, all love relationships are not findings but re-findings. Mike's dream womb opened my dreamwork to help me re-find and welcome my mother, Dr. (M)Other, and aunt. Bringing these words to life has been difficult. I have had to rip Mike out of his place as a background object of primal support to put his work in the foreground. My background and foreground Mikes are at times concurrent, at times representations of each other, and at times each other's no-breasts, at times open, and at times obstructive containers. I love them all with all my might.

Note

1 Notik, G. About Mitzvah Tank https://www.mitzvahtank.nyc/about retrieved 7/27/2023.

References

Bion, W.R. (2018a). Transformations. In W.R. Bion, C. Mawson, & F. Bion (Eds.), *The complete works of W.R. Bion* (Vol. V, pp. 115–280). Abington and New York, NY: Routledge. (Originally published 1965)

Bion, W.R. (2018b). There is blood everywhere. In W.R. Bion, C. Mawson, & F. Bion (Eds.), *The complete works of W.R. Bion* (Vol. I, p. 29). Abington and New York, NY: Routledge. (Originally published 1992)

Eigen, M. (1986). *The psychotic core*. Northvale, NJ: Jason Aronson, pp. 215–250.

Eigen, M. (1996). *Psychic deadness*. Northvale, NJ: Jason Aronson, pp. xviii–xix, 49–54, 139–148, 201–212.

Eigen, M. (1998). *The psychoanalytic mystic*. London and New York, NY: Free Association Books, p. 84.

Eigen, M. (1999). *Toxic nourishment*. London: Karnac.

Eigen, M. (2001a). *Damaged bonds*. London: Karnac, pp. 43–61, 77–92, 158.

Eigen, M. (2001b). Mysticism and psychoanalysis. *PSA Review* 88(3): 455–481.

Eigen, M. (2005). *Emotional storm*. Middletown, CT: Wesleyan Press, pp. 96–119.

Eigen, M. (2011). *Contact with the depths*. London: Karnac, pp. 17–30.

Eigen, M. (2012). On Winnicott's clinical contributions to analysis with adults. *Indian Journal of Public Administration* 93(6): 1449–1459.

Eigen, M. (2016). *Where are we going?* Unpublished paper, Graduation Address at NPAP.

Eigen, M., & Phillips, A. (Eds.). (1993). *The electrified tightrope*. (Originally published Eigen, M. (1981). The area of faith in Winnicott, Lacan and Bion. *The International Journal of Psychoanalysis* 62: 413–433).

Elkin, H. (1972). On selfhood and the development of ego structures in infancy. *Psychoanalytic Review*, 59: 389–416.

Ferenczi, S. (1929). The unwanted child and his death instinct. *The International Journal of Psychoanalysis* 10: 125–129.

Freud, S. (1910). The antithetical meaning of primal words. *The Standard Edition of the Complete Psychological Works of Sigmund* 11: 153–162.

Freud, S. (1912). A note on the unconscious in psycho-analysis. *The Standard Edition of the Complete Psychological Works of Sigmund Freud* 12: 264.

Freud, S. (1913). On beginning the treatment (further recommendations on the technique of psycho-analysis I). *The Standard Edition of the Complete Psychological Works of Sigmund Freud* XII: 121–144.

Freud, S. (1914). Remembering, repeating and working-through (further recommendations on the technique of psycho-analysis II). *The Standard Edition of the Complete Psychological Works of Sigmund Freud* XII: 145–156.

Kara-Ivanov Kaniel, R. (2013). Therapist from the depths: A conversation with Michael Eigen. Therapist from the Depths: A Conversation with Michael Eigen - Tikkun.

Meltzer, D. (1976). The delusion of clarity of insight. *The International Journal of Psychoanalysis* 57: 141–146.

Meltzer, D. (2008). *The claustrum*. London: Karnac Books. (Originally published Roland Harris Educational Trust 1992)

Swinburne, A.C. (1866). "A leave-taking" was published in poems and ballads, first series, in 1866. Retrieved 7/3/2023, https://www.poetryfoundation.org/poems/45296/a-leave-taking

Tausk, V. (1933). On the origin of the "influencing machine" in schizophrenia. *The Psychoanalytic Quarterly* 2: 519–556.

Winnicott, D.W. (1969). Additional note on psycho-somatic disorder. In C. Winnicott, R. Shepherd, & M. Davis (Eds.), *Psycho-Analytic Explorations* (pp. 115–118). Cambridge, MA: Harvard University Press, 1989.

Chapter 9

Unwanted Nearings and Therapeutic Clearings

Holding on, in a Difficult Encounter, to Michael Eigen's Clinical Wisdom

David Smith

On Unwanted Patients

> …as I become a little less frightened of being open, I become more and more aware of how I grow with certain people, and how interacting, especially with so-called 'difficult' patients, promotes my own development. For example, if there's a person I cannot help, for whom anything I do strikes out, that person is forcing me, if I'm going to help them, to find a way of being with them that I hadn't exercised before. And if I fail to find it, it will be a failed treatment.
> Michael Eigen, *Interview with Anthony Molino* (1997, p. 140)

Michael Eigen presented *On Working with "Unwanted" Patients* (Eigen, 1977) at both the New York Centre for Psychoanalytic Training and the Institute for Psychoanalytic Training and Research in 1976. It was subsequently published in the *International Journal* in 1977. The paper summarizes ten years of clinical work with difficult patients in the New Hope Clinic in Brooklyn, a setting Eigen describes as providing him with "rich fare," throughout what he characterizes as "years of discovery" (2020, p. 83). And one of Eigen's key discoveries here, as he attests to 20 years on, when he references the paper in *Psychic Deadness* (1996, p. 217), is a certain capacity for tolerance within himself for what he terms the "contradictory demands of difficult patients." In *The Electrified Tightrope*, Adam Phillips' gathering together of Eigen's early essays, Eigen (1993b, p. xviii) notes that "most of these patients exhibited what might loosely be called masochistic lifestyles, but what was at stake was severe narcissistic injury." Aware of the potential for such challenging clinical encounters to foster mutual growth, Eigen's primary concern is with the therapeutic use that can be made of a range of negative states in the therapist, and here he makes specific reference to "irritation, discomfort, revulsion, rage, hate, pain of various sorts, impatience, deadness, impotence, frustration, panic, horror."

When, in 1977, Eigen undertook his analytic sessions with Bion in New York, Bion had just read this recently published paper, which Eigen describes as being partly concerned with hostile dependent relationships. Discussing the state of his own relationships with girlfriends, Eigen suggested to Bion that he guessed that the

DOI: 10.4324/9781003322986-9

time had come for him to meet someone new and was left bemused and speechless by the directness of Bion's response: "And have another hostile dependent relationship?"

In what Daws (2023, p. 64) describes as "a transformative paper articulating *psychic distaste* in the Other," Eigen explores "the therapeutic use of the therapist's negative states. Staying with, tolerating, transforming that which is unwanted...." The paper sets out an early version of what will become an enduring emphasis in Eigen's writing on the evolutionary nature of psychoanalysis. In one of his most recent publications, *Psyche Singing: Dialogues with Michael Eigen*, he writes (2020):

> It may be that people we can't help now and who keep getting angry and impatient with us are going to force an evolution of self or force an area of development that is much needed but just beyond reach at this moment. Here we can dip into, locate, and find a certain faith in what *might* happen, if not this moment, with this person. This too can be part of psychoanalytic faith. (p. 207)

Eigen suggests (2020, p. 210) that the persistence of the so-called borderline patient has forced the therapy field to evolve to the point where many therapists have, by this stage, found within themselves the response systems that such patients need in order to grow. Daws (Bloch and Daws, 2015, p. 108) makes a helpful distinction between the "hard to reach patient" and the "hard to reach interface between therapist and patient," underlining Eigen's emphasis on the importance clinically of finding the place where you can work from, rather than staying with the place where you cannot work from.

In his introduction to *The Electrified Tightrope*, Phillips (1993b, p. xiii) suggests that what he calls "the absorbing preoccupation of Michael Eigen's remarkable psychoanalytic essays" is "the capacity to *experience* [italics added], for the therapist and the patient both, how it can be sustained, and the diverse and subtle ways it can be sabotaged...." Phillips quotes from Eigen's first book, *The Psychotic Core* (1993a, p. 320): "It is difficult to overestimate the role omniscience plays in deadening one's capacity to experience. If one knows what is *going* to happen ahead of time, one does not have to experience it." The question of why a person might foreclose and kill off his or her vital capacity to experience is a key one for Eigen, who shares Phillips' belief that psychoanalysis is not about cure but about finding new ways of being alive, new ways of living.

For Eigen, aliveness is a key indicator of growth, and he emphasizes (1993b), within the context of a clinical encounter that has potential for both mutual growth *and* co-created insanity, the need for the therapist to be alive and real in engaging with the patient:

> Therapist outbursts *can* be helpful. Offhand remarks in a context of persistent struggle and hard work *do* change lives. Can one know ahead of time whether

letting go of self will amount to worthless indulgence or stimulate aliveness? It is inhuman for the therapist always to be on good behavior[.]…..I fear there are still many therapists who take themselves so seriously that they fail to envision a time when they and their patients can laugh good-humoredly about the traits that drive each other crazy. (p. 277)

Eigen's privileging of aliveness very much resonates with, and is deeply influenced by, Winnicott's emphasis on the real and the true self, and might put us in mind of Winnicott's prayer (quoted in Phillips, 1989, p. 19): "Oh God! May I be alive when I die." And it's an emphasis that is also very much shared by Thomas Ogden (1997):

I believe that every form of psychopathology represents a specific type of limitation of the individual's capacity to be fully alive as a human being. The goal of analysis from this point of view is larger than the resolution of unconscious intrapsychic conflict, the diminution of symptomatology, the enhancement of reflective subjectivity and self-understanding, and the increase of one's sense of personal agency. Although one's sense of being alive is intimately intertwined with each of the above-mentioned capacities, I believe that the experience of aliveness is a quality that is superordinate to these capacities and must be considered as an aspect of the analytic experience *in its own terms*. (p. 26)

In a 1997 interview with Anthony Molino, Eigen, while acknowledging the limits of what is possible clinically, emphasizes the importance of sticking with the process:

…..but I rather like siding with this feeling of "good to the last drop" in psychoanalysis…..like a bug that never stops moving…..There's just a sense of never giving up…..never giving up on a case…..not giving up on anyone…..Who knows better?" (p. 123)

Later, in the same interview (Molino, 1997), Eigen underlines his faith in the evolutionary potential of psychoanalysis, using the touching image of a baby bird persistently pecking away at its mother in a bid to evoke the particular type of maternal responses and feeding capacities required for the development of both the baby and mother bird:

Well, there are certain patients who have to keep pecking away at the therapeutic field until, somewhere along the line, the field develops the capacity to help this particular set of birds develop. And when one of them arrives in the office and you cannot help them, when you can feel their anger or their drive to get help pecking away at you, it's not always easy to recognize that we've yet to evolve a corresponding capacity to respond to their particular kind of pecking[.]…. And when that actually happens with a patient, after weeks or months of being stuck, it's marvelous! When all of a sudden, because of an internal shift in one's own being, the case moves on: because the therapist's being has actually changed and has entered another phase of living in response to getting pecked at in a way never experienced before. (p. 140)

Clinical Material: Katie

Katie's clinical presentation resonates very much with Eigen's own depiction of the "unwanted" patient. Eigen portrays a very hostile form of needy and demanding dependency, characterized by powerful, masochistic resistance to any attempts to help relieve the pain and suffering linked to a chronic and deeply felt sense of injury and grievance. Katie is a woman diagnosed with borderline personality disorder who entered therapy with me at the age of 25. With a long history of self-harm and suicide attempts, Katie had worked through a series of therapists, psychiatrists, psychologists, doctors, nurses, and Lifeline telephone counselors, both in her native country and here in Northern Ireland. All of which had reinforced in this very isolated, fragile, unloved, and evidently unlovable young woman a bitter and very painful sense that nobody out there wanted or cared about her and a deep conviction among mental health professionals that she was essentially untreatable.

My phantasy was that Katie's experience with me would somehow be very different, and I had an early, very fanciful notion that this relationship would somehow be the stuff of a French arthouse movie. In reality, I soon found myself appearing, three times a week, in a regular shitstorm, playing a part that I'd be ashamed of and embarrassed for anyone to catch a glimpse of me in through the keyhole, let alone on the big screen. We seemed to fight all the time, throughout a couple of years, which was characterized by Katie presenting me, infuriatingly, with a constant stream of *faits accompli* along the lines of "I told them where to stick their fucking job/their fucking course/their fucking friendship!" Everything was a done deal by the time the session came around, with no pause in the action, no pause for thought – nothing in Katie's experience for us to reflect on together, only endless confirmation of how hostile and unreliable the world about her was. It's hard to convey quite how much this wound me up and did my head in. It was often unbearable for me to stay in the room listening to Katie's uncontained hateful anger, overwhelming distress, indignant hurt, and deeply pained sense of being repeatedly wronged, combined with her stubborn refusal to hear anything I might have to say about what was going on. Many times I pictured myself holding open the door during a session and shouting at her to get the fuck out of my room and not to bother coming back. And I felt like I was genuinely and frighteningly close to acting this out at times. Or I would imagine myself walking out of the session and away from the therapy – and possibly from therapy itself.

Katie was heavily overweight, and I came to see her physical form as an embodiment of the solid block I was coming up against in the room – a block which I didn't tire of relentlessly banging my head against. Katie routinely presented in a state of unregulated distress, all over the place, which rather than me being able to contain it, more often than not, left *me* feeling unregulated and distressed myself. In a neat but awful inversion of the container-contained model of therapeutic intervention, we seemed between us to have developed an uncontained-uncontaining model of therapy.

A key aspect of Eigen's clinical approach is his welcoming of the deepest, at times annihilated and unwanted states of the other, described by Bloch and Daws (2015, p. xxxviii) as "an act of radical courage on the part of the therapist embodying what Bion means when he talks of F in O." Daws (2023, p. 68) suggests that patients deemed "unwanted" reflect their own category of difficulty and that the psychic distaste associated with the "obnoxious negativism" and cynicism characteristic of hostile dependency engenders a stifling and foreclosing "atmosphere of muted rage and resentment," in turn provoking "interpersonal and therapeutic recoil, distaste, frustration, even non-involvement." While much of this rings true in this case, there have been times when the word "distaste" feels like a huge understatement. Emphasizing Eigen's "basic love approach," Daws underlines the importance of "staying the analytic course" in order to have a chance of providing a supportive and facilitating environment in which growth is possible. And Eigen himself (1993b) underlines the way in which, as the therapist accumulates more and more experience of such cases,

> he begins to telescope and develop increasing control over its negative impact... he reduces the intensity of dislike or distaste a patient can invoke in him...he becomes more sensitive to the *various nuances of negative feelings the patient can stimulate, and his interventions become more highly differentiated.* (p. 15)

The length of Katie's arm was also covered, hideously, in so many self-inflicted scars that I was initially confused as to what I was looking at and trying my best not to look at. I thought for some time that they were horrendous burn marks. She continued, for a very long time, to cut herself regularly and to take some perverse pleasure in displaying her latest wound – as if there was a certain triumph in showing me how useless I was. She once brought in a painting to show me with an intriguingly odd texture and feel to it. And as I held it in my hands to study it, Katie told me with a certain relish that she had painted it in the blood she had collected from her cuts. I was disgusted and felt quite sickened, and as I washed my hands after the session, I felt quite determined that this was time for me to wash my hands of Katie altogether.

Through all of this, I tried my best to hold on to two things that I'd picked up from Katie's hugely troubled history, which was characterized by neglect, abuse, and trauma, with repeated and ongoing exposure, in Eigen's terms, to *damaged bonds* and *toxic nourishment*. Firstly, the awful, deeply upsetting image of Katie being repeatedly pushed away by her mother with the words "You and your fucking cuddles!" when Katie would attempt, as a toddler, to climb up onto the settee alongside her. And secondly, the idea that there was a little girl inside of this infuriating and quite repulsive woman who had been sexually abused without any experience of parental protection and care. These were not at all easy to keep in mind, as it was impossible to associate the woman in the room with either cuddles or infantile vulnerability. What helped me more than anything to stay in the room was my supervision and the regular and vital meetings with a steady mind outside of this terrible mess that I found myself caught up in – at enough of a distance to offer me support, containment, encouragement, and some digestible food-for-thought to sustain me in the ongoing struggle with Katie.

Desperately seeking something transformative, I undertook some training in one of the treatments of choice for working with borderline patients, mentalization-based therapy, and made the journey over to Los Angeles to play the part of Katie in numerous role plays there. It was a part that, to my surprise, I enjoyed playing, and I found myself taking some perverse pleasure at seeing just how hard it was for my fellow trainees to work with me when I was in this role. And I also discovered that I was good at playing the part, to the extent that Peter Fonagy paid me the very dubious compliment of saying that I was a natural at playing a borderline! It was becoming harder for me to distance myself so fully from those unwanted aspects of my own personality, which I was inclined to find so distasteful in Katie and which my encounter with her was bringing me uncomfortably near to, including my own tendency to nurse painful grievances and hurts, in turn hurting myself more and keeping myself in a painfully wronged, let-down place in the process. While I definitely found the mentalization model to be theoretically very helpful, I did not find it so useful as a technique – at least as I practiced it, which took the form of a much more active but equally fruitless form of toe-to-toe close combat, which I didn't have the stamina or the heart (and maybe the technical skill) to maintain.

Around this time, I also discovered the writings of those often New York City-based analysts associated with the relational turn in psychoanalysis, including Michael Eigen. And I've been particularly inspired and sustained in my work with Katie by the honesty, wit, and playfulness of Stephen Mitchell's writings and his encouragement of the therapist's open acknowledgment of his or her own mistakes and enactments within the therapy, bearing in mind, also, Bernard Cullen's mantra that there can be no therapy without enactment. This, in turn, freed me up, counter-intuitively, to be able to begin to reflect openly with Katie about the times I thought I'd maybe gotten things wrong or had let myself get caught up in something quite unhealthy in our intersubjective interaction. Counter-intuitively because I had found myself up until this point locked in an embattled, war-of-attrition, don't-give-an-inch mindset, and freeing because it allowed me to relax a little – my step back in turn allowing for the creation of a small clearing in which I could start to reflect and to gather myself a little. It also had the unforeseen consequence of somewhat wrong-footing Katie, helping both of us in the process to begin to wonder together about what sort of madly repetitive dance we'd been caught up in for so long.

The relational school's re-description of borderline personality disorder in terms of chronic relational trauma has been a very useful one for me in terms of helping me to keep working with Katie and to contain my strong inclination to write her off. As has been Gwen Adshead's encouragement to think more in terms of fluctuating levels of personality function and dysfunction rather than the much more rigidly set concept of personality disorder, which often serves to repeat and reinforce the let-down suffered by those who have been relationally traumatized in early childhood by writing them off as untreatable. I've also found Adam Phillips' observation on the amount of love-testing that goes on between patient and therapist a very helpful idea to keep in mind when feeling tested to my limits, as it helps me to see beyond the "bad" behavior to the underlying basic human need to feel loved, held on to, and wanted.

About three years into the therapy, Katie did something she never did and reported a dream. From the beginning of the treatment, she had repeatedly told me that she would kill herself before the age of 30, as she could never imagine being able to bear the pain of living beyond that point. In the dream, she found herself on a moped, surprised to realize she could ride this steadily out on the road. She noted a speed limit of 30 mph on the road. Still, she discovered when she looked at the speedometer that she had gotten the bike up to 32, and, again to her surprise, she was doing OK. Not only was Katie surprised that she was doing OK, but she was also enjoying herself! I took a lot of heart from this dream, which was very out of keeping with what her conscious mind was telling us in the sessions – and which I think can be thought of as an unconscious expression of some sort of what Eigen terms *analytic faith* generated between the two of us.

Gradually, and often in a one-step forward, three-steps-back kind of way, there began to emerge the first signs of Katie having at least heard *something* of what I had been trying for so long to say to her. And very slowly, over time, it became clear that she was beginning, very much against what part of her felt to be her better judgment, to internalize some of the healthier and more reflective aspects of the therapeutic encounter. And crucially, this was combined with something a bit more playful becoming possible between the two of us, replacing the deadly earnestness that had characterized our long period of stalemate. So that Katie might now come into the room, still in a very agitated way, too distressed to speak for a few minutes, but then say something like:

> I was ready to tell a colleague to go and fuck herself this afternoon, but in my head I could hear you saying 'Hold on now! Why don't you hold fire, and let's see what we can make out of this between us.' There, you've just under 47 minutes now – over to you, wise guy!

There was a very moving moment at the end of a session in which Katie had talked angrily about the latest version of her all-too-familiar story of being misunderstood and uncared for, this time by her manager. My attempts to intervene and introduce some thinking into a very knowing narrative were met with repeated blocks, with Katie hurt and angry that I was, to her mind, typically siding against her and being weirdly protective of her manager. I said that I couldn't care less about the manager but that I was very concerned that Katie's rigid stance, built on certainties and absolutes, was damaging only to Katie herself and threatening to undo a lot of her good work. The session was very hard work and painfully repetitive. As it wore on, I had no sense of being able to reach Katie at all until right at the end of the session, when she suddenly started to talk about *Amnesty International*, how heartened she'd been to read about them employing satellites to monitor human rights abuse across the world, and how much it meant to her that they never give up on working relentlessly to protect us. When she got home, she said she would donate to them. Tired by this stage, and without thinking, I instinctively responded by saying, "Thanks very much – I'm going to take that as a compliment." Much to my surprise, Katie immediately began to cry, and, wiping the tears from her cheeks with her hands, she said (somewhat begrudgingly), "You know, that's surprisingly touching. " The image of the satellite seemed to reflect the technical position I had adopted after years of getting drawn into close fighting – a more distant presence within the room but still close enough to monitor and engage consistently with what was getting played out between us there.

Reflecting on his "Unwanted" paper, Eigen (2020, p. 111) notes that it is "mainly about patients who make you want to distance them. They may arouse disgust, be too hostile, or any number of things that make them more difficult to be with." He talks in terms of "highly toxic" psyches and outlines his own technical development in relation to working with what gets stirred up in such cases:

> What do I do with these feelings? There were periods I might have expressed more of these feelings, trying to mold and use them therapeutically. I still might today if I thought it would be useful. However, I've learned that a lot more can happen if you don't prematurely blurt out your psychic garbage. Hold on to it and get through any way you can. I think over time a sense of complexity deepens.

Eigen places great emphasis on the fluidity of the human psyche and the shifts that inevitably take place in both patient and therapist if things can be waited out in the consulting room:

> The psyche doesn't stay in one place. There is always more. Moods and attitudes shift[.].....Psyche is both blocked and moving[.].....And just because it's a toxic situation for you doesn't mean that it is or always will be that way. Life-saving openings can come[.].....The psyche never stops. (2020, p. 112)

And in response to the question of how much weight to give to one's response to the patient in the present moment, he suggests, "Take it seriously, give it respect, give it it's due, but don't absolutize it. Don't literalize. It's not the whole world" (2012, p. 112). Eigen's deep analytic faith and his willingness to get to know un-wanted states of mind, combined with his steadfast refusal to "concretise destruc-tiveness and treat it as an unchanging or unchangeable power" are crucial for Eaton (2015, p. 144), who stresses the way in which Eigen's "deconcretizing attitude… slowly expands possibilities for thinking and feeling, lessening intimidation and anxiety," and in turn allows for the possibility of radical evolutionary change, in which unwanted aspects of experience can be communicated with and destructive-ness played with. Key for Eaton is the provision of a welcoming, receptive space for the unwanted parts and experiences of both the patient and the therapist.

A couple of years ago, Katie came to a session on her way home from the Christ-mas market and took great pleasure in showing me a couple of beautiful, intricately decorated bowls that she had bought there – one for her younger brother and one, to my delight, for herself. Unlike the gruesome earlier painting, these bowls were a pleasure to hold and to behold, and I felt like a father receiving and handling something very special and important from a young child. I wondered to myself what Katie would give me for Christmas, but was surprised a couple of weeks later when she presented me with what I can only describe as a very sexy little box of gift-wrapped, hand-crafted French chocolates, which prompted my normally Zen-enough wife, who has seen and put up with a lot by this stage, to ask, "Where the fuck did you get them?"

We're now ten years into what I think (but who knows?) promises to be a lifelong relationship. And Katie has made remarkably good and steady progress in her life over these years. She's six years into a job that she enjoys and does well, with some good and well-established relationships with colleagues and an enduring friendship with a good, steady guy called Dave. She has recently committed to something that she never imagined and taken out a mortgage – and, with it, a 25-year commitment to the flat that she's been living in for the past ten years. She attends still life and other art and creative writing classes, loves playing football regularly, and joins colleagues on monthly social nights out. She has just seen her first play, booked a ticket to her first gig, and recently treated herself to her first-ever stay in a hotel with a trip over to London to see the Leonardo da Vinci exhibition. I was very touched when she told me that she would never in her life have dreamt of a trip like that, only that she has learned from me over the years that she has to work at her relationship with herself, to be good and kind to herself, to look after herself, and to treat herself. In recent months, Katie has wanted and begun to lose weight. A mark-edly more human shape is beginning to emerge from her previously solid form, which is in itself a source of great anxiety about the potential emergent sexual de-sire and appetite of both herself and others. What Katie perceives as sexual stirrings in her vagina as she tries to sleep at night are met with a firm, anxious slap – in an instinctive attempt to get rid of such an unfamiliar and unwanted sexual feeling. All of these aspects of her life continue to take some managing emotionally. Still, there's a sense that they don't represent quite the same treacherously dangerous minefields that they did for so long, and a lovely sense of Katie being much more alive and open to the experience of life, whatever it may bring her.

Such work necessarily entails a huge commitment in terms of the time, mental energy, and introspection required to do justice to the challenge of working with an "unwanted" patient, in a bid, in Eigen's evolutionary terms, to find and develop within the therapist the resources that might prove to be mutually useful to both the patient and the slowly evolving therapist. According to Eaton (in Bloch and Daws, 2015):

> Part of the difficulty in welcoming a patient's unwanted experience is linked to the pain of welcoming unwanted states that arise in ourselves, states that are often troubling, even shocking, but that, nonetheless, record the emotional impact of our "contact with the depths" evoked by another person's suffering. (p. 142)

As challenging and deeply unsettling as this is, Eaton goes on to emphasize (Bloch and Daws: 2015, p. 144) the enormous potential for psychic liberation in making ourselves at home with our unwanted demons: "By welcoming unwanted aspects of experience, we break the spells we have lived under for sometimes very long periods. We emerge into new relational spaces as well as into new qualities of mental space." For my part, I've found a lot of love for this woman over the years, and, far from unwanted, her three weekly appointments have become very steady points in my week, which I can find myself looking forward to, often now enjoying the company of a woman who has tentatively and increasingly been coming alive and into her own over several years. Of course, there's no plain sailing here, and it's still annoyingly hard work at times; this isn't Hollywood or its French arthouse equivalent after all, but (much better than that, I think) it's real life, for good and for bad.

Working with Unwanted Therapists

If the projection of unwanted thoughts, feelings, perceptions, and aspects of the self is a characteristic of patients with primitive personality organizations, it is also true that a key universal challenge in terms of mental health comes in how we manage what is unwanted within ourselves in terms of affects, experience, reality, and ideas. Bollas (1987, p. 161) emphasizes the importance of "the maintenance of a receptive space for the arrival of news from within the self," but for all of us as human beings, there are things that we don't want to know and can't bear to hear, either from within or from without. Unwanted aspects of mental life are banished from consciousness and projected out into others in an active process of ridding ourselves of unwanted parts of the self, which others are compelled to carry for us. According to Bollas, this projective identification process is "a highly active unconscious activity aimed at keeping what we cannot bear to have in ourself inside the Other." The uncomfortable reality is that unwanted patients may be the ones in whom we, as therapists, locate our own unwanted parts, from which we are trying to escape. And Phillips (pp. 135–136) describes the very human attempt to escape from one's self as "Man's preposterous project", arguing that in psychoanalytic theory, *that which the subject wishes to escape from but cannot is considered to be his essence.....because we try to escape only from that which is by definition inescapable.*"

It is perhaps an obvious point to make here, but I think an important one is that patients do not fit neatly and stably into two distinct groupings of "wanted" and "unwanted"; rather, they will tend to move in and out of these very subjective categories. Which prompts me to wonder about what might make the difference here for me. And on reflection, I think it's clear that this certainly doesn't come down to the level of disturbance alone. That may be an obvious factor that comes into play, but I have worked with much more psychotic people than the case I'm discussing here, including a number of schizophrenic patients, without the same awful responses getting stirred up within me. Similarly, getting caught up in complex enactments, struggling with complicated countertransference feelings, or having disturbing thoughts and feelings pushed into me – being made to actually *feel* painful and disturbing feelings rather than more straightforwardly *hearing* about them – all of these things are difficult enough but regular enough aspects of therapeutic relationships, and on the whole, tend to be more manageable than what I'm struggling with so much in this case.

I think that what is unbearable for me in what I'm trying to describe here has less to do with the patient herself and more to do with a relational component – that is, with what gets stirred up within me in relation to a patient like Katie and how I'm left feeling as a therapist. This leaves me thinking more in terms of unwanted therapists (or therapist self-states) than unwanted patients, in the sense that the therapist I become in these encounters – paralyzed, inhibited, deadened, fearful, self-loathing, unkind, irritable, impotent, clueless, humorless, lifeless, impatient, deadly serious, lacking in insight, lost, timid, hateful, and hopeless – is painfully far removed from the playful, kind, insightful, creative, and enlivening therapist I would much sooner like to see in myself. It's as if something dies inside of me in such encounters; my creative faculties are somehow lost to me, and I can no longer be me, no longer be real and true to myself. I somehow lose the key capacities within me for empathy, thought, reverie, play, humor, curiosity, and concern, and I no longer feel alive in the room. And all of this puts me in mind of a couple of lines from Philip Larkin's powerfully unsettling depiction of the state of death in his late poem *Aubade* (2012, pp. 115–116) – a state of "total emptiness" in which there is "nothing to think with/Nothing to love or link with...." Death here, for Larkin, is a destination that we're all inevitably bound for, "And shall be lost in always." These are lines that resonate very deeply with my experience, for a very long time, in relation to Katie – finding myself horribly and alarmingly lost and trapped, seemingly with no prospect of ever finding a way out of this profoundly unwanted place – with an awful hollow feeling of having no capacity for thought, for love, or for making the kind of links required in order to find a way through and out of these deadly and deadening experiences.

I think, with Katie, that she had me so actively disturbed, and at times so frightened at the prospect of her killing herself, that I maybe had no choice but to desperately and regularly seek some help – from local supervision to transatlantic training, and from the embodied balancing and breathing practice of yoga to analysis of my own. The clinical encounter was a form of death by a thousand cuts, if you like, which constantly left me disturbed and needing some psychological first aid. And this, in turn, puts me in mind of Eigen's image of the bird pecking away at its mother until it finally gets the response it needs. What's crucial, if we're to survive this kind of experience of being buried alive in the consulting room, is the ongoing creation of what we might think of as a therapeutic clearing – a vital pocket of space in which the therapist can breathe, think, regain one's balance, and feel. This involves drawing both creatively and heavily on all of the key resources available to us as therapists, such as supervision, personal analysis, a community of colleagues, training, theory, and spaces like this current volume – all of which represent different versions of a clearing in which we can gather, shelter, regroup, reconnect, recharge, replenish, and restore. Taking care both to maintain and to regularly withdraw to such spaces outside of the consulting room is vital if the therapist is to be able to keep the psychoanalytic faith, to stay alive, and to co-create, with the patient, a clearing within the therapy itself in which ongoing mutual aliveness, growth, movement, and evolutionary progress are possible.

References

Bloch, S. and Daws, L. [editors] (2015). *Living Moments: On the Work of Michael Eigen*. London: Routledge.

Bollas, C. (1987). *The Shadow of the Object*. London: Routledge.

Daws, L. (2023). *Michael Eigen: A Contemporary Introduction*. (Routledge Introductions to Contemporary Psychoanalysis). London: Routledge.

Eigen, M. (1977). On working with "unwanted" patients. *International Journal of Psychoanalysis*, 58: 109–121.

Eigen, M. (1993a). *The Psychotic Core*. Northvale, NJ: Jason Aronson.

Eigen, M. (1993b). *The Electrified Tightrope*. (Ed. A. Phillips). Northvale, NJ: Jason Aronson.

Eigen, M. (1996). *Psychic Deadness*. Northvale, NJ: Jason Aronson.

Eigen, M. (2020). *Dialogues with Michael Eigen: Psyche Singing*. (Ed. L. Daws). London: Routledge.

Larkin, P. (2012). *The Complete Poems*. New York, NY: Farrar, Straus and Giroux.

Molino, A. (1997). *Elaborate Selves*. New York, NY: The Haworth Press.

Ogden, T. (1997). *Reverie and Interpretation: Sensing Something Human*. London: Karnac.

Phillips, A. (1989). *Winnicott*. Cambridge, MA: Harvard University Press.

Phillips, A. (2013). *One Way and Another: New and Selected Essays*. London: Penguin.

Chapter 10

Raging against Love – Surviving Injury-Rage Patients

A Personal Reverie

Richard Raubolt

I have worked with unpleasant people.... The subset I'm trying to describe is one I have not done well with. I'm picturing a group of angry, needy women who always want more. I never (rarely) give enough or I give the wrong thing. I just don't get exactly what I'm supposed to give or withhold. I can try to get off the hook because I am a man.... But many of these women have been thrown out by women therapists who couldn't or wouldn't take them...I sit through anything. **They attack, demand, go after their needs, seek by attacking. I clam up. They leave.... Some stay for a while. They see something good and insist I give it to them. I would if I could, but I click off, a steel sheet across my chest. They keep banging, bloody against the metal. I try and try, but there is little I can do....** (Eigen, 2007, p. 96)

So, Eigen (2007) writes, and I experience. From the beginning, rage is there but silent, cold, and tucked in the corner with injury-rage patients. When I have chosen not to confront such patients, they may be content to let the momentum build. This uneasy peace does not last.

Like shards of glass haphazardly forged together, posing raw, jagged danger, patients with injury rage leave me feeling:

You will pay for every betrayal
every phone call you miss
every email unread.
every impatience
every hesitation
every dead ass interpretation
every bead of sweat
every dinner with your family
I love you so much.

Eigen (2002) warned, but I did not hear. I had not yet read:

Rage substitutes for growth, fills in holes, masks deficiencies. It is allied with a sense of helplessness, disability, frailty. It hammers others into helplessness...It

DOI: 10.4324/9781003322986-10

freezes others' spontaneity, immobilizes and attempts to control others. It tries to squeeze reality into one's own narrow frame of reference. (p. 10)

Many injury-rage patients may present as interesting, perhaps quirky, and intelligent. They can possess a quick, sharp wit and reveal a motivation to engage in "talk therapy." Many have had various therapies previously with a few therapists, but commonly report failures. They may come with a true, even desperate, need to break off bad relationships with partners when they find themselves caught in negative spirals. They may present with genuine sadness, regret, helplessness, and childlike vulnerability. Painfully, they may present with overwhelming feelings of helplessness and a gnawing hunger to experience love. Tragically, injury-rage patients can find themselves unable to *express or receive intimate* and tender feelings as basic trust in the motives of others is often compromised, if not traumatically shattered.

Soon, however, the unsuspecting analyst may find, through a slight, an early sign of what is to come. A slight, a misperception, or a word not quite right (but not wrong either) earns an unexpected and virulent rageful reaction, catching one off guard. To be sure, not only would one be caught off guard, but the analyst may even be attacked for being sanctimonious and false. Attempts to provide clarification can be described as being deceitful and self-serving, coupled with accusations of vindictiveness or a wish to do harm on the part of the analyst. Subsequent psychoanalytic efforts to explore the meaning of such reactions can be stonewalled. Injury-rage patients, so capable of delivering withering, sadistic attacks, can leave the analyst feeling hesitant, lost, silent, and even questioning their motives. Vicious but bloodless enactments make for intense affective storms and lay bare the full intensity of rage, only partly obscured from the beginning of treatment.

Paradoxically, they claim:

My love knows no boundaries.

So, to the analyst:

You must love me with no boundaries.

Recalling such patients, I felt:

From the beginning, on **my side of the couch,** unconscious and taking shape darkly in the shadows, I was reflecting their terror:
I am dead to them
I am dead on arrival.
A possession.
Inanimate – an object.
Functional.

I could only offer muted patience.
Compassion generous, without complaint.
Attention unwavering, without question.
Redemptive love, without restriction.
I was to provide what they never had and wouldn't, couldn't, ever have…
This analytic dyad whitewashed bad under the guise of good
… and I thought
masochistic surrender
ever forgiving
timeless availability
empathy for damage unleashed without protest.
… and inside, I howled against my assigned role
You demand I exist for you.
You demand I exist only for you.
Must I exist only to murder your love?

Yet my analysands' wounds were visible. They had been hurt badly, very badly, many times. The yawning wounds from parental inability to love are pursuing them now into adulthood, forming tough layers of skin all but closing their eyes, pushing ever deeper into isolation and despair with only the sparks of rage offering any signs of life.

Eigen (2002) provided a perspective I was struggling to comprehend:

> Rage can lead to change. It can force others to hear that something is wrong, call attention to oneself or one's cause, stimulate the need for help. (p. 10)

And he warns:

> But it is also part of abuse and continues the affliction. It runs deep in all directions, allied with righteousness and cruelty, dominance – subservience, freedom – slavery. (p. 11)
> What directions was their rage pulling me?
> Killing me and demanding I survive ala Winnicott?
> Were my analysands' screams of fury the twilight of a child's long need to be seen? Heard?
> Were my analysands' words empty echoes of pretend love that was bringing to haunt us both?
> Could I hold a singed ember long enough to cool the burning torture of the analysands' self – hate?
> How close to their core seething would I dare approach?
> Did I have any right to ask these questions?

And yet, as I was considering these questions, others began to tumble over them, crowding them and pressing for attention:

Would rage ignite new life?

Could my analysands tolerate me being beside them as they fought to live?

Was I rigidly cast in their play of repetition?

Could they survive their self-collapse?

...and they thought I thought

Oh, Dr. R I love you to pieces, bits, and pieces

Don't you fucking dare let me down

You will find only bits and pieces.

...and I thought what they thought

You will be cruel.

You will hate me.

You will laugh while hurting me.

You will reject me with every lying word.

How could you? How could you? How could you? How could you? How could you? How could you not? How could you not? How could you not? The paradoxes of rage that grow and shrink; take turns and contradict, preserve and destroy.

I will wish you dead. No, really dead.

I can find myself in their possession, trapped by the relentless, destructive pursuit of hope (Stark, 1999, 2017). When I offered a little kindness or a tender word, it was hurled back as disingenuous and most likely memorized. I wanted life, but I was assigned to the *death watch*. There was enough oxygen for only one, and there was no sharing. Instead, my words set off explosions, claiming abandonment. I didn't "get" my injury-rage analysands, so in this binary thinking, I wasn't paying sufficient attention and wanted them gone. Frequently each became an enemy of health. With scalding rage, injury-rage patients cut into my person, spitting my every word back with spite and viciousness.

There are no patients, not in these dyads. Some analysands have even joked they were serial killers who would pick apart my words until I lapsed into silence, and then they could possess me, steal my mind, and love me to death. Injury-rage patients can claw their way into my unconscious even as I try to confront, clarify, contain, and interpret. *But most of all, as I sought empathic attunement, this resulted in an infiltration and contamination of my dreams and a dismantling of my thinking.* Attuned to my every breath, they know when they have pushed too far in quitting therapy with such a "heartless, cold therapist." After waiting a few days, they would plead to come back, mouthing the magic words that they needed me, and it was a terrible mistake they made that only I could repair. This is an enactment of the idiosyncratic version of Freud's *fort-da* narrative: I could be thrown away, "fort," only until the aggression is undone by making me reappear, "da," taking pleasure in the game of repetitious enactment much like Ernst, Freud's grandson. These narratives are saturated with sadomasochistic satisfaction. Staging this incessant play of disappearance/appearance, expressed as the wish that I love only them and they love only me forever, becomes a form of physical imprisonment.

In treating injury-rage patients, an essential question about empathy emerged for me: what are the limits beyond which empathy cannot go? For example, Stark (1999) and Carveth (1997) have suggested that empathy, as practiced analytically, requires the analyst to de-center from his/her own perspective and immerse him/herself in the patient's perspective. By implication, this process is one-dimensional and a step removed from authentic engagement. Carveth (1997), in addressing this concern, writes:

> ...but of course empathy is not enough. Having thoroughly understood my patient, I may decide, all things considered, his reality testing is off, and I will confront him. He may feel mine is off. Out of our dialogue, one or both of us may shift ground. (p. 4)

Reliance on the provision of empathy exclusively may serve as a defense against the authentic engagement necessary for the development of mutuality. Yet I find myself doubting whether authenticity based on mutual recognition is possible with any kind of consistency. To give or receive empathy can be experienced as a threat to maintaining the maternal introject that provided the only love, distorted as it was. Any feelings of empathic attachment are commonly dismantled and dismissed with raging outbursts to avoid anxieties about dependence. At such times I have become aware of thinking that more than not being in the treatment, injury-rage patients could be *aggressively against it*.

These patients that I have experienced over the years have demonstrated severely tattered self-cohesion. In its stead was an engulfing, entitled, and impulse-driven fragmentation that could explosively take command of the therapy hour. Still, I remained committed to finding a way to invite my analysands to consider what damage they might be causing themselves. This required going beyond empathy, and if authentic relating was unavailable, where did that leave treatment? (Where *did that leave me?*) I did not forget that the fundamental objective of the analysis is for the patient to become an analyst to her/himself. Relationally, patients and analysts must each change, or neither will. They are both in therapy: changing and growing together (and separately).

Belatedly, I began to realize that patients who are addicted to rage are not in therapy as much as they use the process to accumulate even the slightest perceived grievance to justify further retaliation. Intersubjectively, empathy is thought to offer the necessary glue whereby disruptions can be repaired, while for injury-rage patients, relying on rage to settle perceived scores undermines any attempt at reparation and leads to greater destructiveness. Injury-rage patients' present with blinding rage, though they experience no choice. They feel they are fighting for their lives; it is to destroy or be destroyed. Injury-rage patients are like moths drawn to the flame, where they mimic the obstructive objects (Bion, 1959) that have created much of their misery, persecution, and barely tolerable aloneness that is their daily existence. This, by now, internalized ego-destructive object perpetuates an atmosphere of intense emotional pain. Eaton (2011) describes the analytic ambiance with such patients as follows: "Chronic self-attack, including attacks on linking, blocks the growth of a sense of personal agency that would ordinarily allow a person to receive help and to cooperate in her own analytic transformation" (p. 17).

And as Eigen (2002) opines:

> Without a perception of how damaging rage is, there is little reason to change. The sense of damage must be acute, heartfelt … a rendering of soul that recoils in horror upon seeing what rage does. And that soul must seek help. (p. 15)

As continued attempts to destroy me as their analyst intensified, the therapeutic process lost meaning and instead was restricted to nightmarish enactments of false accusations and paranoid vindications. In order for love and hate to be real, to exist as two sides of the same coin, they must be titrated, circumscribed, and bound by physical and psychological realities. Otherwise, and outside the boundaries of ordinary and mutual reality, the analytic dyad enters the territory of fantasy and/ or delusion. Such territory can be visited, explored, and enacted if it is temporary and the real relationship with the analyst remains intact. To be real, love must also include experiences of sadness and loss while remaining capable of containing and withstanding disappointment. I believe my injury-rage patients are unable to tolerate such losses; instead, they live out cruel, suffocating fantasies while attacking my own, at times, tenuous grip on reality. As a result, I failed to recognize how powerfully and quickly projective identification emerged as a primary defensive style when the therapeutic relationship became skewed and imbalanced. It became a defining way of transforming delusion into a self-constructed and unassailable reality. "I hate you, so you hate me (delusion), now that I know you hate me, I hate you even more (reality)."

The Sound and the Fury: Persecutory Attacks on the Analytic Container

Given the intrapsychic and interpersonal realities of injury-rage patients, it is no surprise that the analytic container may be battered by relentless assaults, shredding the analytic relationship through threats, projections, and hate-driven accusations. The phone may even become a weapon, and cumulative voicemails may become a vehicle of war. The full range of emotions can be on display, seemingly competing with others for expression, i.e., some were attacking, some were pleading, some were childlike, some were sarcastic, some were accusatory, some were desperate, and some were threatening. These were presented with such breathless intensity that I have to write with no spaces between "some were," to approximate what it felt like to be on the receiving end of such vitriolic exchanges. The objective of this mission may be to fill a mailbox so that the analyst remains unavailable for other patients. If an injury-rage patient couldn't possess the analyst, no one else would either. Paradoxically, the injury-rage patient may effectively dance on the edge of therapy, not really "in" or rather only "in far enough" to brandish the threat of quitting. Sometimes, it may feel that the injury-rage analysand only continues the analysis because they believe the analyst wants the analysand to quit. Strangling the container and tearing at any appearance of cooperation, the analytic drumbeat rhythm of a day may be flooded with conscious and unconscious themes evoking therapeutic fear and concern – suicidality mixed with sarcasm, provocation, resentment, and punishment. And so, sadomasochistic repetition ensues – endings and do-overs – blood pooling on the floor, and I, as an analyst, kept cleaning it up. I frequently succumbed and vowed for one last time to try again. I had not heeded Eigen's (2002) call for caution when the tide turns and regret is hinted at, or, more plainly, spoken clearly. Rage can feed off any underestimation of its' power and metastasize into something far more virulent and destructive:

> A problem is that feeling sorry is not enough and can be a danger sign. One feels sorry for the destructiveness then the sorrow ebbs and the destructiveness builds, akin to an addictive cycle. I don't know what makes this tick, but both sides of the cycle go together, reparation-destructiveness. One is tied to both, need both, wallow in both. (Eigen, 2002, p. 47, italics added)

Upon reading an earlier draft of this chapter, Gianotti (2018, personal communication) emphasized the importance of maintaining a stance anchored firmly on the side of containment. In a personal communication (Gianotti, 2018, personal communication, example, April 4th), she wrote:

> A holding environment of empathy is only as solid as our ability to hold the dialectic tension between empathy and the need for containment of toxic rage, rage that threatens to kill the body of the patient and the contagion effect that spreads into the body of the therapist.

Even though I knew this to be true, at times, I did not know how to go forward with my injury-rage patients or how to stop.[1]

It is also important to note that, given the vexing difficulties in treating injury-rage analysands, none of my immediate colleagues that I consulted had any clearer ideas about how to proceed with the treatment questions I was posing: mixed in with the rage, injury-rage patients may still somehow remain seeking health, as much as they are able to, or was this just one of many repeat performances? Do injury-rage patients regress and take with them whomever they can as well? Is the analyst a mere "whomever?" As a psychoanalyst, I do not like dismissing what patients tell me, with or without words, or blindly pursuing any ray of sunshine amid emotional storms. Nor is it my frame of reference to focus on the pathological trailing edge to the detriment of a drive toward health.

Parenthetically, as I was completing the final draft of this chapter, I came to read Robert Grossmark's article (2012), *The Unobtrusive Relational Analyst*, where he writes of similar doubts:

> I found myself continually confused. At first I panicked and would ask questions in a futile attempt to gain clarity, interrupting the flow of words. Explanations did not help. I learned that I had to settle into this felt world of confusion and near psychosis, and somehow to find some way to get comfortable, or at least survive and keep my own mind intact. (p. 635)

Upon reading this description, I felt he and I had seen the same patients, and I welcomed the company. I came to realize, however, that upon further reflection, our appreciation and understanding of dynamics and history were quite different. For his patient, there was emotional deadness or, perhaps more accurately, profound confusion about existence in time and space. While rage was present, it was less relentlessly directed at his destruction. In a personal communication (2019) with Grossmark, he offered the following cogent insights regarding one of my vexing injury-rage patients:

> It seems from the get-go that your patient could not tolerate anything that did not come under her omnipotent control. The patient's initial rage came when you spoke from an Other place, outside of her/his inner reality...anything you did which created even a drop of separateness or anything that asked his/her to *think* would result in wild destructive rage. So, the more you became a separate person and set limits the more her/she would escalate her desperate hatred. It is indeed a punishing knot. (Personal correspondence, 2019, day)

I have seen troubled patients in my years of practice. With injury-age patients, I kept telling myself to trust the process. As long as they were talking, I was talking and looking for some threads to grab hold of that would move us into a different way of relating. I kept asking myself if, through this intensely negative transference, they needed me to hate them in order to be seen as they experienced themselves. Bollas (1984) describes such a patient as

> ...seeking his/her double in the confusion and anger in the analyst and if able to access this frame of the analyst's mind the patient will have constructed a negative self-object, ... an object, not differentiated but carrying his projections and identifications. (p. 231)

Might it not be considered from this viewpoint that the expression of empathy lay in hating a patient, for only then could they feel genuinely seen? Could there be some residue of hope – a raw, broken search for intimacy, not yet taking shape but with this possibility existing within the ferocity of their attacks? As theoretically satisfying as these considerations might be, I could find no evidence of such an unfolding but only escalation that was damning the analytic pair. As such, my mind began filling in the empty spaces, doing my best to anticipate from what angles and over what grievances would the subsequent firefight be launched. I never had to wait long to face the analysands' growing fierceness. Fierceness, rupture, distancing, and the repetition to continue therapy finally leave the analyst refusing to continue the analytic process, nourishing further attack on the analyst for abandonment.

From My Side of the Analytic Couch: Seeking to Understand, Seeking to Recover

In retrospect, I have come to realize that therapy with injury-rage patients can begin and end without mutual recognition. I will sometimes feel that I do not exist as separate from the thoughts and feelings assigned to me. I "existed" only in so far as I empathically provided a corrective emotional experience, i.e., love. Such patients need some type of corrective *relational* experience. Sensing how traumatized and fragmented these patients are, I have adopted a modified analytic approach and offered empathic resonance and love for the pain and rejection and, as I discovered, the aggressive but ambivalent self-loathing/hatred they experienced. Judiciously, I also provided some disclosure of personal biographical information, feelings of hesitation and specifically my "stiffness" in language, doubts about the success of the treatment, and, most pertinently, revealing vulnerability. I believe such disclosures can be clinically valuable if the patient can metabolize the revelations. By this, I mean the patient must be able to take in the information, reflect on its' relevance, consider the reasons, assess the accuracy, and accept it as a gift from the therapist.

   In the treatment I have described here, anything but exquisite attunement and agreement may be met with bouts of rage; even brief periods of silence needed to establish some reflective space may be experienced as acutely rejecting. Rather than being able to use my attempts to understand their internal world or consider what might be happening within the psychoanalytic pair, an injury-rage patient may slip into a seemingly bottomless malignant regression. I offered soothing and empathically informed understanding while failing to appreciate how *any* empathic lapse, no matter how slight, is usually greeted with hatred and stated wishes and threats to destroy me. When feeling trapped by the projective nature of such destructiveness and my growing concern with analysands safety, I double down with patience, gentle clarifications, interpretations, and periods of patient quiet. In retrospect, by unwittingly participating in masochistic/sadistic enactments, I opened myself to my injury-rage patients by seeking to deny my hatred and demonstrate I could survive their rages and *appear* available. I was choking the life out of myself. I also came to realize that this response not only fueled many injury-rage analysands' aggression but also made me a participant in my own emotional murder!

   Since my attempts at containment through limit setting, interpretation, and confrontation were experienced as selfish rejections, I found myself ingesting a toxic brew of withering rage, accusations, and threats. I was losing myself, and I was no closer to finding my patients. Stewing in my own juices, I became resentful and internally enraged at the assignment of the role as my analysands split seductively, rejecting bad object. These emotional undercurrents would surface and lead me to seek and establish some semblance of control. Misunderstandings and misinterpretations of emails and texts only lead to "meltdowns," so I requested, yet again, and in various registers, that my analysand/s bring these feelings/experiences into the therapy room where we could talk together and seek some understanding. I told my analysands that if they continued to send emotional texts and emails, they would remain "unread" until their next session. This precipitated crisis after crisis, leading a number of analysands to quit or threaten to quit therapy – more times after establishing this boundary. And each time, I was accused of being dangerous, hateful, and out to destroy the analysand.

After a "cooling off period," some injury-rage analysands would beg me to take them back into treatment, claiming I was the only one who "got" them and thus wanted another chance and therapeutic work. In a disguised fashion, these enactments expressed a delusional belief I admittedly shared that they could not destroy me, but I certainly wasn't helping either. I came to learn, painfully so, that the "second chances" were not about changing how therapy is used, but instead, they provided injury-rage analysands further opportunities to see how much I could tolerate before I would lash back with much-anticipated vengeance. The only way I could be in the room with various injury-rage analysands was to be totally immersed in their sadomasochistic object-relations world. There was no space that was not an enactment of this aspect of their mind and being. It seemed impossible to *Be*, and to be with them – this can be captured in the fort-da metaphor – such was the force to dominate totally.

I was aware of Winnicott's paper (1969), where he wrote that the analyst must survive the patient's destructiveness if there is to be a developmental leap forward, i.e., from object relating to object use. Exploring the nuances of this paper is beyond the scope of this presentation. I only note Ogden's (2016) reminder that Winnicott's clause "These attacks may be difficult to stand..." contained an important caveat, which I missed, attached as a footnote: "When the analyst knows the patient carries a revolver, then, it seems to me, the work cannot be done" (Ogden, 2016, p. 1259). From nearly the beginning, my injury-rage patients brandished revolvers that carried their malignant rage as ammunition.

Mills (2006) has implicated such intense repetitive enactments as being reflective of death work as defined by Freud. Let me quote Mills at some length:

What we analysts face every day is inherent self-destructiveness of patients who can neither find amity nor reprieve from psychic conflict and the repetitions that fuel their suffering. These inherent capacities for self-destructiveness are not merely located from external sources, for they are both interiorized and internalized, thus becoming the organizing death -principles at work on myriad levels of unconscious experience. In the same article Mills cogently writes: "We see it every day in the consulting room. From oppressive guilt, disabling shame, explosive rage, contagious hate, self-loathing, and unbearable agony, there is a perverse appeal to suffering, to embrace our masochistic *jouissance* – our ecstasy in pain. (p. 13)

Fairbairn (1943) offers us an entirely different therapeutic lens through which to view such self-destructiveness. He identifies intense internal attachments to bad objects that make separating and extricating from compulsive repetitions difficult. Many of my injury-rage analysands, who rely on splitting as a significant defense, continued to unconsciously assign to me either the role of the libidinal bad object that they needed to excite them and/or the anti-libidinal one that was hated because it rejected them. Such an internal defensive structure originally occurs as a result of failure in "good-enough mothering," where, according to Winnicott (1945), the mother gradually moves from total immersion in her infant's needs to responding less and less completely according to the infant's ability to cope with her failure(s). When the mother is incapable of meeting this developmental need, the child will have difficulty surrendering demands for omnipotent control of future object relations. Instead, s/he relentlessly pursues what was not available by attaching to an exciting object spellbound with the hope his/her specialness will be recognized and the accompanying emotional supplies (love) will be delivered. Since this love is believed to be available but is withheld – again – aggressive retaliation occurs as the only alternative to unbearable rejection.

Stark (1999, 2017) has also cogently presented the dynamics of this sadomasochistic dance as presented in the clinical setting when she writes:

The patient's relentless hope (which fuels her masochism) is the stance to which she desperately clings in order to avoid confronting certain intolerably painful realities about the object of her desire and its limitations; and her relentless outrage (which fuels her sadism) is the stance to which she resorts in those moments or dawning recognition that the object is separate, has its own center of initiative, and is not going to relent. (2017, p. 12)

With my former analysands, I have sketched the subtler aspects of their masochism, their persisting struggles, and their suffering from wrestling with their hoped-for love from me. What is more dramatically displayed and frequently present with such patients is their sadistic rage at each perceived betrayal, disappointment, wrong, or slight they experienced. Every time such patients perceive a refusal to accede to their demands, they become infuriated. Analytical exploration can be dismissed as just so much theory, detached, and, as a result, failed to titrate the unbearable pain being presented. Attempts to help digest the history and meaning of symptoms, especially as they were enacted between us, were seen as self-serving on my part and greeted me with additional explosiveness. Empathy was dismissed as disingenuous and at odds with the rejection believed to be the running undercurrent of therapy, and silences were experienced as withholding and aggressive indications that justified rage. I believe this rage is what Eigen (1999) identifies as "*injury rage*," which is cumulative over one's life. He describes it thus:

> Its sediments in the belly of one's being and corrupts muscles, nerves, veins. It not only stiffens one's body, it poisons one'd thoughts...Cumulative rage helps nourish a pessimistic, depressive, semi-malevolent counterpart or undertow to one's official, happier self. (p. 48)

The impact and reality of dis-ease can permeate every exchange, including misinterpreting emails and voicemails; if I would not, could not, soothe analysands by my surrender, they set out to destroy me. I could find no middle ground. There was no "good enough." There was only all or nothing at a pitched intensity level I had never experienced. In the end, a misinterpretation can provoke the needed mercy killing of therapy and save both the analysand and me. I usually find I can breathe again. Or I think I can.

For many analysts working with injury-rage dynamics, the unconscious connection may continue even after termination, similar to Bion's notion of a destructive force that keeps destroying long after all has been destroyed (1965). Even in my work with injury-rage dynamics, connections continued after the cessation of therapy, and I have received emails and texts for, at times, months after termination. Transference/countertransference binds remain uncanny and accurate. I would wonder when or if I would continue to hear from an analysand, and then I would within a day. These were unpleasant, accusatory, damning, and threatening. Injury-rage patients may even threaten or contemplate filing complaints with licensing boards or suing the analyst for abandonment. To prepare for either eventuality, the analyst may have to rely on institutional containment in the form of legal protection, which, for many analysts, is a trauma in itself. Cumulative rage and rage injury spur cumulative attacks in the form of, as mentioned, countless emails, texts, and phone calls. Subjectively, I even reached the point where I was hesitant to answer my phone or read my emails. At times, analysands have been on the verge of successfully turning me against myself and into the victim they themselves felt to be. Gradually and with resistance, I became aware of my own growing anger and rage. Initially, the raw intensity of these feelings was deeply unsettling. Consultation helped provide a safe container to allow exploration and detoxification of my countertransference reactions. Consultation also served to recognize and appreciate the self-protective survival reactions necessary for treating injury-rage patients.

Note

1 As *I wrote these words, I heard Beckett's in my head: "And what I'm doing, all-important, breathing in and out saying, with words like smoke I can't go on, I can't stay, let's see what happens next"* (Beckett, 1995, p. 102).

References

Beckett, S. (1995). *Samuel Beckett: The Complete Prose, 1929–1989.* Texts for nothing, 100–121. New York, NY: Grove Press.

Bion, W. R. (1959) Attacks on Linking. In *Second Thoughts*, 93–109. London: Karnac, 1984.

Bion, W. R. (1965). *Transformations.* London: Heinemann.

Bollas, C. (1984). Loving hate. *The Annual of Psychoanalysis*, 12, 221–237.

Carveth, D. L. (1997, December 28). What is valuable in self-psychology and what isn't? One analyst's opinion. https://www.yorku.ca/dcarveth/Kohut.pdf

Eaton, J. L. (2011). *A Fruitful Harvest Essays after Bion.* Seattle, WA: Alliance Press.

Eigen, M. (1999). *Toxic Nourishment.* London: Karnac Books.

Eigen, M. (2002). *Rage.* Middletown, CT: Wesleyan University Press.

Eigen, M. (2007). *Feelings Matter.* New York, NY: Routledge.

Fairbairn, W. R. D. (1943). *The Repression and Return of Bad Objects.* An object-relations theory of personality, 59–81. New York, NY: Basic Books.

Grossmark, R. (2012). The unobtrusive relational analyst. *Psychoanalyst Dialogues*, 22, 629–646.

Mills, J. (2006). Reflections on the death drive. *Psychoanalytic Psychology*, 2, 373–382.

Ogden, T. H. (2016). Destruction reconceived: On Winnicott's the use of an object and relating through identifications. *International Journal of Psychoanalysis*, 97, 1243–1262.

Stark, M. (1999). *Modes of Therapeutic Interaction.* Northvale, NJ: Jason Aronson.

Stark, M. (2017). *Relentless Hope and the Refusal to Grieve.* e-Book. Bethesda, MD: International Psychotherapy Institute.

Winnicott, D. W. (1945). *Primitive Emotional Development.* Pediatrics to psychoanalysis, 145–156. New York, NY: Basic Books.

Winnicott, D. W. (1969). The use of an object. *International Journal of Psychoanalysis*, 50, 711 716.

Chapter 11

Transcendent Intuition

Linking Fragments to Psychic Attunement across Time and Space

Keri S. Cohen

In order to appreciate and understand Eigen's work, one is drawn to the life and work of Wilfred Bion. Eigen's work is steeped in Bion's life and writings, among many others. Eigen has been teaching Bion's work for decades and has devoted at least the last 10–15 years to teaching Bion's *A Memoir of the Future.*

In *A Memoir of the Future*, Bion writes,

> that…intuitions that are 'blind' must lack completion, and that the 'completion' which is not 'complete' or is 'unfulfilled', nevertheless exists… it is the 'job' of the link or synapse to join….but no substitute can do what the link does… sooner or later any substitute for the real thing is bound to fail through instability. (Bion, 1991, pp. 387–388)

Intuition provides opportunities for links, creating space between two people to develop a link. Drawing on Bion's work, Andre Green states, "the real analytic object is neither on the patient's side nor on the analyst's, but in the meeting of these two communications in the potential space between them" (Green, 1975, p. 12). Intuition begins in that space, where one may seek attunement with an Other. It opens room for a link to a new experience rather than a repetition borne from a mind filled with memory, desire, and expectation. For Bion, a deep focus of intuition begins with the capacity to embody a state of mind where one is open to the Unknown.

Eigen's work, like Bion's, is attuned to trauma and fragmented experience, remaining open to not knowing and using intuition to welcome a new integrative experience representative of the unknown to transform into new links. This develops capacities to feel an event or traumatic event dispersed along different frames of experience on the time and space continuum. It opens up the possibility of the context of simultaneous happenings in the mind and the environment. Remaining open to not knowing breathes the possibility of life into the analytic dyad. "Two people in the room waiting on the emergence of unknown emotional reality, everything expressible" (Eigen, 2018, p. 72). Without this context, one shrinks into a narrow plane of existence, defined by memory and expectation of function. Repetition ensues, and intuition is obstructed. Among his many other writings, Eigen devotes his book, *Psychic Deadness* (Eigen, 1996), to this topic.

DOI: 10.4324/9781003322986-11

Jeffrey Eaton, in his seminal paper, *The Obstructive Object* (Eaton, 2005), describes the following:

> ...chronic self attack...perpetuates an atmosphere of intense mental pain, violence and self attack...Chronic self attack, including attacks on linking, blocks the growth of a sense of personal agency that would ordinarily allow a person to receive help and to cooperate in his or her own analytic transformation. According to W.R. Bion, some patients give evidence of living with an internal object that operates as a *projecting identification rejecting object*. Bion names this ego-destructive internal object an *obstructive object*. (p. 355)

Bion expands Freud's statement that "There is...more continuity between intra-uterine life and earliest infancy than the impressive caesura...of birth would have us believe" (Freud, 1926, p. 109). Bion imagines the fetus exposed to pressures in the womb, noises, disturbances going on, and possibly an argument. These pressures, Bion suggests, turn into

> characters of the personality, aware of fear, hate...then the fetus may turn in hostility towards these disturbing feelings...fragment them, destroy them, evacuate them...I can imagine the fetus...tries to get rid of its personality to start off with, and then after birth learn all the words and phrases people consciously use. (Bion, 1987, p. 318)

Conscious words substitute as a defense against intuitions, damaging or attacking links to capacities for mutual emotional attunement. Intuitions are used as a link with the mother. Reciprocally, both infant and mother reach for quality experience.

Original fetal disruption narrows the capacity for the fetus to experience future trauma triggers within a broader context. The fetus, or newborn, becomes unable to see in the context of infinite possibilities. This repetition or quantity threatens future stability or quality of experience, setting up a rigid response to the environment. The use of intuition floats experience across a broader context, creating possibilities to access new emergent experiential healing processes.

Arnaldo Chuster states, "...the mind of the fetus develops in the 'perversion' of having to cope with certain situations that will appear in after-birth, but in a certain way have already arrived" (Chuster, 2014, p. 107). He emphasizes remembering the "embryonic mental medium, where some facts occur that prepare the individual to live in the 'gaseous' medium" (Chuster, 2014, p. 108).

When intuition is obstructed, psychic attunement fails, hindering the capacity to develop emotional growth and psychic vitality, which transcend experience and time. Intrapsychic life is obstructed.

Fragmented feelings and dissociated experiences add challenges to forming a positive link between the analyst and patient. One learns to hold both the feeling of trauma alongside intuition as a guide toward linking the plethora of concurrent, emergent, affective experiential feelings in the background environment. The patient builds the capacity to add links to experience, a mental space where, creatively, one again gains freedom from the tyranny of trauma, the environment, and of the self.

Capacities are missing in order to function. The patient's transformation enables an internal link, opening capacities for deeper intrapsychic healing work. To a large extent, Eigen's work aims to help form and develop missing capacities in his patients' lives. He helps patients transcend the dead parts back to life, even if just for moments of existence. Moments grow, and Eigen fiercely believes in moments.

Clinical Vignette

Greg, a middle-aged man, began therapy after separating from his wife. He had a restless and racing mind, laying awake at night, unable to sleep due to anxiety. He was physically restless, with the energy of a young man. Greg was bright, articulate, and emotionally intelligent, but despondent, without hope of ever trusting anyone to partner in an emotionally intimate relationship. He often expressed his distrust in others, yet he desperately yearned to trust others so he could form friendships, especially a relationship with another woman. Instinctively, he understood he required this to survive but could not welcome following his intuition.

Greg's grief and feelings of rejection were palpable. Greg grew up with constant feelings of not belonging, feeling discarded, and bearing witness to his father's tirades, alcoholism, and marital affairs. His parents divorced and then remarried each other five years later, while he was a child. His father continued his behavior following their second marriage. Throughout his life, Greg felt ostracized by his mother and sister. His mother and sister formed their own dyad, which strained Greg's relationships with both of them. His father died when Greg was in his 20s. He was a forgotten child, feeling discarded from his family and from his internal life. His parents could not function as containers for Greg, and Greg internalized a rejecting object. These feelings filled his loneliness and his unwelcoming internal life.

Greg mostly kept to himself, having no real friends, cautious about trusting the outside world. As a young man, Greg found his way to alcohol and trouble. He joined the military as a way to save himself. Afterward, he worked in blue-collar jobs in leadership positions while raising his children with his wife. Greg remained faithful to his wife throughout their marriage.

He often teared up in sessions with me, feeling overwhelmed, anxious, and at a loss for his life. He felt only his children kept him alive. Sometimes, he called them to his apartment out of desperation. Greg's coworkers were crass, and his interests went beyond drinking at bars and chasing women. Work exhausted him emotionally. He enjoyed exercising, spending time with his grown children, and having more intellectually stimulating discussions.

Some early common phrases:

"If it weren't for my kids, I don't know if I would be here."

"My stomach and ulcer are eating me alive. I am in so much pain. Sometimes I can't move or eat."

"I didn't know what to do or where to go. If I didn't come here, I felt I would die. I have so much bottled up inside. I feel like I can't take it."

"I have no real friends. I talk to nobody. I spend a lot of time alone."

"I am lonely, but I am scared to get close to people. I don't trust people. I have a really hard time initiating conversations, especially with women."

"I didn't get close to my wife or to her family."

Greg could not trust himself to pursue social experiences. The link to his intrapsychic life was broken during his childhood, quite possibly never forming. He died in childhood. He substituted alcohol for the void, but developed an ulcer. Emotional turmoil/indigestion interfered with physical digestion. His ulcer nearly killed him. Alcohol as a substitute link for emotional intimacy and psychic attunement failed.

Alcohol and an ulcer could not provide a background support with which to develop a link to nourishing psychic attunement. Greg needed to clear space in order to feel his trauma along a different time and space continuum. He protected himself, preventing the mourning of his life, which obstructed the space to grow a capacity for a positive link to internal and external objects. Therapy provided an opportunity. Greg felt he was losing time. "Sometimes we hide ourselves to survive. To make pain go away we simply make ourselves go away…" (Eigen and Daws, 2019, p. 183). Furthermore, "Over time, a traumatic emotional experience becomes dispersed so it is seen through many lenses. If time becomes a pressure point, this ability is compromised" (Cohen, in Fuchsman and Cohen, 2021, p. 32). Greg felt time as a pressure point, leaving no time left to catch up to himself. A viable link was desperately needed to open and mitigate the original breakdown (Winnicott, 1974), his childhood, and the marital disruption which narrowed his plane of existence. Greg was running out of time to welcome himself into the world.

He was fighting against repetition. He feared becoming his father, unable to see across the time and space continuum that individuation from his father occurred many years ago. Greg built a wall between the reality he lived as a boy, young man and the perceived future relationships he yearned for. His ability to welcome trusting relationships through emotional intimacy was obstructed. Greg knew this on some non-verbal level, but fear and hostility toward his own disturbing feelings threatened to keep him stuck in a repetition that was not originated by him. He became a proxy for his father in his mind. Greg attacked an unformed link by attacking the potential space between the obstructive and the welcoming transformation of inner psychic attunement.

Events of his father's life merged into Greg's inner life. Trapped inside and across the time and space continuum, Greg internalized his father's fragmented trauma. Greg felt responsible for his father's actions and sabotaged his own potential out of fear of emotional collapse. Original emotional collapse likely occurred as he formed in and out of utero (Winnicott, 1974), narrowing his field of experience and ability to expand.

He denigrated himself, his softer feelings, his longing for a better life through fear of risking further loss. He was blocked by the sins of his father, punishing himself for his father's misgivings. His insight was informative, yet fear of emotional intimacy and vulnerability kept him stuck.

Greg's work included gaining freedom from the tyranny of himself and the persecutory nature of time as he saw it.

Time was stolen from him, creating current time pressures to reconcile disappointments of his father's behaviors with his disappointments from his own life.

Therapy provided an opportunity for Greg to listen and begin welcoming himself alongside his evacuated fragmented trauma. Building a positive link within himself through unobstructed intuition, without feeling persecuted by the time and space continuum, felt arduous to him.

Alcohol evacuated disturbance, but it nearly killed him. He went from external (alcohol) to internal (fragmented trauma and fear) obstruction. Listening to his positive inner voice began to grow in and out of sessions, but a despondent realization of loss and fear coincided, making acting on his newfound voice difficult. Eigen remarks that

> We are not at-one with ourselves, a gap part of our being. But the gap and relationship with our self-awareness can take on all sorts of emotional tones and attitudes. We may experience ourselves not just as dis-unity, but toxic, beset by psycho-spiritual deformations and aberrant....a less self injurious way of being is worth seeking if only our experiential capacities are up to it. (Eigen, 2021, in Fuchsman and Cohen, 2021, p. 14)

A recent opening has allowed for palpable movement. Greg said, "I don't want the responsibility of a woman." I asked him if he meant that he had been carrying the responsibility of his father's misgivings and was conflating the two. This brought tears, but also an embryonic opening filled with potential growth. "Bion describes therapy as a pendulum moving between wholeness and the parts that are ruptured, in a movement between fracturing and assembling" (Eigen and Daws, 2019, p. 174).

Slowly, obstruction is lifting. Greg has begun to learn from his experience, building intrapsychic attunement. With a welcoming attitude toward time and care, a link to trust between himself and an Other will grow. He is growing a capacity toward a relationship between container and contained (Bion, 1963). A thinking function has begun as he internalizes his own container-contained functioning capacity. Bion spoke of therapy as a place to introduce the patient to herself (Bion, 1991). Greg is growing a *welcoming internal object* (Eaton, 2015). He is making a break from repetition with compassion and patience for his journey. Greg expresses moments of freedom, where intuition, intrapsychic communication, and feelings are free from tyranny of the self. Recognizing that he conflated responsibility for his father and a woman has opened space to form a link. Internal contact has begun.

A recent vignette illustrates a transcendence, a beginning, welcoming intrapsychic life, clearing the obstructive internalized object. Loneliness is slowly transforming into some relief, a sense of peace. Greg has long talked of biking with a local bike club. Recently, he began going for long bike rides in the countryside alone. His tone, affect, and mood describing his experience took on a different texture and meaning. Although his lack of overall trust steered him away from joining the local club, his intuition welcomed a new affect, feeling tone, transforming his intrapsychic life from obstruction to moments of welcoming peace. Greg began containing his aloneness in a well of emotional freedom, a step toward trusting himself, an awakening to inner life, to inner psychic attunement, a meeting of the Self.

Greg's intuition lacks the frenetic feeling of loss and capacity from when we first began. He is growing a capacity to contain himself. He has mourned much loss along the way. Mourning has cleared space for growth of capacities. Greg has moments free from racing thoughts. He has had nearly six months free from stomach ulcer pain. Greg no longer feels as if he will die from his "bottled up" feelings. Time's persecutory feelings still affect him, but often time unfolds organically in service of transformation. Greg is beginning to simultaneously hold his feelings of psychic deadness (Eigen, 1998) and form a viable link to help him mitigate his original breakdown. Intuition and experience borne from intuition have become links, the real things, not substitutes. "No substitute can do what the link does" (Bion, 1991, p. 388).

Greg seems more trusting of himself and his journey, integrating evacuated fragments into his psyche, building psychic attunement. Seeds have been planted for someday when he will be ready for a relationship with an external welcoming object (Eaton, 2015), a woman.

Greg is becoming his own welcoming object, a virtuous start, building a link to a more fruitful inner life.

References

Bion, W.R. (1963). *Elements of Psycho-Analysis*. London: Heinemann.
Bion, W.R. (1987). *Clinical Seminars and Other Works*. London: Karnac.
Bion, W.R. (1991). *A Memoir of the Future*. London: Karnac.
Chuster, A. (2014). *A Lonesome Road: Essays on the Complexity of W.R. Bion's Work*. Rio de Janeiro: Trio Studio Grafica Digital.
Eaton, J. (2005). The Obstructive Object. *The Psychoanalytic Review*, Vol. 92, No. 3, pp. 355–372.
Eaton, J. (2015). *Living Moments: On the Work of Michael Eigen*, ed. Bloch, S. and Daws, L. London: Karnac.
Eigen, M. (1996). *Psychic Deadness*. Washington, DC: Rowman & Littlefield.
Eigen, M. (1998). *Psychic Deadness*. London: Karnac.
Eigen, M. (2018). *The Challenge of Being Human*. New York, NY: Routledge.
Eigen, M. (2021). Rebirth: It's Been around a Long Time, in *Healing, Rebirth, and the Work of Michael Eigen*, ed. Fuchsman, K. and Cohen, K, pp. 3–15. New York, NY: Routledge.
Eigen, M. and Daws, L., ed. (2019). *Dialogues with Michael Eigen: Psyche Singing*. New York, NY: Routledge.

Freud, S. (1926). *Inhibitions, Symptoms and Anxiety: The Standard Edition of the Complete Psychological Works of Sigmund Freud, Volume XX (1925–1926): An Autobiographical Study, Inhibitions, Symptoms and Anxiety, the Question of Lay Analysis and Other Works,* 75–176.

Green, A. (1975). The Analyst, Symbolization, and Absence in the Analytic Setting (on Changes in Analytic Practice and Analytic Experience). *International Journal of Psychoanalysis*, Vol. 56, pp. 1–22.

Winnicott, D.W. (1974). Fear of Breakdown. *International Review of Psycho-Analysis*, Vol. 1, Nos. 1–2, pp. 103–107.

Chapter 12

Welcoming Faith, Forgiveness, and Destruction

Being-with Sara

Brent Potter

> *Life lives in faith, faith permeates life, every single cell. That does*
> *not exclude faithlessness, no-faith, the empty bottom.*
> *And psychoanalytic faith? The work of faith in sessions?*
> *...many sessions are crises of*
> *faith. Is life worth living? With what quality? How? Or is a soul too*
> *crippled to go on, too infected with ill spirit?* (Eigen, 2014, p. xii)

In what follows, I recount my psychoanalytic work with Sara. Working with her brought the phenomena of aphiemi, faith, destructiveness, goodness, badness, stuckness, and metanoia to light in poignant and meaningful ways. It is impossible, of course, in a single paper to do proper justice to the phenomenon. I hope and pray that the reader finds a window into the qualitative world Sara and I occupied together for quite some time.

Sara sought Christian counseling, stating,

> I have struggled with anxiety/depression privately for a few years. What is making it a little more complicated is figuring out how to parent adult children and re-examining my life. What makes me seek help is that my youngest son told me that he is attracted to men. I am struggling with this as a mom and as a Christian.

She had no history of receiving mental health services. Culturally, Sara describes her family as being of German descent and as part of a family with close adherence to "very conservative Lutheran churches." Sara is in a marriage of 31 years and has two male children (21 and 25 years old). She has had no previous marriages or romantic relationships in her history. Sara's primary work capacity is as an administrator overseeing physician education and training at a major hospital. In addition to these duties, which are voluminous, Sara has taken on a separate contract to be the lead COVID educator for the region. She has worked as a nurse, in one role or another, since she was 18 years old.

When asked about more specificity in how her depression and anxiety manifest, Sara described these as more global, generalized affective states. She denied any

DOI: 10.4324/9781003322986-12

acute anxiety, such as panic attacks, or acute depressive episodes. "I am sorry," she said:

> I can't describe these things. I am not even sure if it's really anxiety or depression or includes both of them. It's like a black 'blah' mass that is always in me; makes me feel terrible inside. I don't know; I don't know. I am really here to talk about my son's attraction to men. I am worried he will lose his salvation. That is what I am here to talk about.

Sara comes from an intact family. Her parents own a large house with land and a few horses. They live close to her, and she has frequent contact with them. Sara has one younger sister who, with her seven-year-old son, lives with them. Sara reports having "…a really exceptional childhood. It was happy, my family was happy. My dad was the typical stoic German dad, and my mom was always busy taking care of my sister and I." Sara reports no significant losses, medical events, or deaths during her childhood. The only conflict she reports is with her sister:

> My sister and I were and are opposites. Where I started working as a nurse as soon as I could, got married as soon as I could, and built a life for myself and my family, she just seemed to date men that were bad for her. We're just the opposites on everything.

Despite their opposing views, Sara goes out of her way to be accommodating and tolerant of her sister.

Curiously, Sara cannot recall any significant or long-standing friendships from her childhood up to the present. She cannot recall any teachers who left a positive impact, mentors, nor other significant people of influence in her life. When asked about this, she responded, "Funny, I've never thought about that. You know, I basically went to school, got licensed, started working, and got married, and that was it. I haven't really had time for anything else." Sara describes work and her family as being "…the centerpieces of my world." When asked about her marriage, Sara described it as favorable yet remarked that her husband was "…very stoic, like my father." Sara's husband suffered a car accident that, roughly a decade ago, left him with chronic back pain and some limited mobility. Sara stated that, at that time, she then had to be the primary income provider. She had always worked, but she found that, at that time, she began working 90–100 hours per week. This would essentially become the norm.

When asked about relational coping, Sara described herself as being "…conflict avoidant, a peacekeeper." Concerning stress, Sara said, "I keep it in. I've seen a lot of things in my years. I keep it in. I think it may have something to do with that black 'blah' mass that I keep inside." While successful at her job, Sara admits that she often has a hard time holding healthy boundaries in the workplace, both with employees and supervisors. The kinds of boundaries she has a hard time maintaining are instances of her being asked to work too much or take on too many projects: Sara cannot describe anything resembling a healthy work-life balance, and she states that she has "accepted how my life is." Concerning diagnosis, Sara stated that she felt that persistent depressive disorder may be a fitting diagnosis.

Psychoanalytic Process

Sara arrived precisely on time for her first appointment. She could have come immediately into my office, as the door was open, but she politely sat in the waiting area for me to come out and welcome her. She sat smiling in a chair and seemed to have an upbeat comportment. "Ok, so I've never done this. What do we do?" I explained that this relationship was like other relationships but had the features of being professional and always providing a safe and consistent space for her to tell me whatever she would like. As mentioned, Sara explained that she worked a lot and suffered from what she thought was anxiety and depression linked to her son's possibly being gay. She was very curious about what I thought about Biblical ethics and homosexuality. I responded,

> When I talk to Christians, I don't know where they are coming from, in a sense. I mean, saying 'Christian' is sort of like saying 'Asian food.' Certainly, it sets out a certain area that differentiates it from others, but it does not really say much specifically. But I just don't know what your beliefs are and where you come from. I'd love to know, though. Please tell me.

Sara told me of her faith and dedication to conservative Lutheran churches she had attended and her family's commitment historically. She said, "But, you see, I have no one to talk to." Of course, I was curious to know why. She explained that she had found her son's personal diary. Therein, he expressed attraction toward men. "I am worried he is going to lose his salvation. I think he's going to go to hell. This world is so brief, but he'll spend an eternity there." I had to take a minute to silently absorb the gravity of her grave concern. I had to move past my knee-jerk response of feeling her belief was overly dramatic. I wanted to feel the impact of what it would be like if I believed this about my own child. "This must be unbearable for you." Sara responded by telling me the whole story. I felt I somehow passed a test. Believing that her son may be damned, she went to speak to the lead pastor of her church. "He told me that my son would likely go to hell and, more, that he was not really a member of our church anymore. From this point on, he was not allowed to partake in communion." Dejected by her encounter with the pastor, she appealed to her fellow nurses and co-workers, who told her she was overreacting. "There is absolutely nothing wrong with him being gay. It is perfectly normal." In both cases, Sara felt her experience was hugely invalidated, that no one "got" her. Her belief was solid that her son's salvation was at risk, and she felt powerless to do anything about it. Telling Sara that a homosexual lifestyle was completely normal and healthy was no more helpful than the pastor ejecting him from the church community. I sat with her and listened, both of us deepening our rapport.

Faith/No-Faith

Neither Sara nor I had all the answers. We had to struggle with faith and no-faith moments together. I read to her Keat's definition: "Negative Capability, that is when man is capable of being in uncertainties, Mysteries, doubts, without any irritable reaching after fact and reason" (Oxford Reference, 2021). While this didn't offer her a literal solution to her situation, it provided some relief and, more importantly, opened a new dimension to our work. We explored our faith capacity for our work and lives. Her Christian conception of faith melded reasonably well with Bion's psychoanalytic-mystical notion of faith. Faith is a kind of openness to what appears in life, an ability to sit with pain, unknowing, confusion, and darkness without reaching for practical, ready-made solutions, for certitude (Symington & Symington, 1996).

Goodness and the Black "Blah"

My feelings for Sara were warm. Sara recounted being a nurse since the age of 18. She described horrific stories of emergency pediatric nursing, and her decision to leave due to its graphic and soul-crushing nature, her move to administration, and her recent struggles with the COVID pandemic. With the advent of the pandemic, all nurses (administration or otherwise) were required to provide direct service where needed in the hospital system.

> We had a child die alone. Who knows where his parents were? When a child dies without parents present, we all line the hall as the body is carried out in a kind of ritual. Then we try to comfort each other.

I found emerging in me a growing sense of her bravery and her willingness to face things head-on. I thought about my experience, personally and professionally, of trauma and traumatic situations. Another point of connection between us. I, of course, did not share much of my experience but would make notations like, "Over the last roughly three decades, you've probably spread more goodness than anyone could possibly know." Sara's transference to me seemed warm too. I felt I was becoming a kind of "third" space wherein she could be heard in a way she could not elsewhere in her past and present. I didn't explicitly express this to her, as I did not need to. She commented to that effect with some frequency, often with a tone of pleasant surprise.

During this time, I was attempting to link several items in my mind – her son's loss of eternal salvation, internal black "blah" (of which she rarely spoke), sustained exposure to pediatric trauma, being a passionate mother, having a sister so opposite, overwork, anxiety/depression, invalidating experiences with church and co-workers, faith/no-faith, etc., and I inquired as to the source of her pain. "Is your suffering only about your son?" At this time, Sara began discussing her internal black "blah," a formless mass of unnamed negative affect. Sara discussed her suicidal thoughts, something she felt very guilty of having. Sara and I discussed what and who dies when one kills him- or herself. Sara struggled with the question. Was she skilling the sense of "I" that she experienced herself to be? Was she killing the black "blah"? Was she killing the pain? Was she killing off the contagion to keep everyone else safe? Was it just one person or thing she would be killing off in suicide? We wrestled with these questions together for quite a few sessions. Sara bravely stuck with the difficulty and decided that she was unaware of many possibilities that existed in the fantasy of suicide. My stance was neutral but supportive during this time. The fact that she maintained this comportment seemed to give her the freedom to engage with these questions. After much consideration, she concluded that she felt there was a combination of things she was trying to kill off in the suicide fantasy. She was able to discern that her "self" was not one of those things meant to die.

She still could not quite describe it nor articulate it when she began experiencing the black "blah." I noted her frequent use of the phrase "I don't know" as a way of simultaneously blotting out some part of what she was feeling as well as her best articulation of that black "blah." Curiously, the discussion of her son's possible homosexuality went away. I took the matter to supervision. We metabolized her experience together, making the mass digestible by breaking it down into nameable and then named bits. Sara affectively became more able to state things like "I was sad," "That made me angry," or "I felt so much anxiety," and the dark mass gave way to "I don't know if I can experience love." We have moved from a literalized space of what to do about her son's possible homosexuality to the dark space via the growth of our mutually indwelling faith capacity. This darkness gave way to its aspects being named, producing a more differentiated, discerned, tolerable affective state.

Underneath that was a fear that she could not experience love. But this did not make sense to me. She seemed to love her family, especially her children. "I don't know if I actually love them or if I am taking care of them and everyone else, so they can't feel the way that I have felt all of my life." Interestingly, I received a rare text from Sara during this time:

> I want to thank you for all of the work we're doing together. I feel like I finally have someone to talk to. I wish I had a mini-you that I could carry around in my pocket while I was growing up.

I remarked on this next session, thanking her for her kind text and asking if she would like to provide more context. She politely declined, and I honored her resistance on this point.

Dream 1: Confrontation with the Shadow

It was around this time that Sara presented her first dream.

> There is a man. He is all black, like a dark ghost. In the dream, no matter where I go, no matter how fast I run, I keep running into him. I run faster and faster, but then he just chases me in a car. There is no escape from him. I woke up scared.

I inquired as to her affect and associations with this. Sara was able to name "fear," but little else. She had no associations whatsoever. I was curious if this represented a shadow aspect of our work. She was increasingly dependent on our work and was motivated by caring for everyone else's needs. Maybe this was some unnamed fear of me – would I leave her? – or a feature of our work. Perhaps this figure was a personification of something we were missing. I decided to make a notation of this but to interpret this in a more Jungian direction. Somehow, I felt that the deep dive into a Kleinian interpretation might not help her as much as a more Jungian interpretation. She had just come out of the whirlwind of her internal black "blah" space, and I decided to interpret more toward something positive, easier to understand. Sara had responded favorably to psychoanalytic educational material. I recognized that such information could be used as a defense against emotional life, but (on the other hand) I thought that a Jungian route would foster more curiosity in her. I explained to Sara that after some months of analysis, it was common for patients to begin having dreams of shadow figures. I further explained that, in Jungian psychology, the beginning phases of analytic work comprised a confrontation with one's shadow (Jung, 1981). The shadow, I explained, was simply that which was not in the light of our consciousness, outside of the "light" of the ego. It was not necessarily bad but was constituted by the unnamed, ignored, or as-of-yet unknown aspect of ourselves. Sara took great interest in this and did much research on her own. Our work during this time seemed to deepen and broaden our experience. The internal black "blah" space was being named and changed.

Sara and I further explored the personification of her shadow, her "badness" which could apparently magically infect others. *Shadow as contagion.* I wondered if this contagion fantasy reflected grandiosity beneath the surface, like, "I am so bad that my badness can infect others. I must protect others from my badness." Or perhaps this was a paranoid-schizoid remnant fantasy (or phantasy?) of omnipotent control like, "I am in charge of other peoples' emotional states." Somehow both seemed to fit and not fit. It fit relative to what I recalled from Klein's work on primitive developmental states (Ogden, 1989). I thought of interpreting this back to Sara, but decided against it. Instead, I wanted to continue opening the field of our experience. I reflected to her that, in the Bible, one person's sickness was not just his or her own. One person's sickness was often the sickness of a larger area. One person's sickness was linked to the sickness of a community, a city, an organization, or a society; even the world could be sick. One person's malady was linked to broader maladies. One did not necessarily cause the other; they were simply reflected and linked somehow. Over some sessions, Sara and I discussed not only her "badness" but a phenomenology of "badness" itself. As with her naming of affective states, this also seemed to take the burden off her. There was Sara's "badness," Brent's "badness," the badness of the hospital where she worked, etc. Badness is an environmental condition but not the only or most important one.

We struggled with "badness," but the conversation organically led to "goodness." Badness and goodness go together just like shadow and light. Pairs were organically forming (given in no order): Brent/Sara, goodness/badness, faith/ no-faith, shadow/light, homosexual/heterosexual, salvation/damnation, no one to speak to/one person to speak to, etc. Opposites do not necessarily contradict each other; they can complement and make room for each other. We were making room for each other and complimenting each other. Through this, Sara reflected that she was not all bad inside but could also experience and give love. According to her, she was always doing this but did not have the words for it or to explicitly understand it until now.

Dream 2: Loving, Living, Legacy

I asked several times if Sara was curious about where and when her shadow emerged. By her description, her sense of "badness" had always been present. I recalled that she reported an unremarkable history for trauma or loss. Sara acknowledged that she felt compelled to look out for everyone else's needs but her own. Surely, this did not come from nowhere. I did not press the matter and waited. By this time, we had established a good working alliance. We developed our own silly language, a kind of "couple's language," and often had moments of laughter, especially as we compared stories of raising toddlers. My feelings of warmth and respect for her continued. I felt that her transference, too, was warm but perhaps a bit idealistic. She said nothing specific that I can now provide as evidence for this assertion. It was more of a feeling.

Along with it was a concern I carried in the back of my mind that, as with most people, she would feel the need to take care of or please me too. It seemed consistent in all of her relationships (including her professional life), so I also had reason to keep an eye out for this dynamic in our relationship. It was during this time that Sara had her second dream[1]:

> "I am in the hospital being euthanized by my own choice. They have given me in the injection, and I am waiting for the poison to take effect. I am wondering, 'What should I do with the time before I die? I think I should be doing something important like writing a will, or calling some loved ones, or leaving something behind for someone else. But I have nothing to give. The dream shifts. I am high above in a hot air balloon. Below me is a crowd. I don't know if it is a rock concert or a war. The dream shifts and I am sitting on the couch with my parents. I am not in the hospital. I have the opportunity to euthanize myself, I have the injection. I don't use it. I think to myself, 'I have to find someone to love deeply something worth really living and fighting for, and some things of value to leave behind." Sara describes waking up and dubbing this dream, "The three Ls, loving, living, and legacy."

Sara and I spent many sessions understanding this dream relative to the other work we had engaged in. Sara felt that the euthanasia aspect of the dream reflected her suicidal thoughts, and I agreed. I added, though, that she was going through a large change, a metanoia, and that often such images accompany such a change. Part of her was dying off to a new way of knowing and being in the world. Sara and I discussed how suicide is a literalism for personal transformation. I referred her to Hillman's (1998) *Suicide and the Soul*, and she appreciated it. I asked for her affects and associations around the hot air balloon and the crowd below. She said she had no idea what that was about. I intimated that the hot air balloon afforded her a broad visibility, a bird's-eye view. The crowd below may suggest a collective or social element to the dream. It seems that the image of the crowd vacillates between creativity and celebration (rock concert) and literalism and violence (war). Of the many discussions we had, Sara felt that the Three Ls were the main takeaway from the dream. Sara told me that she felt she had not been living her life to the fullest. Even though she was married, she did not feel she was loving fully. She had possessions to leave behind but remained unsure of what significance she could or should leave. Of the three Ls, she mainly struggled with what to live for. I pointed out that, in fact, the dream "her" had the opportunity to kill herself but chose not to. Since this was the more pressing area, I asked her to elaborate on it.

Balance, Bodyhood

For the first time, Sara recounted her numerous health conditions in the past and those that followed her into the present. Sara had mentioned a few of these things in passing historically, but not in any sustained fashion. About seven years ago, she said, she simply collapsed at work. Mercifully, she worked at a hospital, so she was able to receive attention immediately. It took some time for the doctors to figure out what was going on. Tests revealed that she had stomach cancer. While not immediately terminal, it is a kind of stomach cancer that will invariably return and ultimately be terminal. For the time being, Sara was stable, having gone through chemo and multiple other treatments following her diagnosis. More recently, though, she reported having been diagnosed with premature osteoporosis and a lump in her breast. Sara and I utilized the time to discuss what we were missing and what may be being bodied forth. Boss (1977) noted that we are always already bodying forth our existences. An often-ignored dimension in psychoanalysis is our bodyhood's role in our wellness and unwellness. Remaining a two-person cerebral pursuit, psychoanalysis seldom pays enough attention to the body. So, Sara and I engaged in many discussions concerning her numerous health conditions, her present conditions, and her inevitable (by her admission) stomach cancer regrowth. During this time, I suggested that she read Mate's (2011) *When the Body Says No: Exploring the Stress-Disease Connection*. Sara found this especially helpful, as Mate described at length a certain personality type of caretaker. This person, Mate shows, takes care of everyone except himself or herself. In short, this produces long-term stress, which, in turn, is expressed (or bodied forth, in Boss' terminology) as cancer or other manifest diseases. Sara could identify with this character and, in combination with our work, operated as a very helpful adjunct.

In time, the conversation came to center around her work ethic. Sara had previously said she "worked a lot," but upon further examination, it became apparent that her work was literally nonstop. Sara described the two departments she managed as well as an additional contract to be the lead educator on COVID for the region. She worked from sunrise, took her work home with her in the evening, slept, and began again the next day. There was zero work-life balance. While producing an incalculable amount of good during her decades of work, she was dissatisfied with her work. She felt it was killing her slowly. I felt protective of her, as if I needed to convince her to discontinue working. I restrained myself, resting instead on faith in the process. Especially during the apex of the pandemic, I was simply there for her, supporting her. During these times, I was not sure if what I was doing was in-depth psychoanalytic work. I took it to supervision, and my supervisor supported this comportment. My supervisor supported me, and I supported Sara. Sometimes, my supervisor told me, the analytic work is simply being an encouraging, solid, caring presence. I was hoping to be informative to Sara, not judgmental about her work ethic. After all, I was working a full-time regular job as well as a private practice. While not as extreme as Sara, I was undoubtedly working too much. I would have been a hypocrite to suggest she work less.

As time went on, I sought to work less. Sara saw that I was maneuvering toward more self-care. I did not discuss this with her explicitly, but she seemed to take in what I was doing. These elements combined to produce something new in her. Quite out of the blue, Sara began a session by showing me some pictures on her phone, "I am thinking of starting a bed-and-breakfast. I may buy one of these houses." I contained my surprise but certainly expressed interest in what shifted for her. Sara said she did not really know what changed: "Something is just [long silence] different." Sara said her husband was on board with purchasing another house, as he always wanted to start a Christmas tree farm. Spontaneously, I said, "Yeah, I can just see him driving around on his riding mower. Your sons are there, working on things. They don't have to work, since they now work for you." Sara picked up on the fantasy and played along. We laughed, and this playful space became an ongoing part of our work. Without direction from me, she began working less, going to work later, and coming home earlier. She kept a journal of the days she did not bring work home with her and would proudly show it to me. The image that came to mind for me was of a plant beginning to sprout out of the ground. In fact, Sara never did purchase a house, but her parents said they were downsizing and would sell her their home and land for a nominal fee. Apparently, they were waiting for their elderly horse to die before moving. Sara is planning her bed-and-breakfast, and her husband is going to use the land for his Christmas tree farm. It was during this time that Sara had another dream.

Dream 3: Invisible Supports

I am driving to Linda's, following reading her obituary online. How did I come across the obituary? I am not sure. But there I am. I am at Linda's house. I go up to the front door. I walk in, no knocking. There are men inside, dressed in black suits. One approaches me and I say, 'I am not totally sure why I am here, but I was a friend of Linda's.' The man replied, 'She had so many friends.' He smiled. 'Please do what you would here. Take your time.' I walked all over the home, revisiting the many rooms and areas where I had spent so much time. I went into the garage, the yard, just everywhere. I came back into the house and found the three men trying to carry a grand piano. 'It's taking up too much space and no one uses it here.' 'Oh,' I replied, and then offered to help them with the piano. They accepted my help. I recall helping them lift and move the piano but then the dream shifted to my looking around the house again. I was looking for something personal, something with her [Linda's] handwriting. And I found it. It was a little yellow post-it with her handwriting on it. I was so happy, became tearful, and woke up.

Sara was tearful as she explained the last section, yet she had a subtle smile on her face. I thanked her sincerely for sharing the dream, but I had to ask her to please provide some context from waking life to help me understand the dream. Sara responded that there were some things that she kept secret from everyone but that, now, she felt comfortable enough to share with me. Before meeting her present husband, she had one significant relationship from roughly the ages of 15–18 years, just before meeting her (now) husband. Sara explained that she never felt totally connected to her parents, especially as an adolescent. Something was missing at home. I mentioned that it was interesting that she never talked about her upbringing other than to say it was exceptionally nice in every way. As it turns out, Sara had fallen in love with Amos (Linda's son). She explained that he gave her attention and somehow filled a void. Interestingly, Sara stated that what was even more important to her was that Amos' family "…adopted me…" Sara described the family as welcoming her with open arms, having Sunday dinners without fail, extended relatives who would come to visit from California, and Amos' older sister having a baby with whom she could play. By her description, it seemed that the family provided her with a sense of belonging, love, warmth, engagement, and normalcy. Without any explanation, Amos, one day, simply told Sara that the relationship was over. To this day, Sara said, she does not know the reason. More than Amos, Sara said she suffered greatly from the loss of her "adoptive" family. For whatever reason, the family discontinued contact with her as well.

I felt a sinking feeling in my stomach as her story constellated a memory of my own past. I reflected to Sara my gratitude for sharing this and my sincere apology that she had to endure such a tragedy. I was mostly quiet, listening to her. I thought to myself that Sara must have been mis-attuned in her relationship with Amos to miss such an impending dramatic separation. I suspected she was more in love with the family than Amos. I suspected that she must have been disconnected from her own affective life to a degree not to notice any disturbance in the relationship. Sara went on to explain that, in waking reality, she had read about Linda's (Amos' mother's) death two or three months ago. Sara said that she had Googled the old town where she and Amos dated. Apparently, coincidentally, she came across Linda's obituary. Sara described a sense of shock upon reading the obituary. Linda was 70, but somehow, Sara said she imagined she would always have time to speak to Linda again. Linda and Sara were especially close. Sara endorsed my comment that perhaps she was more connected to Linda than to her boyfriend. Though she and Amos had never been sexually intimate, she never told anyone about the relationship. It was better, she said, that her husband thought he was the only romantic relationship she had ever had. Moreover, Sara blamed herself for the breakup, even though there seemed no evidence to that effect.

Over the following sessions, we explored the dream. I asked her about the image of the house in the dream, what it looked like, and what she felt when she pulled up and saw it again (in the dream). Sara acknowledged, in fact, that she would like to see the house again but that she never literally went there. She had looked up the house online. Sara expressed, again, a sense of shock that the house had sold following Linda's death. Sara described seeing pictures of it and was startled by the contrast of "Linda's home" where so much had taken place and "empty sold home." Sara was able to name her feelings: "shocked," "sad," "nostalgic," "happy," and give thought to them. As in the dream, in waking reality, Sara did not fully understand why the house was such a captivating image to her. She did not understand either why she had such a pull to go to the house. When asked about this, Sara relayed that the house was "…such a place of life, so much happened there." We sat together with the juxtaposition of "so much life" to a "house for sale."

While the juxtaposition was a lot to bear, I pointed out that she had a lot of support in the dream. The man in the dark suit welcomed her to the house and allowed her to make herself at home and do what she felt she needed there. Sara had a strange expression on her face and was sitting silently. I sat with the silence until it seemed to become absurdly long. "What is it?" Sara responded, "You said that my mind is on my side a little bit ago. I've never thought about that." I was affirmative with the dream, wanting to attempt to expand her mind via the imagery:

> Yeah, well, it seems your mind *is* on your side. Your mind drew you to Linda's house where the men welcomed you. It is possible that you're getting more support than you know, that things may be better than you suspect.

Sara and I went on to talk about the piano, the clunky, weighty object that was not being used, taking up too much space, "You're getting rid of things you don't need in your life, making room for something new." Sara was surprisingly engaged in the conversation. She was not only able to name and differentiate her feelings, but also able to list off many of the things she would be getting rid of (or would like to get rid of) in her life. Sara seemed to be internalizing the self-reflective aspects of therapy that, until recently, I had carried for her. Her level of insight improved, her ability to think abstractly/symbolically, and her faith capacity grew. During our discussions, I pointed out to her that the third person carrying the piano was probably my supervisor, who had been especially helpful in my understanding of how to proceed. Sara commented to the effect that she had forgotten I had a supervisor. She added that she was being supported even when she was not thinking about it. We discussed the goodness that she invariably spread throughout her decades of service as a nurse. In a sense, she had emanated goodness to countless others, known and unknown. Moreover, she too was supported by invisible presences more often than she probably realized.

Openness and Expression

The work continued. At one point, Sara felt so moved as to impart that not only was her husband a "repeat of my father and Amos," but that he had at least one affair. Curious and a bit perplexed, I asked if she would feel comfortable telling me more. While she was struggling to recover from her stomach cancer, her husband had an affair with a co-worker:

> It was about seven years ago, so I don't remember all of the details. I am pretty sure he confessed to it. I am not exactly sure, but I don't think I suspected anything. He confessed. But it was the way he confessed. He blamed me for being unattractive and forcing him to have sex with someone else. Then he never mentioned it again.

I had many pressing questions, but there were simply not a lot of answers. Sara did not know how long the affair lasted, if it was the only affair, what exactly led to the affair, etc. After being, by her description, verbally assaulted by her husband, the topic went dead. Sara never spoke of it again until this very meeting. It was yet another example of critically important events and experiences simply being "x-ed," to use her word, out of her life. We were involved in our own *perichoresis*, but Sara aptly gave testimony to what happens when anti-perichoresis forces are at work, when the primary background presence of identification becomes tyrannical.

Reorienting to the World

Again, I was concerned for Sara while she was venting because there was a risk of it going out of control. The mind is a tremendous magnifying-minimizing machine. It is relatively easy to produce one of these states. It is often exceedingly difficult or impossible to turn it off. Eigen (2021) notes:

> Our minds are partly magnifying-minifying machines we use the term "to blow up" to characterize certain "exaggerated" states. On the other side, I remember a patient who said she had a disappearing machine that made thoughts and feelings vanish…Our mind can maximize states and move towards zero at the same time, as well as develop maximizing-minimizing rhythms, a little akin to crescendo-decrescendo in music. Our mind can act like a plus-and-minus

infinitizing machine blowing oneself up in both directions, intense and overflow and null. Maximum emotion and minimum emotion. Emotion moving towards infinity and emotion moving towards zero. (p. 36)

While dangerous, fortunately, the relational frame was able to contain Sara's affective output. More importantly, though, is that she expanded her affective range, saying, "I can have a huge emotion and survive." We survived. Not only did we make it through, but our relationship grew stronger for having had the experience. Sara was able to become irritated and angry with me from time to time. The increase in affective and relational range/scope was impressive and, I thought, signs of wellness. Of her own accord, Sara wondered about her husband and if she could also express her rage towards him. Through some sessions, we explored her fantasies about how that conversation would go. Maybe it would be explosive: "I should just let him have it!" Maybe it would be simpler and easier to continue with things as-is. After all, she had gained a lot out of our work together already. Maybe what had been done to that point was enough. Where we landed was that she should probably best process the marriage dynamics in marriage counseling. This felt right to Sara and I, as this would allow us to continue our relationship and have another staging ground for marital work. We were able to do some work on interpersonal effectiveness, limit and boundary setting, and assertiveness training. She was being a lot more assertive with her husband as well as with people at work (both patients and co-workers). Sara was surprised to learn that most people, including her husband, responded well to her comportment.

Growth

Sara continued to show what I considered to be signs of improvement. As mentioned above, she had an orienting moment and was able to reorient toward her relationships and the world more authentically. She was more assertive and confident, held healthy boundaries, was more spontaneous, was more available to her affective life, and was less reactionary to it. Sara came to be able to see me in a more realistic light. I went from being the person she wished she could have carried in her pocket throughout childhood to a more mature, differentiated view of me. Sara was able to use our relationship to generalize thoughts, dynamics, feelings, fantasies, and relatedness to the outside world. Recalling that her presenting issue was her son being gay, we found ourselves on a very different journey. I was usually the one to take the initiative to ask about her son. I thought I was responsible for helping the patient recall her reason for coming to treatment. In fact, her son's possible homosexuality, while a serious concern, was not an area that Sara was organically drawn to work on in any sustained fashion. Instead, a host of other issues arose. The host of issues, Sara learned, was not without a pattern.

Multiple functional failures of primary background presences echo throughout her history and into the present: father, uncle, Amos, me, and husband. I asked her why she initially noted a very unremarkable, even idyllic, childhood. Sara intimated that these and other items seem to exist as fragments residing in a liminal space. She knew they were true but did not really want to know they were true. Sara chose the optimistic healing fiction. The hermeneutic key to supporting Sara's process rested in my interpreting her experience and concerns in the immediacy of our experience. I would do so often and do so in such a way that it did not take Sara more than one step, as it were, to understand what I was trying to impart. Sara grew her capacities of faith, play, and acceptance. Her possibly gay son, for example, may or may not be gay. Sara could now simply let that be, at least to a healthier degree, and let it be what it was. Her faith capacity allowed her to await something new to emerge. Taking her son's potential situation up in this way is less terrifying and tormenting to her. Sara learned that these capacities could be broadly generalized to many life contexts and relationships. To my surprise, Sara began taking photography classes. She is not simply sitting in a class somewhere. She hired an expert photographer for private lessons. Sara's capacity for play allows her to go out on her own, to be inspired by images around her, to capture them, and to display them to others. Sara and I talked a lot about her experience of play and reverie while walking with her camera. Our discussions caused me to wonder about her ability to be alone. Aloneness and primary background presence may go together. Eigen (2011) notes,

> As we grow, the aloneness that received nurturance supports us. A background aloneness, elusive and poignant, touches our beings. Part of what we do for each other, all through life, is to support the aloneness that informs and supports us. (p. 93)

Sara was receptive to my reading some of this and other quotes. We wondered together how her aloneness capacity may have been damaged early on. More important was the emphasis that Sara could grow and enjoy the capacity to the fullest today. Aside from her photography, Sara and her husband continued fantasizing about what they would do when they acquired the new home. As mentioned previously, Sara's parents are waiting for their last elderly horse to die before they sell the house to her. The point being, Sara and her husband remain in a state of reverie and imagination, together with a kind of playful negative capability. While I am unsure what Sara and her husband talk about with the marriage therapist, Sara is clearly asserting herself, processing her pain with him, and continuing the marriage.

Other areas of improvement are her self-report of zero suicidal ideation, and she refers to her depression now as having "receded into the background." It seems reminiscent of what Eigen (2005) refers to as psychic background radiation. The failing and tormenting background presences could be thought of as psychic explosions. Through the psychoanalytic process, the tremendous force of those explosions faded, becoming less harmful and more oriented toward aliveness. But as with the Big Bang, there remains a background radioactive presence, a lingering element of the primary explosion. Sara has increased her focus on her physical health. Sara recognizes now that *she* is terribly important in her experience. This may sound odd, but recalling McWilliams psychoanalytic diagnosis, depressive personalities believe the solution to every issue is the absence of themselves. One could hear such a person saying something like, "The world would be better off if I were dead." Sara once shared a similar worldview, believing that she had to protect others from her contagious badness. The world, she thought, would be better without her. She compulsively performed good deeds to gain some semblance of goodness and self-esteem. Sara now understands her agency and its importance to herself and others. She matters. Sara committed, of her own accord, to never let anything be "x-ed" out again. Even if it is painful or confusing, it can still be held, named, given shape, and understood.

Note

1 As a side note, I often asked her about any dreams she recalled and encouraged her to keep a dream journal. She was resistant to both, and I did not press the matter.

References

Boss, M. (1977). *Existential foundations of medicine and psychology.* New York, NY: Jason Aronson.
Eigen, M. (2005). *Emotional Storm.* Middletown, CT: Wesleyan University Press.
Eigen, M. (2011). *Contact with the Depths.* London: Karnac.
Eigen, M. (2014). *Faith.* London: Routledge.
Eigen, M. (2021). *Eigen in Seoul, volume 3. Pain and beauty, terror and wonder.* London: Routledge.
Hillman, J. (1998). *Suicide and the soul.* Washington, DC: Spring Publications.
Jung, C.G. (1981). The archetypes and the collective unconscious. In R.F.C Hull (Ed. & Trans.), *Collected works of C.G. Jung* (Vol. 9, Part 1, pp. 3–42). Princeton, NJ: Princeton University Press. (Original work published 1968).
Mate, G. (2011). *When the body says no: Exploring the stress-disease connection.* Indianapolis, IN: Wiley Publishing.
Ogden, T. (1989). *The primitive edge of experience.* Lanham, MD: Rowman & Littlefield Publishers.
Oxford Reference. (2021). *Negative capability.* https://www.oxfordreference.com/view/10.1093/oi/authority.20110803100227203
Symington, J. & Symington, N. (1996). *The clinical thinking of Wilfred Bion.* London: Karnac Books.

Chapter 13

A Cup of Love

Gagandeep Kaur Ahluwalia

As a student of Psychoanalysis and a freshly minted therapist, one can often feel trapped by the idea of the psychoanalytic encounter. The desire to chase the profound is both sublime and mundane at once. The idea of wisdom is often much larger than the chaotic grasping that occurs when you begin to truly work with your clients. Eigen, in *Coming Through the Whirlwind*, writes about the "possible catastrophic elements of any human interaction" (1992, p. xiii), reigniting the mind to ponder Bion's initial words from his paper *Making the Best of a Bad Job*: "when two personalities meet, an emotional storm is created" (1994, p. 321). To think of these storms, one must imagine the meeting. Who is meeting whom is a question that is perhaps answered in therapy? When I imagine this meeting, I imagine a shaken can of a carbonated drink both of them are trying to open. When it is opened with just a crack, a large amount spills on both people. The work of two personalities meeting involves witnessing and excavating by the therapist. Both await storms that will be created from the pressure systems of the emotional storm. This paper is a modest attempt to present the meaningful influence of reading Eigen and psychoanalysis to the practice of becoming psychoanalytically minded.

I was in the throes of such a storm in my first meeting with a client a few years ago. I started my independent practice during the Covid lockdown in the summer of 2020. During my training, I had access to the university clinics. I was acclimated to working in the clinic, but working out of my room online as I started my career was a scary but exciting endeavor.

By the end of the summer of 2021, I had lost half my family to COVID. I took a few months off work. The pandemic was devastating in so many ways – on memories of our lives, internal and external worlds, relationships, states of mind, and *being*, not to mention the economic, physical, and mental health fallout. Everything was finding itself being split into a pre-pandemic and a post-pandemic era. We live lives forcefully altered by grief, loss, despair, and destruction, both internal and external. Carrying all this and, at the same time, having one's own forceful immersion in grief is painful. In fact, to call it pain is entirely off the mark. It's constant dissociation, numbness, a selectively functioning mind and body, and a steep learning curve to navigate a chaotic adjustment to a new reality. Loss changes a person's timeline of living. Loss removes a love object, leaving a haunted void in its place

DOI: 10.4324/9781003322986-13

that constantly aches and burns. It changes the course of life for people. It alters futures. It makes a person more than they were before loss while simultaneously amputating parts of that person. There is no anesthesia for the pain caused by this hollowness. Loss and grief have textures. The loss of a parent impacts differently than the loss of a child, a partner, or a sibling. The death of a person is also the death of some aliveness in those who survive it. The abrupt dead-ending of what life could have been causes a quick change in life's permutations and combinations for what you can do with it and yourself. It sticks to everything like a second skin, not allowing whatever is touching you to permeate fully, to sink into you, and to touch you. It obstructs your experience and your response to it. In my work after my encounter with loss, there is a third present constantly, a second me, an incomplete, not-me that interrupts and impinges on the space the first me works from, feels from, and responds from. The *not-me*ness of my *I*, who returned to work, went unnoticed until grief consistently confronted me in my clinic. This paper is a narrative of the meeting of the obstruction of the therapist with that of the client. A narrative of what erupts when a known grief meets an unknown one. This narrative is an excoriated wound for both the therapist and the patient.

Collisions of the Real and the Virtual

I worked online for almost a year before my family fell ill. There was already a flux in how one dreams in therapy. The curiosity with which I would approach my clients' questions regarding my health was now a genuine concern that demanded to be addressed instead of only being opened psychoanalytically. When I resumed work a few months after the second surge of COVID-19 in 2021, after the personal losses I incurred, my work field was already in a completely unknown landscape. When my family contracted the virus, I had to let my current clients know I would be unavailable for a few weeks until we recovered, or at least tested negative. And then, as things progressed, I had to let them know I could not resume any time soon. I distinctly recall feeling conflicted about disclosing any of this to my clients. It felt unethical to do so, but at the same time, with the shared reality of what life had become in the pandemic, it felt wrong to not disclose it. We were already deprived of bodies, touch, and physical presence. It felt wrong to obliterate "touch," "holding," and "presence" by considering not sharing this with my clients, who had already been with me for a little over a year, and in some cases more than a year. The unpredictability of the aftereffects of COVID-19, the longer recovery times for some people, and death for so many were undeniable factors in letting people know I had contracted the virus. In the first wave of COVID-19 (in the year 2020), many of my clients fell ill, and they were all afraid to call it by its name as that would mean acknowledging the genuine possibility of death. I experienced a similar hesitation, unwilling to believe during that first week that not all of us would come through it alive. I suppose the difficulty of a modicum of self-awareness at a time like this was in the desire to hide from it all and being unable to overlook the truth of my feelings underneath this desire, making it nearly impossible to hide.

Early in the pandemic, a colleague had fallen ill. She mentioned struggling with disclosure during her illness and recovery. I admitted I was unsure what I would tell my clients if I got sick from COVID-19. She said, "I think you should tell them the truth, trust me, you don't want them to randomly pick up the phone and see a text or an email telling them you died." I couldn't deny the truth of her words. Usually, when we are ill, we let our patients know we are unwell and will have to cancel. It's a vaguely specific message, informing people that there is an illness and stopping further queries about it, thereby keeping the boundaries in place. In a world where the pandemic has shut down the world and driven everything online, where everyone is unsure of when an otherwise common symptom could be what kills you, panicked curiosity bled out of us all at finding out someone had a fever – "what is it? Did you do the swab test? How bad is it? Have you measured your pulse oxygen?" A therapist may disclose an illness they have that could cause their death in the near or distant future. But COVID may or may not kill you. It may or may not have severe symptoms. It may or may not impact you in serious, severe ways. The pandemic has pushed us into a world where, as therapists, we were deconstructing and remaking boundaries and rethinking ethical concerns around them.

Resuming work with clients who were already aware of the upheaval in my personal life was more fluid than beginning work with a new person. For the longest time, I considered not taking on new clients at all. Realizing I was deeply conflicted about my own capacities and their depletion, I brought my concerns to my supervisor (Dr. Shalini Masih), who, in her wonderful, inherent wisdom, advised me to "live through this as I've lived through other things so far: with empathy and courage."

Losing someone or something is not a new experience. Our whole lives are built around losses. Growing with those voids and going through the sense of suspension of time and life, and oddly being tethered to the fabric of life and time, one finds one swaying in a soft dance with both deadness and coming alive. I was watching myself live life through a vignetted lens; so much of me had already faded into the background. Was there even enough of me left to be called by my name anymore? This grief can feel a little psychotic:

> The sense of self can expand to include all existence or shrink even to exclude itself. Animals, also, are concerned with boundaries and may fight over territory. But in human life, the stakes are raised to a new level. The very fit between the self and its sense of space and time can be thrown into question and well-nigh obliterated. Psychotics are riddled with profound boundary problems, which raise basic issues concerning the nature of our relationships to ourselves, others, and the cosmos. (Eigen, The Psychotic Core, p. 139)

I had to find a bridge between the various fragments of myself by acknowledging the almost absolute destruction posed by COVID and the psychosis-like experience of my current self. I could no longer hope to be who I was; I had to go forward holding my shattered objects and find new places to put them, finding different ways to connect the pieces of me.

This did not go unnoticed by my clients. Those in the know offered me care in different ways and forms. One client offered to have food delivered to me. Another suggested supplements to her diet helped her recover from COVID. One client offered to bring me a puppy to "help me stay connected through this." I chose not to interpret these offers psychoanalytically but responded to their kindness and engagement with empathy for carrying me in their minds. I decided I would have faith in my clients' faith in me and in my supervisor's faith in me, and I opened myself up to working with new clients.

And that is when Saira[1] found me.

The Eye of the Storm

Saira came to therapy with me for closure regarding her feelings towards her previous therapist. Highly suspicious of therapists and psychoanalytic processes, she would come to sessions angry and armored up, rejecting all interpretations and feeling angry at the slightest appearance of connection with me. I, too, struggled initially to connect with her. Her previous therapist had abruptly ended their work as she began developing a solid, trusting love toward him. She was hopeful of his return, but when she was able to acknowledge it was doubtful, she started to look for another therapist who could help her deal with the feelings evoked and left unaddressed from losing him and the space she shared with him. As mentioned, she rejected most communication from me in sessions quite angrily. It didn't matter if it was an interpretation, an intervention, or even a hmm-ing acknowledgment. Anything that alerted her to a therapist's presence, she would attack and then me. I recognized that her anger was directed at the therapist and the process of therapy. Her rage was connected to a deep hurt of being opened analytically and then left waiting and exposed, to fester and to suffer. She would almost immediately feel apologetic after yelling at me. She could not tolerate herself in her grief or acknowledge grief at all; nonetheless, it was thrust upon her consistently, but she refused to allow any of it to touch her. And yet, all of it is under her skin, slowly sinking into her bones. Over a year after beginning work with me, she developed a near-constant pain in her neck that refused to let go of her. Every ache and every pain was described as a possibility of death approaching, simultaneously a death being re-experienced. It is interesting to note here that I have had a constant painful stiffness in my neck since the day of the *Bhog*[2] for my father and brother. This pain in my neck has moments of flare-ups and moments when it is bearable. It has become a constant companion. I understand my pain as my body's response to feeling burdened by a life without two significant relationships. For my client, her neck pain is a source of fear. She's afraid she will die. This pain is a reminder that she's alive and in pain. I sensed in her a more profound desire for an absolute decathexis – a wish to obliterate all existence, physical and psychological. The fear she experiences is the swaying between psychic aliveness and psychic deadness. The lure of being alive was calling to her as much as the bait of relief from all pain in deadness.

She had been in a heterosexual relationship for nearly ten years with a man who abruptly ended their relationship in 2018. She survived the breakup. In January 2019, however, she found out through a mutual friend's social media that her ex-partner was in a serious, committed relationship and experienced a breakdown within hours. Something in her "cracked," and the pain that burst through was uncontainable. She sought a therapist. That therapist had to abruptly stop working with her, which ushered in experiences of pain, abandonment, loneliness, heartbreak, paralyzing fear, and a fury that physically hurt her without language to construct a response. She did not have an apparatus with which to reflect or recognize it. There is no skin to touch it safely.

Michael Eigen guided my work with Saira unconsciously, like a spirit guide in my ear, laying markers after each session as I reflected on my numerous missteps and mistakes. It led to a meaningful recognition; these mistakes and misdirections were where we perhaps needed to go together in our work. She needed someone to acknowledge the hurt she'd been suffering – a therapist who could sincerely admit they could have handled something with more grace. Saira was stuck in loops of emotional catastrophes, never having learned to tolerate and transcend painful and frustrating experiences. Each session brought an internal sense of *Groundhog Day*.[3] She could not trust me to be present for her breakdowns, perhaps because she had never experienced containment; instead, she always bore the burden of having to be the container for others. We were stuck in an endless repetition of what happened to her in therapy before me and everything her previous therapist did that upset her. Her previous therapist was cursed in detail. I knew so much about her relationship with her previous therapist, both internal and external. What she could not bring to therapy with me was *herself*. She stayed on the periphery. It was almost like a child showing and telling a caregiver: This is who hurt me; this is how they went about hurting me; this is wrong; this hurts; make them stop; make me better. But at the same time, I rejected any soothing or comfort I could offer her. Her rage was overflowing forcefully, and I was drenched in it. My witnessing it all was also painful for her. 'Don't look at me when I'm hurting like this, but don't you dare look away!' was her unformulated, unconscious communication to me. And my grieving parts understood the value of what my immobility (and a frank admission of my immobility) brought to her: Safety, from therapy, and from the therapist. She had lost that sense of faith in the therapy process and the space of therapy. Her previous therapist had mishandled termination in the middle of a highly alive interaction of erotic transference and countertransference, and she couldn't bear it nor the thought of being analyzed again by anyone. Yet she found herself in therapy because this pain was familiar. The rupturing that occurred here was a familiar one. But I was not him. And treatment with me was uncanny in that it was a known unknown.

She was the bearer of, and perhaps also burdened with, breaking the cycles of transgenerational trauma. She was the family's unwilling, unknowing secret keeper. Her internal objects were these complexly layered yet crudely formed rocky canyons, where so much could get lost before it could be found. *It's a joy to be hidden but a disaster to not be found* (Winnicott's *Communicating and Not Communicating Leading to a Study of Certain Opposites*, 1963). She had been holding so much pain for others that her own sensory experience was lost. Whatever she would find in small bits and pieces would become catastrophes, not mere disasters. She was protective of all her pain and guarded it zealously.

She spoke about her previous therapist, let's call him Neville, in each session. His betrayal, her loss, and her anger would come out frequently. Her feelings would often try to scratch me too, and initially, I sat there, unmoving, letting her scratch me, cut me, hurt me, and hold space for her to express herself. But it hurt me. She could see that it hurt me. And I had nowhere to hide it. She was resisting connecting with me so much; she was fighting for her life as she fought this wish and this desire to feel connected to me. She was so afraid of me and so angry with therapy, and yet this is where she could *be* afraid *for* herself and angry for what she experienced with Neville. In the first few months of therapy, I only knew the basics of her life: the ex-boyfriend, the ex-therapist, the stoic absent-present father, the depressed mother, and a younger brother. About these, I had many details about the ex-therapist and then, to a lesser degree, the ex-boyfriend. Nothing else seemed important. She demanded I fix a specific pain, and if I wasn't going to focus on that, she might as well try someone else.

I was struggling to feel anything when I began to work with her. The devastation of my own internal world was too heavy on my body for me to fully feel sensitive to her heaviness. Grief hadn't even become an emotional experience for me, as the loss hadn't fully sunk in just yet. When Saira's grief was seeping out in session, it was connecting to parts of me that weren't fully formed and ready to be found. I hid deeper into myself, withdrawing myself from active experiencing and retreating to a distantly observing self. I lost my capacity for dreaming and reverie. She expressed her disappointment and hurt through enactments during our sessions regarding my expectation of her being present but my unwillingness to bring myself fully to the session. Upon reflection, I realized she could sense I was carrying something heavy and dense internally, and she would often comment on how unfair it is that she won't ever get any straightforward answers to her curiosities about me, and at the same time, she wouldn't freely ask me any questions. After sessions, I often feel flustered at my inability to establish an alliance or a sense of connection with her. And then, with a heavy heart, consider if I made a mistake in starting work when I feel so shattered, so inadequate, and plagued with a shallowness I could not bear to look at. But she was insistent on my fullness. She would settle for nothing less than a present, alive therapist. A conversation with my supervisor brought something forth for me.

Shalini: Once I asked Mike, what do I do with all this love (that a client is bringing to me, for me)? In classic Mike fashion, he said, "enjoy it."

G: But it's not me she loves.

Shalini: To open oneself to love, is also to open oneself to experiencing loss. Love is risk-taking behavior.

Trying to hold on to and weakly emulate Eigen's acceptance of all experiences of interactions and his ability to reassure, challenge, and encourage is instrumental in what happened in the session with my client next. I remembered how Eigen had written so evocatively and openly about his own feelings about Ruth and Cynthia (about Ruth in *The Call and the Lure*, 1973; about Cynthia in *Coming Through the Whirlwind*, 1992). The words he wrote evoked a reminder of the feeling of awe and fantasy of feeling that freedom in my analytic work, which was enough to lead me to a moment of self-disclosure in a session with Saira.

Symptom of Change

She was stewing in anger because Neville (her ex-therapist) had reached out to her, wanting to see if she wanted to resume therapy with him again. She eagerly responded, and he didn't respond for a month. She eventually texted him late one night, reprimanding him for making promises he could not keep. He responded after a week, and they scheduled a time to meet for a session online. In that session, she communicated her feelings about his behavior. She felt a delight in "putting him in his place." She feared being stuck in limbo if her anger left her or if she gained this closure. "I want to go back to how I was feeling before this call with Neville. I felt closer to myself in that state." I interpreted her feeling like she was cheating on him by being in therapy with me. She said it was the other way around. "I feel like I'm cheating on you, after I spoke to him." I was stunned that she could feel something toward me. More than that, I was surprised she carried me in her mind to feel that way. It was now a triangle, in which I was an active vertex. Triangles are also a mathematical symptom of (or symbol of) change. This was a change, as before I had felt as if Saira had set it up as if she were speaking to a wall.

To Saira, therapy with me felt like a lucid dream. She experienced a passivity in therapy with me, a rituality. With Neville, she would fantasize about the upcoming sessions. She would actively think about what she would bring up in therapy, what she would wear, and how she would talk. Seduction was present. This dynamic was absent in treatment with me. She was at a loss as to what to do with this therapy, unable to acknowledge what she'd lost. Part of her loss was transgenerational. After treatment with Neville, she had lost a sense of herself. Her internal object was a dehydrated, highly toxic, and thorny love. Love that she could not hold, and that could not hold her. It was a continuous loss of love. There is something so unthinkable or unspeakable about this love. It cannot be felt without an accompanying sensation of pain and an experience of acute distress. This love is traumatic. This pain is without end. This pain-love persists. A wish to make the pain stop will also make the love stop. This wish cannot be fulfilled. And what is grief if not love persevering?[4]

It was a moment where Saira could move towards making meaning of her experience. She has suffered through multiple rejections of the love she offered.

In her confusion about my ability to bear her aggression and hate, I recognized something: She had no experience of an object that could bear her aliveness, love, or hate. She was aware of her destructiveness, but only in a sensory, experiential form. While she was quite verbose and lexically skilled, words were yet to become attached to specific experiences. An infant initially cannot distinguish between the Me and Not-me, and therefore, the perception of the world is subjective, but with a supportive environment and a good enough mother, that distinction becomes possible, and thereby the infant arrives at object usage. Saira's knowledge of the external world and its objects was superficial at best, as she had yet to arrive at this distinction when she started therapy with Neville. The abruptness with which he closed work with her caused a significant rupture in her newly developing capacity to tolerate her own destructiveness. When an infant attempts to destroy a not-good-enough mother, if the mother cannot bear such affects and reacts in a way that interrupts the infant's emotional development, object usage may be foreclosed, and the destruction, over time, can turn inwards.

Could I be the mother who could use her intuition and emotional experience to contain this infant's distress? Could I be the mother who could use her internal experience of loss, grief, and absolute and utter devastation to assure the baby that I was emotionally present and alert to her? Allowing Saira to see how I was holding her distress made space in her body for receiving comfort from me without fearing it. I couldn't begin to work *with* Saira before we created a silhouette of a willfully containing mother.

G: It's not your fault
S: It doesn't make any difference, it doesn't help
G: No, it doesn't. and that is also not your fault. There is a sense of loss that you're carrying around that you're finding difficult to bring to language.
S: Why do you always have to make it about losing something. Neville was awful to drop me like that. Why can't you just acknowledge that.
G: I have a favorite mug out of which I drink my favorite beverage, tea. My younger brother bought it for me. It's a beautiful black mug with colourful flowers painted on, in the middle of those flowers it says Cup of Love. I lost him to Covid a few months ago. And the first thing I remember doing after hearing he died, was pack that mug away. I didn't want to accidentally break it and lose something that held that fleeting thought of love and affection that he carried when he went into a store, and looked at a mug and thought, 'oh that's my sister's mug for sure' and bought it for me. I connect with a similar sense of loss to you. Grief can make us yearn. For one last call, more sessions, fantasies of how I would end it, anger at him leaving, of redefining how you lose what you lose instead of it being painfully being ripped away from you without warning. So we go around in ever-widening circles, dancing with our rage and our delight and our hurt.

Saira starts to cry

S: This is triggering for many other losses that I've had.
G: Let's stay with how you're feeling right now.
S: No, we are at the end of the session. I don't want to stay.
G: It's understandable you want to put parts of yourself away because they carry too much love. Having them accessible and visible makes you aware of that's been ripped from you. It's also a way to protect and preserve a piece of what you have lost.

She cried for herself and for me. We ran over session time, but I made no move to alert her of it. I felt I needed to witness these tears and whatever came after them. After nearly 20 minutes, she revealed that her brother had attempted to kill himself twice in the last four months. This was the first time a good internal object was showing itself in therapy, but that too was warped by pain and helplessness – a fearful mistrust of it.

I obliterated two boundaries in this vignette. I revealed to a client my own internal world and personal experience. I also extended the session time by 20 odd minutes. One can ask me why I did it, but I have no clear answers. I only know I was responding from a part of me that was listening keenly to Saira. I was responding to her in a free-flowing state. Maybe grief recognizes grief in others. Maybe grieving parts want to be made whole too, and they call on other such parts to do so. There is a Me that is separate from the Me-in-this-moment. The self feels knotted up. It is, and it is also (k)not. When Bion distinguishes between "learning from experience" and "learning about," he explicitly states that the growth of the mind is directly dependent upon "truthfulness." When one learns through experience, a personal language of achievement is developed, which allows for the development of greater capacities for exploration, to formulate, to think, and to experience. When Freud sets up the uncanny, the unheimlich in a negative sense, uncanny is whatever is not canny; uncanny is something that is *not* home-like, unfamiliar, or uncomfortable. It stirs curiosity: Is all that unfamiliar and uncanny? Cixous posits that the Un, the knot in any analysis of the Unheimlich, is that analysis itself is an Un, a return of what is repressed (*Fiction and Its Phantoms: A Reading of Freud's Das Unheimliche (The "Uncanny")*, 1976). This is where the gaps in translation and meaning-making present themselves in stark light. Heimlich also carries multiple meanings, like that which is obscure, inaccessible to knowledge, secret, clandestine, familiar, amicable, unreserved, a place free from ghostly influences, intimate – which leads Freud to conclude that Unheimlich is unreservedly related to something that is frightening, to what arouses dread and horror, but also can coincide with the stirrings of fear. *What is Heimlich thus comes to be Unheimlich.* That is to say, the uncanny is that 'which ought to have remained hidden and secret but has come to light' (What was hidden, has been found, feels like a disaster). When one's earliest learning from experience – of being loved, held, and contained – is riddled with secrets and scary feelings, what happens when something begins to bring it out? When the obstruction in the way of feeling your experiences is accessed, perhaps also moved, what does it do to the infant? Owing to unfamiliarity with the experience, the sensation of feeling love evokes fear. The infant in distress (distress being a highly intense emotional experience that permeates the infant's sensorial experiences) needs another mind to project these experiences onto/into. In an ideal world, a mind can be found to house and hold the infant's pain. That mind will welcome the projective identification, tolerate the pain and distress, and hopefully, the distress can be spotted and contemplated with empathy and compassion. But to make meaning of this experience, the infant will depend upon the mother and her ability to offer her mind to contain and hold this distress, to use her internal capacity to hold her own emotional experiences and distress. If the mother is unable to pay attention to the infant's cry of pain, unable to offer attention to it, or her mind herself is riddled with her own infantile distress and fails to use her intuition to soothe and comfort, then this emotional experience of distress can become an internal obstructive object. If the mother's internal object world is barren and empty, the infant cannot use it to create its own internal world of vital objects. Grief can empty out otherwise rich internal object worlds, turning alive and vibrant worlds into a post-apocalyptic, barren, desolate landscape. I sense that this grief-stricken internal state is the object world that Saira was depending upon and using to make sense of her distress, but that dependence was also, at the very best, weakly reliable. It's an uncanny, haunted internal object world – things that feel familiar and unfamiliar, safe and scary, alive and dead, simultaneously. In all this, when I offered a tether of real feeling – loss, grief, and anguish – Saira hesitantly grabbed it. Her experience of a mother (previous therapist, maybe her actual mother, or any other love object) rejecting her distress was perhaps being slowly written over by her experience of a mother(me) welcoming her distress while using her own experiences of grief, loss, and pain intuitively, keeping them separated, but not in the way of the uncanny, where what is hidden is a secret that must never be revealed, but in the careful, loving acceptance of what she needed help in holding. The obstructing grief has hampered her ability to tolerate experiences of great pain and emotional turbulence, but miraculously, faith has survived. Faith survived and clung to her mistrust of therapy and of therapists. This moment of self-disclosure was a turning point in my therapeutic alliance with Saira. There was a slow and steady movement towards accepting and attempting to tolerate emotional experiences from us both, together, in session.

Welcoming the Obstruction

After this session ended, I remained seated, and for the first time since my brother passed, I allowed myself to imagine him alive and vibrant, not only as a body on the funeral pyre. For the first time, I was able to peel that tar-like layer of grief from my skin, enough to remember his hugs sensorially. I allowed myself to hear his laughter instead of the shattering silence that had enveloped me. As I was telling Saira about my mug, I was also living through my fear of it breaking. As I was telling her he was dead, I was also, for the first time, living that experience for myself. I hadn't experienced his death, not in the moment he died or the moments that followed. My entire family had COVID-19, me included, and I was the only one who could focus on what needed to be done and what needed to be taken care of. This self-disclosure was a way to let her know that I could hold her pain and mine separately but together. An old Hindi song comes to mind, loosely translated as: *you're the source of pain and comfort. You're what I see, how I see, who I see, and you're also the eye, which is the apparatus through which I see. My love for you is wounded, and is constantly wounding me, I will love you through each sunrise and each sunset, but your name will not find my voice.* (Chahunga Main Tujhe from the movie Dosti (1964) sung by Mohammad Rafi). Something that is forgotten about love and longing is brought forth. Something has been lost that must now be formulated, bursting forth in an endless scream that finds no reflection, echoes, or sound,[5]

> To build a tolerance for ourselves is hard enough, but personal growth also demands fine tuning. Psychotherapy nurtures sensitivity rather than 'spoils' it. It opens channels for new qualities of experience. As we work, we learn to become sensitive to moment-to moment catastrophes without succumbing to them or, more accurately, we learn to come through our succumbing. (Eigen, Coming Through the Whirlwind, 1992, p. xiii)

I still wonder why I succumbed to the urge to share my experience of a life permanently altered by loss with Saira. I was worrying about all the what-ifs and the could-haves. Eigen wrote in Psychotic Core, "*In psychosis, what we ordinarily take as material may be treated as if it were immaterial, and vice versa*" (1986/2004, p. 1). These words flashed through my mind, and I experienced a state of unformulable trust for an extended moment. I burst into sobs that were wrenched from somewhere deep within – a preverbal, purely sensorial place of despair and sorrow. Am I connecting my grief-stricken objects and object usage to psychosis? It is, after all, a break from reality. The loss, ache, and grief are all very real, but the experience is disconnected and unreal. Sometimes the grief is mine, sometimes it's not. I do the work of grieving for both the Mine and Not-mine. An infant born into a grief-stricken object world will assimilate all that desolation as "normal." The grieving baby becomes a melancholic baby. The melancholic baby becomes a melancholic, not-good-enough mother. And the cycle continues.

In her paper *Happy Objects*, Sara Ahmed writes, "Pleasure creates an object, even when the object of pleasure appears before us. The creativity of feeling does not require the absence of an object. We are moved by things. In being moved, we make things" (2010, p. 25). The disjointedness between being a therapist and *becoming* a therapist was highlighted in that moment of grief I experienced after a session. To encounter the fear of not knowing, to let it in, and to explore the aliveness it lends to the process of therapy. My grief unknowingly pushed me into an enactment, but it took one leap of faith to rediscover the emotional experience of becoming a psychoanalyst. The Cup of Love is still sitting unused in the cabinet, but I can sometimes look at it and touch it. The hope is that, one day, it will be full again.

Notes

1 Name changed to protect identity, respecting the confidentiality of the client.
2 Bhog is a ceremonial reading from the Guru Granth Sahib in a gurdwara (temple) for Sikhs, followed by a prayer for peace merging with the ultimate Guru/God for the souls of the departed; it also signifies the end of all rituals connected to the death of a person, post-funeral.
3 Referring to a fantasy comedy film Directed by Harold Ramis, released in 1993. The protagonist finds himself reliving the same day over and over again, with slight variations, until something significant shifts internally for him, and eventually he awakens to a new dawn.
4 Direct dialogue quoted from Marvel's Wanda Vision.
5 This thought came about in a personal conversation with my dear friend and colleague Ms. Epsita Sandhu.

References

Ahmed, S. (2010). Happy Objects. In *The Promise of Happiness* (pp. 25–26). Duke University Press.

Bion, W. R. (1994). Making the Best of a Bad Job. In F. Bion (Ed.), *Clinical Seminars and Other Works* (pp. 321–331). Karnac Books.

Eigen, M. (1973). The Call and the Lure. *Psychotherapy: Theory, Research & Practice, 10*(3), 194–197. https://doi.org/10.1037/h0087572

Eigen, M. (1992). *Coming Through the Whirlwind*. Chiron Publications.

Freud, S., Strachey, J., Cixous, H., & Dennome, R. (1976). Fiction and Its Phantoms: A Reading of Freud's Das Unheimliche (The "Uncanny"). *New Literary History, 7*(3), 525. https://doi.org/10.2307/468561

God

did you see the skeletons behind the fence
their hollow eyes
the bare-boned boy clutching
a barbed wire fence going in flames
God
did you sit on your throne
guarded by six-winged fiery seraphim
who shielded your eyes
lest you see little hearts of children
gassed and cremated turning to ash
Rachel Berghash 2022

Index

For Product Safety Concerns and Information please contact our EU
representative GPSR@taylorandfrancis.com
Taylor & Francis Verlag GmbH, Kaufingerstraße 24, 80331 München, Germany

www.ingramcontent.com/pod-product-compliance
Lightning Source LLC
Chambersburg PA
CBHW050656280326
41932CB00015B/2929

9 781032 346007